Creative Writing

FOR

DUMMIES®

by Maggie Hamand

WILEY

Creative Writing For Dummies®

Published by
John Wiley & Sons, Ltd
The Atrium
Southern Gate
Chichester
West Sussex
PO19 8SQ
England

E-mail (for orders and customer service enquires): cs-books@wiley.co.uk

Visit our Home Page on www.wiley.com

For general information on our other products and services, please contact our Customer Care Department within the U.S. at 877-762-2974, outside the U.S. at 317-572-3993, or fax 317-572-4002.

For technical support, please visit www.wiley.com/techsupport.

Wiley also publishes its books in a variety of electronic formats. Some content that appears in print may not be available in electronic books.

British Library Cataloguing in Publication Data: A catalogue record for this book is available from the British Library

ISBN: 978-0-470-74291-4

Printed and bound by CPI Group (UK) Ltd, Croydon, CR0 4YY

C9780470742914_151024

About the Author

Maggie Hamand is the author of two novels, *The Resurrection of the Body* and *The Rocket Man*, and has published a number of short stories which have been nominated for prizes. She is the author of 16 non-fiction books, and her articles have appeared in magazines and newspapers including the *Guardian, The Sunday Times*, and the *Observer*. She founded the Complete Creative Writing Course at the Groucho Club in 1998 and is also the Director of the award-winning small independent publishing house, The Maia Press.

Author's Acknowledgements

I would like to thank all those people who supported me while writing this book, most importantly my husband Jeremy.

Special thanks should also go to Shaun Levin and all the other teachers on the Complete Creative Writing Course from whom I've learned so much.

Publisher's Acknowledgements

We're proud of this book; please send us your comments through our Dummies online registration form located at *www.dummies.com/register/*.

Some of the people who helped bring this book to market include the following:

Acquisitions, Editorial, and Media Development

Commissioning Editor: Wejdan Ismail

Executive Project Editor: Daniel Mersey

Project Editor: Rachael Chilvers

Content Editor: Jo Theedom

Development Editor: Kathleen Dobie

Copy Editor: Kate O'Leary

Proofreader: Kelly Cattermole

Cover Photo: © Andy Ryan/Getty Images

Cartoons: Ed McLachlan

Composition Services

Project Coordinator: Lynsey Stanford

Layout and Graphics: Reuben W. Davis, Melanee Habig, Melissa K. Jester

Proofreader: Dwight Ramsey

Indexer: Cheryl Duksta

Contents at a Glance

Table of Contents

Part IV: Exploring Non-Fiction 231

Chapter 17: Breaking into Journalism 233

Chapter 18: Writing from Life 245

Chapter 19: Crafting Narrative Non-Fiction 263

Introduction

Creative writing may be fun, but it isn't easy. It requires some imagination, a degree of application and a great deal of effort.

This book gathers together everything you need to know about writing and publishing all kinds of creative writing. It distils my more than 20 years of experience in journalism, novel-writing, teaching creative writing and working in publishing, all in one place. I share the basics – and some of the extras – of writing novels, stories, poetry, plays, screenplays, biography and autobiography. I discuss journalism and blogging and offer pointers on how to get published.

I try to give you the essence of what a life's work spent in loving reading and writing literature in all its forms has taught me, to help you avoid repeating some of my mistakes!

This book aims to help you gain confidence in your ideas, to inspire you and provide the knowledge and skills you need to get started on your writing journey.

About This Book

Most people who write start off by spending a lot of time alone, puzzling out how to tackle the various difficulties and challenges that writing brings up. How do you know what to write about? Where should you begin? What point of view should you tell the story from? How do you write dialogue that leaps off the page, invent intriguing characters and describe places and objects so that the reader can see them? Should you write your story as an autobiography, or turn it into a novel? And how do you write plays, screenplays and poems, or sell an article to a newspaper?

Unfortunately, if you sit alone in your room, never reading about how to write or sharing your concerns with others, you may find yourself simply going round in circles. You may spend weeks making elementary errors you could have avoided had you known more about how writing works. Most people tackling things in this way find writing so hard that they soon give up, which is a great shame because something unique is then lost to the world.

This book helps you avoid some of the common writing pitfalls and offers practical advice about how to write creatively, no matter what form that writing takes. Each type of writing has its own rules and techniques, challenges and rewards. In this book, I provide the rules and techniques – you get to reap your own rewards.

Reading a lot and thinking about how writing works is vital if you want to write well – reading is the best teacher of how to write. I refer to many different books, plays and films as examples of good writing to illustrate some of the points I make. I also suggest a lot of books to read. I don't recommend a book, film or play unless I've read it or seen it, so inevitably these are very personal lists. You may not like some of these works, but almost all are highly acclaimed, so I'm not alone in thinking they're great.

How to Use This Book

This book is intended to be a companion for you as you explore the process of creative writing. I include exercises to help you try for yourself some of the techniques I describe. I believe that you learn to write by writing, and not just by reading a book about it. Try out the exercises and see what happens!

Reading some of the books, watching some of the plays and seeing some of the films I suggest is a good idea. Setting yourself some simple targets, such as reading a poem a day and finding some time to write each week, is also helpful.

You can read this book in a number of ways:

- ✔ If you're a complete beginner, thinking about writing creatively for the first time – or perhaps the first time since you left school – this book gives you the grounding you need. You can start at the beginning and work your way through to the end.

- ✔ If you have a great idea and some experience of writing but have got bogged down, this book can help you to get unstuck. You can select the areas in which you feel you need guidance and read those first.

- ✔ If you've written a lot and sent your work out but you don't seem to be getting anywhere, this book can help you ask the right questions about what you've written, and find the right answers.

- ✔ If you want information about how to get your work into print, this book has the information and tips that you need to approach agents, newspapers, theatres, film studios and different kinds of publishers.

Foolish Assumptions

In writing this book, I make some assumptions about you – the person who's reading this book. I assume that you:

- ✔ Enjoy reading books and magazines or watching films and plays, and that you think about what you read and watch.
- ✔ Have a fairly serious intention to learn about and do some writing.
- ✔ Have a reasonable amount of self-discipline and are prepared to create some time to write.
- ✔ Don't expect to write a work of genius right away and make a million from the first piece of writing you attempt.

Conventions Used in This Book

This book uses various typefaces to highlight different bits of information. For example, I use _italics_ when a term is first defined, **bold** for a key term in a bulleted list and `monofont` for website addresses.

You also see grey boxes from time to time. These _sidebars_ contain information that you may find interesting but isn't essential to understanding the text. So, you can read them if you want to, but you aren't going to miss anything crucial if you skip them.

How This Book Is Organised

Creative Writing For Dummies is divided into six parts.

Part I: Getting Started

These chapters take a look at what you need to be able to write, including the motivation, tools and techniques – and also the rewards!

Part II: Introducing the Elements of Creative Writing

This part of the book gives you the nuts and bolts you need to write creatively. It looks at the difference between autobiography and fiction, shows you how to create characters, handle point of view, write dialogue, invent your own world and plot your way through a story.

Part III: Writing Fiction

These chapters look at all the different kinds of fiction writing: short stories, novels, plays, screenplays, children's books and poetry. They define the different genres within fiction and consider how to connect with your readers.

Part IV: Exploring Non-Fiction

These chapters cover all the different kinds of non-fiction writing, which are still essentially creative, such as journalism, autobiography and biography, memoirs and journals, narrative non-fiction, travel writing and even the new big thing – blogging.

Part V: Finding an Audience

The chapters in this part guide you towards thinking about your writing in more commercial terms, and help you to identify a market for it. They describe how the world of publishing works, and look at how to get an audience, agent or publisher for your writing.

Part VI: The Part of Tens

This standard part, found in every *For Dummies* book, contains lists of writing tips and books you should read and why.

Icons Used in This Book

The little drawings in the margins, called *icons,* highlight information that's especially interesting, important or both.

Important advice is highlighted with this on-the-target icon.

This icon indicates information to keep in mind while you're reading a chapter or for the rest of your writing life.

Information highlighted with this icon helps you to avoid mistakes and points out approaches that can get you in trouble.

This icon marks illustrations of points I explain in the text. Sometimes an example makes an explanation come to life.

These exercises help get you writing and encourage you to try out some of the techniques I talk about.

Where to Go from Here

You have several options at this point:

✔ You can flick through the chapters and read something that interests you, which highlights an area that you're having problems with or covers an aspect of something that you're working on.

✔ You can start by reading the contents and selecting those parts of the book that seem most relevant, missing out any areas that don't seem useful to you at the moment.

✔ You can start at the beginning and read through to the end. Don't worry if you pay greater attention to some bits than others – your focus clearly depends on which kind of writing you're most interested in.

- ✔ You can keep it on your desk and use it as a reference book, to refer to frequently while you're working on your writing.

- ✔ You can take this book and use it any way you choose, such as picking chapters at random, reading it from back to front, using it to sit on while you meditate or even throwing it across the room when you're feeling frustrated with your writing. Don't worry – we've all done it!

Finally, whatever you choose to do with this book, I hope you find it useful. Enjoy!

Part I
Getting Started

'Is that all the help I get? Keep
using the Computer Grammar Checker?
A fine muse you are!'

In this part . . .

*W*riting is a skill, and like any skill you need to find the best way to do it well. Even published writers continue to hone their skills. The best way to start improving your writing skills is by reading a lot, especially the kind of work you'd like to write yourself. You need some tools – pen and paper, a notebook, a computer or a laptop – and you need to find a place to write and a time and routine that suits you.

This part gets you started and gives you some much-needed support and encouragement.

Chapter 1

You and Your Writing

reative writing starts with you – with your imagination, personality and interests. Only you know what you want to write about and how you like to work. Only you can choose to spend time working at your poetry or prose to help your words communicate to others.

Listen to yourself, not to others, and be prepared for surprises. This chapter encourages you to get started on a journey of discovery and to develop the attitude you need to carry your chosen task through to the end.

People often ask, can everyone write? Well, (almost) everyone can write, in the sense of creating a sentence and then stringing another after it, and so on. However, in contrast with other artistic skills, such as playing the violin or painting in oils, or crafts like pottery and carpentry, people sometimes fail to realise that writing for an audience – writing to communicate to others – also requires study, hard work and practice.

We all spend our lives telling stories, and in that sense everyone does indeed have a book in them – or, if not a whole book, then at least a tale or two – but that doesn't mean to say everyone is prepared to work at it in such a way that, as a piece of art, it communicates itself to other people. This book gives you all the tools you need to take yourself seriously as a writer and develop your craft as best you can.

Writing as Well as You Can

A world of difference exists between writing for yourself and writing for others. Both are perfectly valid, and can be approached in much the same way. Whether you're aiming to record your experiences for your children, to write for therapy or personal development, or to get a novel published, you want to write as well as you can. Doing so doesn't mean you need to think of yourself as a genius, but it does involve stretching yourself and learning as much about writing as you can.

When you start writing, don't think too much about whether your work will get published. After all, on passing your Grade Three violin exam, you may congratulate yourself on having got so far, but you wouldn't rush off a letter to the Wigmore Hall to ask if you could put on a solo recital. Considering other people's opinions of your writing – whether they like it, or will be interested in it or whether it will suit the current market – is death to true creativity.

J. R. R. Tolkien spent years writing a history of an imaginary country, inventing languages and mythology and timelines and maps, purely for himself. He never thought anyone else would be interested in it. When his publishers asked him for a sequel to *The Hobbit*, he used this material as the basis for *The Lord of the Rings*, a work that went on to become one of the bestselling novels of all time. Completely unexpectedly, something in the deep recesses of Tolkien's imagination connected with a vast number of people, all over the world. Yet at the time his publisher, Stanley Unwin, was so convinced the novel wouldn't sell that he cynically offered Tolkien a profit-sharing deal – because he believed no profits would accrue!

By digging deep into yourself and your imagination you'll find the thing that you really want to write about, that gives you the greatest pleasure and presents you with the greatest challenge – and paradoxically this subject is most likely to be the one that most interests others. So write for yourself and forget about what other people think until much, much later in the process.

Examining Why You Want to Write

Before you begin to write, ask yourself why you want to do so. If the reason is that you think writing's the easiest way for you to become rich and famous, a bit of a reality check is in order. Every year nearly a quarter of a million books are published in the UK alone. Admittedly this total includes everything from computer manuals and academic tomes, through cookbooks and knitting manuals to celebrity memoirs and mainstream fiction, but it still represents a huge amount of competition.

In addition are all the *backlist titles* that have been in print for years and are still selling. Of these books, very few sell in sufficient numbers to make anyone much money. In the fiction market, about 25 titles make around 65 per cent of the income, leaving a lot of writers making very little money at all.

Of those books in print, very few are by writers who are household names. To achieve that degree of recognition, your book needs to be filmed, shortlisted for the Man Booker Prize or become one of those rare runaway bestsellers that everybody dreams about but hardly ever happen.

Most writers earn very modest amounts, and the majority have other sources of income from work or supportive partners. So if money and fame are your main motivation to write, you're likely to be extremely disappointed.

Here, however, are some good reasons to write:

- ✔ Something is nagging away at you that you need to write down, an event from your life, perhaps, that has haunted or puzzled you.

- ✔ You keep hearing a character's voice in your head, and you want to find out who it is.

- ✔ A situation keeps coming to mind – *what if* this were to happen, how would I feel, what would I do? – and you want to explore it.

- ✔ You always loved writing stories at school and realise you'd like to feel that pleasure again.

These are all good reasons to write because the impulse is coming from you. This impulse isn't dependent on anything outside yourself that you can't control, such as the vagaries of editors or the whims of newspaper reviewers or prize judges or the economic situation at the time your book is published. Your desire to write is dependent only on your imagination, commitment and willingness to learn and develop your craft.

Various theories are propounded about why people write – as a wish-fulfilment fantasy, a form of therapy or a way of achieving immortality and living on after death – and any of these might apply to you. But, ultimately, *you want to write because you want to write*. And you have to want to. No one's putting a gun to your head and demanding that you produce your masterpiece. Enough written work already exists in the world, and people can probably do without your contribution. But then, as the famous choreographer and dancer Martha Graham said:

> 'There is a vitality, a life force, an energy, a quickening that is translated through you into action, and because there is only one of you in all of time, this expression is unique. And if you block it, it will never exist through any other medium and it will be lost. The world will not have it. It is not your business to determine how good it is nor how valuable nor how it compares with other expressions. It is your business to keep it yours clearly and directly, to keep the channel open.'

(Agnes de Mille, *Martha: The Life and Work of Martha Graham*)

Identifying the Kind of Writing You Want to Do

If you're drawn to a particular form of expression, then go with it. Some people like to work in miniature, others love the grand gesture – temperament decides. If you love children and reading aloud to them, or have a story in mind for your own children or grandchildren, then go ahead. Many of the best children's stories have started that way. Or if you love a grand canvas and big novels with sub-plots, twists and turns, go for that. Don't let other people talk you out of your natural way of writing.

Thinking, 'I really want to write poetry, but no market exists for it, so I'll write a novel instead', is pointless. You may turn out to be a very fine poet but a hopeless novelist.

If you don't know what kind of writing you want to do, just try out various forms. Get stuck in and write whatever comes up. If you feel that you'd love to write but don't have any ideas, then just open yourself up to people and situations around you. For example:

- ✔ **Sit in a café and watch the customers.** Invent a story about who they are, where they come from, why they're there, who they're thinking of, what they want.

- ✔ **Look at your daily paper.** Pick a small item from the News in Brief section; use it as the basis for a story.

- ✔ **Go into your garden.** Find a flower, tree or view and describe it. Turn the writing into a poem.

- ✔ **Find an old photograph.** What does it make you think of? What does it remind you of? Where does it take you in your imagination? Write down your thoughts.

As to the form your writing takes, no rule states that you can't write both prose and poetry – many writers do. Don't worry about length when you start; sometimes you start writing a short story and then discover after 20 pages that in fact the tale's so long and complex that it justifies a novel. Or, conversely, you may start what you think will be a novel and discover that it peters out after two or three chapters and doesn't have enough material to amount to more than a short story.

Don't worry too much about your audience either; you may start writing for young children and then find your material is actually adult fantasy. None of these details – length, form or audience – matter. Just write, and let the material take you where it will. You can always go back and change elements later.

Discovering Your Own Specific Talent

Most of us have a particular talent for something – and the same applies to writing. Some writers love plot; they enjoy working out time-lines, organising different strands of their story and weaving it all together. They plot their story on cards or use a computer program to map it out.

Other writers love description; looking at something and finding the best way to capture it in words, and using images to convey its essence to the reader. Some have an ear for dialogue, for how people speak, accents and dialects, and for the silences that lie between the words. Some writers have a wonderful visual sense; others an ear for the rhythm and sound of words.

When you start out writing you really may not know what you're good at. Trying something new is the only way to find out. Don't rely on the same techniques that worked for you when you were at school or when you were working as a copywriter; or that you use in letters or emails to friends. Stretch yourself. Try different ways of writing. You'll never discover that you're brilliant at writing dialogue if you never try it, or that the first-person voice gives you huge freedom, or that your story works much better if you set it in a different time or place. You'll never find out that you're a poet if you never try to write a poem.

As you write, keep these principles in mind:

- ✔ Trust yourself.
- ✔ Write what you want.
- ✔ Try out new ways of writing.
- ✔ Don't expect to write brilliantly straight away.
- ✔ Learn from other writers.

Practising Your Writing

Creative writing's a skill, and if you work at it, you'll improve – becoming a good writer is as simple as that. Writers also use a range of techniques, which you too can learn.

Part of the problem with writing is its solitary nature. When you're working on your own a strong possibility exists that you'll be reinventing the literary wheel. Through long hours and hard work you may stumble on the truths that other writers have discovered long before you. By talking to other writers, reading books and perhaps going to creative writing courses, you can save yourself a lot of time and trouble.

Putting in the hours

No substitute exists for finding time to write. Whether playing the violin, excelling at tennis or developing computer software, all the outstandingly talented people put in a great many more hours than their less successful peers.

You have to really want to write. Writers become writers by writing, not by wanting to write, thinking about writing or planning to write!

Lots of practice makes perfect

Anders Ericsson studied violinists at the Berlin Academy of Music in the early 1990s. His study concluded that a violinist had to practise approximately 10,000 hours to become really good.

Strikingly, Ericsson and his colleagues couldn't find any violinists who were *naturals* – musicians who became outstanding performers without practising for the hours that others did. Nor could they find what are sometimes called *grinds* – people who practised harder and longer than everyone else and yet didn't succeed. Every student who put in the hours played at a high level.

Now, 10,000 hours of writing is an awful lot – if you wrote for, say, five hours a day, five days a week, 50 weeks a year, it would take you eight to nine years to put in that many hours.

In practice, of course, many successful writers have written less than this – and other writers may have written more without ever getting into print. However, without doubt, the more you write, the better you become at it.

Reading and re-reading

What teaches you most about writing is reading. Reading is so important because it demonstrates what you're trying to do; you unconsciously absorb the rules of narrative when you read, and how the author achieves certain effects. Some writers don't read because they say they're afraid of being influenced by other writers. In practice, you're more likely to find that you've inadvertently done what someone else has if you aren't aware of others' work.

If you're attempting to be a writer, try reading more slowly – reading with more attention. When you come to a passage where you can actually smell the cabbage soup on the stairs, where time seems to have slowed right down and your heart is beating extra fast, stop and look back; try to figure out how the author achieved this feat. You are, after all, just reading words on a page. If a character walks into a room and you can see the whole scene before you like a photograph, or if you feel you know a character inside out, how she thinks and behaves – again, stop and look back. Look at the words the writer used, what he did to convey this sense of reality. Or if you read a poem and find that you're crying or suddenly feel happy, or realise that you're seeing something in a new way – again, re-read the poem to see why this has happened.

Re-read a short story or novel that you've read before; not so long ago that you've forgotten it or so recently that you remember it in great detail. Choose a book that you remember in outline, and in particular how it ends.

When you first read a book you often gulp it straight down just to find out what happens; the second time you don't do that because you already know. Already knowing what's going to happen can help you to see how the writer prepared for it, how she slipped in hints or how he concealed something important to keep you guessing. Re-reading in this way really helps you learn how a narrative works.

Read, read and read! Whether you choose newspaper articles, magazines, advertising slogans on the back of cereal packets, classic novels or contemporary potboilers, fact books or letters and journals, read widely – and think about what you're reading and the effect the words you read have on you.

Overcoming Obstacles

When you sit down to write, you often find that a whole host of things distract you. First, you become aware of all the chattering that goes on in your head, and the long lists of things to do that you feel you should do before you can justify the time spent on writing. Second, you may become uncomfortably aware of being alone, of having to manage without any help or input from anyone else. Third, you may suddenly discover that when you finally get the chance to write, you don't know what to say or you can't put it into words.

Everyone experiences these obstacles, so in this section I look at them in a bit more depth.

Silencing your inner critic

Many people say that when they first start writing they're convinced that what they write is rubbish. A voice in their heads tells them their work is useless and nobody will read it.

If all the students I've taught in my writing courses had given me just one penny for every time they said their work was rubbish, I'd be a wealthy woman.

Your inner critic torments you with thoughts like:

- ✔ You're not a real writer, you're just playing at it.
- ✔ You haven't got any talent.
- ✔ Why bother starting when you'll never finish?
- ✔ You should be doing something better with your time.
- ✔ Writing is self-indulgent and selfish.
- ✔ This will never get published, so what's the point?

Parents, teachers, friends or colleagues who've told you 'you could've done better' or 'this isn't good enough' over the years are part of the problem. You've probably experienced an education system obsessed with results and tests, where every piece of work was marked and graded. As a result, you now compare everything you write with the work of others and assess it in terms of a range of A* to D-.

One of the flaws of this approach is that grading a creative piece of work is almost impossible. Consider the Impressionist artists who were turned down by the Paris Salon in favour of far more conventional artists of the day. Those artists are now forgotten, while Manet and the rest are recognised as geniuses. Obviously not every piece of rejected writing is a work of genius – far from it. However, judging creative work effectively, especially something innovative and new, isn't easy.

Most writers, no matter how acclaimed, will tell you that the critical voice never goes away. Even prize-winning, many-times-published writers find the same voice nagging at them when they're writing. Being aware of the voice isn't a bad thing, though; if you're aware of it, you can deal with it.

Good methods for silencing your inner critic include:

✔ Just tell the voice to shut up and go away – out loud if it helps!

✔ Use a meditation technique – when the voice comes into your head, just say to yourself 'that voice', and put the thought aside. The voice will return over and over again, but don't get upset, don't beat yourself up, just gently put it aside and get on with what you're doing.

✔ Try to counter negative thoughts with positive ones. Talk to people who are supportive and encouraging. If your friends or family suggest that you're wasting your time or that you'll never get published, just don't talk to them about your writing. Talk to people who know what writing involves and can help you along the way.

✔ Give your inner critic a name. Call it something stupid or a name you don't like. Think of it as a boring, tedious figure you might meet at a party. Then get rid of it.

✔ Just get on with the writing. Decide that you can deal with the voice later.

Thinking creatively

Being led to believe at school that only one right answer exists for every question can create a creativity-blocking problem for writers. Remember putting your hand up in class and giving an answer that made everyone laugh? The 'right' answer was the one in the teacher's mind or in the textbook. But your answer wasn't necessarily wrong – maybe it was just more original and creative.

No artists or scientists ever came up with something new by doing what was expected of them. They all broke the rules and produced the 'wrong' answers according to the theories and expectations of the time.

Suspend logical thinking. Logic can kill the creative flow of new ideas. Of course, you do need to apply logical thinking in many situations, but writing isn't one of them. Think laterally, backwards and back to front – or don't think at all.

Letting the Ideas Come

Most great ideas don't come when you're sitting at your desk trying to feel inspired. Putting pressure on yourself and hammering away at something isn't conducive to coming up with a solution. You're concentrating so hard on the problem that your mind has no space for an answer to emerge.

Use these tips to help you come up with ideas:

- **Take time to relax.** Going for a walk, reading a book or relaxing in the bath may inspire a really great idea. Or you may suddenly find a solution to a problem blocking your writing. Alternating periods of working at your writing with relaxing activities is important.

- **Realise the importance of doing nothing.** Make some empty time in which to think.

  Today people are so surrounded by noise and activity that they seldom get time to let their minds free-wheel. Even when on the bus or train, people use mobile phones, listen to music or read the paper. Try doing nothing but staring out of the window, watching the world go by. Or try sitting in the park for half an hour at lunchtime, observing the pigeons, trees and people. Or sit at home on your own with a cup of coffee for just 20 minutes and relax.

- **Remember to play.** Ideas can also be generated by play. If you can make your writing fun, you'll find dreaming up good ideas much easier. If you think of writing as a game to enjoy, rather than a task to be completed, you'll find yourself becoming more creative.

- **Ask 'What if?'.** Many great innovators were successful because they asked 'What if?' and didn't stop with the first answer that suggested itself. 'What if?' is a great question for a writer. What if a man discovers the secret of extending life? What if someone tries to steal the recipe for the drug from him? What if a rival pharmaceutical company decides to have him killed?

- **Don't be afraid to make mistakes.** All creative activity involves making mistakes. People who don't make errors never achieve anything. Sometimes mistakes can ultimately be fortunate; you may not only learn from them, but also reinterpret them to write something much more original than what you'd originally planned.

Offering Tips for New Writers

Many new writers fall into common traps that can block their writing or make the process more difficult. Instead of finding out the hard way, through trial and error, take note of the tips in this section to avoid these pitfalls and get your writing life off to a good start.

Don't worry about publication

When you start out, worrying about whether anyone will like or dislike what you're writing is pointless. Don't fret about what genre your work fits into or what kind of sales it may achieve. And thinking about which publisher to send your piece to before you've even completed it really is a waste of time.

The minute you start thinking about sending your work to an editor, agent or publisher, you can feel that person sitting on your shoulder and criticising every word you write. You start altering it to squeeze it into narrow genres, make it the right length or ensure the material's less revealing of yourself.

Writing what you want and enjoying the process is what's important.

Write for yourself

When you start writing, at some point you'll ask yourself 'Who am I writing this for?' You may decide that you're writing a piece for your friends, ex-lover or dead grandfather. Maybe your novel's intended for posterity, for your children's grandchildren. Or you may desire to share your experiences, joys and pains with people your own age or in your current situation. Agents and publishers may be lurking at the back of your mind. Or possibly you're setting your sights on a huge global audience.

No matter who you think you're writing for, the mere fact of thinking of them probably hurts your writing. Thinking about who'll be reading what you've written is the fastest way to completely freeze up.

You are writing for yourself. Always bear in mind this quote from writer and critic Cyril Connolly:

> *Better to write for yourself and have no public, than to write for the public and have no self.*

You always write best about your own private obsessions and things that interest you. Many well-known writers have said that they wrote their books because they were the kind they'd have liked to read themselves but couldn't find in bookshops or libraries. Follow this approach and write the kind of book you'd enjoy.

Draft, don't edit – yet!

Many beginner writers don't realise that writing is actually all about re-writing. When you begin, you're drafting, not producing a final script. *Drafting* is producing initial material that you then work with, refining, editing and polishing as you go. Drafting is a bit like producing clay, which you then shape into your pot or sculpture. Without the clay, you have nothing to work with and can't be creative. So when you begin, simply get some writing done, whatever it is, and no matter how relevant or irrelevant it seems to your final project. At the beginning stage of writing, you really don't want to think too much about what you're doing; you can always go back later. Just keep writing, and see where your drafting takes you. Don't be critical at this stage. (See Chapter 10 for more on rewriting and editing.)

Don't write too fast

Writing too quickly is one of the biggest mistakes many beginning writers make. They rush along, typing away at a rate of knots, with their eye on the end point – aiming to complete a whole novel, memoir or biography in a few weeks. Generally, this approach won't work. A few writers manage to write very quickly, but usually only when an idea has been incubating for a long time and they've been bursting to get it down on paper. For most writers, the process is much slower.

Writing quickly, in long bursts, means that you won't enjoy it. Your shoulders get stiff, your fingers feel like they're falling off, you dislike what you've written and you run out of steam.

You need to *slow down*. Advance in small steps. Relish the process of writing. Try writing longhand, enjoying the feel of the pen on the page. Try writing in a place that you like – perhaps in bed in the morning, in front of a roaring fire or in the garden. Think about the words you use and the way that you use them.

Initially writing brief pieces, short stories, vignettes or poems can be helpful. Polish these efforts and really make them work. Even if you want to embark on a long project, think in terms of breaking it down into short and manageable scenes or chapters. Then get writing.

Pace yourself

At first, writing little and often is important. Just get down some ideas, a few lines or phrases, a paragraph or two. Don't expect too much of yourself to begin with. Even if you aim to write a whole book, going slowly is still the best approach. Consider, even if you only write just one page a day, after 365 days you'll have 365 pages – enough to make a complete first draft. If you launch into a whole chapter or section right at the beginning, you may well find you can't sustain this writing pace and become discouraged or run out of steam.

You may feel that you can complete a short piece in a morning. But even a line or two of poetry, a phrase that works, a beautiful or surprising image, can be a real achievement.

At least to begin with, little and often works best. Aiming to write for ten or fifteen minutes every day and achieving it is better than setting yourself the target of writing for a whole morning or evening and then feeling that you've fallen short. As you get into the writing process, you'll find that you can keep at it for longer.

Set yourself targets, but keep them simple.

Put aside your ego

Forget your ego. If you're writing for fame and fortune, to get your own back on people you feel have slighted you or because you want to show off your skills, you're not likely to produce your best work.

Instead, put aside all thoughts of what will happen to your writing. Try moving forward humbly, taking small steps, advancing bit by bit, working hard and trying to learn as much as you can from the people who've gone before you. Enjoy the journey and do the very best that you can.

Playing with Words

The English language is one of the richest in the world, with a huge vocabulary to draw on. Apparently English contains over half a million words – and yet a normal working vocabulary uses only about 15,000 of them.

Most writers could benefit from expanding their vocabulary. You don't have to use long, obscure words when a more familiar one is appropriate, though – doing so can just seem pretentious; but, as a writer, having more words at your disposal is useful. Words are your tools, and some you may not know will do the job far better than the ones you do.

If you're reading and come across a word you don't know the meaning of, *stop and look it up*. Too often you may think you sort of vaguely know what the word means and move on. You only realise you don't really when someone else asks you to define it.

As a writer, you should really love words. Collect good ones and store them away for future use.

Try these playing with words exercises. Write down a list of words that you really like and love the sound of. Construct sentences around them.

Get a dictionary and find a word you don't know. Read the definition. Write a couple of sentences using the new word.

Making verbs stronger

Using strong verbs is one of the quickest ways to invigorate your writing. You may be tempted to be lazy and use an obvious word such as 'went'. Think of stronger words, depending on *how* the person went: did she stroll, rush, limp, hobble, leap, ride, glide, shuffle?

Avoid using the passive voice. 'The man stroked the dog' is stronger than 'The dog was stroked by the man'.

Taking out adverbs and adjectives

An *adverb* is a part of speech used to provide more information about a verb (a word describing an action); for example, 'Mary sings *beautifully*' or 'The midwife waited *patiently* through the labour'. Deleting the adverbs is one of the best ways to strengthen the verbs you use because you have to make them work harder.

Taking out all the adjectives also makes your writing more punchy. An *adjective* describes a property of a noun; for example, 'The *hairy* dog stank'. Think about how you can communicate what you want to say without using lots of adjectives.

Writing in different tenses

When you start writing, you can be confused as to whether to write in the present or past tense. Try out both ways of telling a story or writing a poem.

Actually, the choice of tense is arbitrary because, in a narrative, the 'past' isn't really past and the 'present' isn't really present. Only the reader's time, as she reads your work, is real.

Using the present tense gives an immediacy to a piece of writing; events seem to be happening now. The present tense can also be useful in a story in which you're switching between two timeframes, for instance a 'now' in which the character is remembering and a 'then' in which the remembered event happened. The present tense is often ideal for poetry, but it can be hard to handle in a long narrative and may even seem clumsy and contrived.

Avoiding cliché

A *cliché* is a worn-out phrase, a figure of speech whose effectiveness has been lost through overuse and excessive familiarity. If you use clichés too often, your writing will seem dull and uninteresting.

However, don't let the thought of using clichés get you down. Most writing uses them occasionally. Only when a text is littered with clichés are they problematic.

When you're drafting, clichés can be a kind of shorthand to help you convey what you mean. You can replace them later with fresher images – if you can't, try deleting the phrases entirely.

Doing writing exercises

When you're learning to write, completing some *writing exercises* – short pieces to get you going and help you try out different ideas and techniques – is a great idea. Try the exercises in this book and see how you get on.

Attending a writing class can be helpful. Your tutor can give you lots of exercises to complete and you may have to read your work to the group, thus gaining useful feedback to help you develop your writing skills.

Writing exercises resemble playing scales to a musician. Often people say they hate practising scales, but I loved them when I first learned the violin.

I knew all the notes so all I had to do was try to make the warmest, fullest, loveliest sound I could. Writing exercises are the same. You know what you're meant to do, so you can concentrate on the way you do it without worrying about creating an idea or fitting it in to what you're already writing.

Exercise pieces don't need to be finished or highly polished. They're simply ways for you to explore techniques in your writing and help you develop more confidence in your craft.

Learning from imitation

New writers are often terribly afraid of *plagiarising* – of copying others' work. As a result they refuse to read good fiction because they don't want to be influenced by it.

This situation's a great pity. Many, many writers have been influenced by the rhythm and powerful language of the King James Bible. Many others have been influenced by reading the work of Shakespeare, Jane Austen and other great writers. You can learn a vast amount by imitating the techniques of great writers.

Oddly, people apply this principle to other art forms, but seldom to writing. Art students sit in galleries copying the works of the great artists into their sketchbooks. They do so to find out how to compose great pictures; how to handle perspective, use colour, create particular effects with pen or ink. Artists are encouraged to sketch, create scrapbooks and think about the influences on their work. And yet writers often expect themselves to come up with everything entirely out of their own heads.

Choose a book by a favourite author. Find a passage of description, dialogue or action. Now imitate it and apply it to your own characters and situation. Borrow phrases, use the same sentence structure and copy some of the words. See what writing a really great piece of prose feels like.

Although this exercise can initially seem really strange and difficult, it can really help free you up to imitate the rhythm, sound and feel of really good prose. Imitating someone else's work means you internalise it and make it feel your own. You don't have to use the same words, situations or images, but you can learn how to use vivid imagery in description and to write rhythmically, powerfully, plainly or colourfully.

Much literature is actually dependant on what has come before – so-called *intertextuality*. Some academics think that all writing is created in reference to earlier texts, whether their authors know it or not. Some famous works of literature that refer to others include:

- ✔ James Joyce's *Ulysses*, which, as the very title gives away, is based on Homer's classic work. *Ulysses* is awash with parody, pastiche, quotations from literature and allusions to many different works.

- ✔ John Steinbeck's *East of Eden*, which is a retelling of the Genesis story, set in the Salinas Valley of Northern California.

- ✔ Jane Smiley's *A Thousand Acres*, which is a subversive retelling of *King Lear*, set in rural Iowa.

Films are also often based on the retelling of works of literature. *The Lion King* is a re-telling of *Hamlet*; the events in *Jesus of Montreal* closely parallel the New Testament passion story. The characters in *The Matrix* have symbolic names: Neo is an anagram of One, and he plays the role of a saviour figure, and the name Trinity has obvious Christian symbolism.

In addition, many books refer to or echo famous fictional incidents. In her highly successful Harry Potter series, J. K. Rowling draws on many different sources, such as Greek and Roman mythology and Christian symbolism.

Developing an ear for good prose

Both poetry and prose need to sound good when read aloud. Writing has a rhythm, which is all-important. Sometimes when you're writing you recognise that you need a two- rather than three-syllable word, or that a sentence should be longer, or that you need to stop just there. Read your work aloud and listen to it. You'll feel when your tongue trips up over words, a sentence is too long or short, a word's missing or it just sounds wrong.

Read poetry, even if you're not writing it. In poetry, the sounds of the words – the rhythm and rhyme – are crucial.

Writing comes in so many different styles that generalising about what makes a piece of good writing is impossible. Read a passage of fancy prose, for example the opening of Vladimir Nabokov's *Lolita*. Look at how he uses words and *alliteration* (words starting with the same initial letter or sound), mixes short and long sentences, and asks and answers questions.

Then read a calm and plain piece of writing, say from a child's book, but which still manages to be powerful. Compare how the two authors achieved the rhythm, structure and emotion in their writing.

To write like the great writers, try imitating them – purely as an exercise.

✔ Try writing a piece in the style of *Lolita* – something complex, original and rhythmic.

✔ Imitate a writer with a clear, unfussy style. Aim for utter simplicity.

✔ Take a poem and adapt it, copying the structure, rhythm and rhyme.

Chapter 2

Getting into the Write Mind

. . . .

In This Chapter

▶ Making a time and place to write

▶ Ignoring distractions

▶ Conquering that blank page

▶ Keeping track of different versions

▶ Embracing the unknown

. . . .

*Y*ou face so many distractions to getting down to write that you need to find the best time and place to do so. Are you a morning or an evening person? Do you work best in silence and solitude or with background noise and people around you? How can you tempt yourself to your desk or computer and reward yourself when you've spent time there? Do you tend to be disorganised and lose track of things and can you devise systems to make you function better?

Unfortunately, many people think of writing as a form of inspiration and wait for the muse to descend and strike them. You may wait a very long time! Thinking of writing as a job like any other can help. You need a routine, a place and some discipline.

In this chapter, I help you decide when and where to write and offer advice to help overcome some common roadblocks.

Finding a Time to Write

Create a time for yourself to write that suits you. If you're an early bird, get up and write while everyone else is still asleep. If you're a night owl, write after the children go to bed or while your partner's watching television. If you have a regular evening alone, make it your writing time. Consider writing in your lunchtimes or keeping a morning or afternoon free at weekends.

Many writers recommend that you write every day, even if you only manage a few paragraphs. If doing so is really impossible due to work or family commitments, just write as often as you can, but at least once or twice a week.

Block out your writing time in your diary and stick to it. If you like, think of this activity as making an appointment with yourself. This time is just as important as any other engagement you make.

Writing in a Room of Your Own

Finding a place to write is equally as important as finding the time to do so. You may be lucky enough to have an office or study in your house, the 'room of your own' that Virginia Woolf thought necessary for writing fiction. You may be able to organise this room exactly as you want it and go there every day to write. But for most people, devoting a whole room to writing just isn't possible.

Even if you have the space to make your own writing room, locking yourself away to write may not be the best plan for you. Graham Greene, when asked why he wrote at his kitchen table, responded that if he had a study it would be a 'room of torture' and he'd never go in it!

The next sections consider possible writing spaces.

Clearing the kitchen table

If you live alone or have the house to yourself during the day, follow Graham Greene's example and work in the kitchen. Just clear some space, wipe down the table and off you go. Or perhaps a table in the living room or bedroom is more useful.

Of course, using the kitchen table doesn't work if you share the house with others or are likely to be constantly interrupted. If you have to keep clearing your writing stuff away, a dedicated space may be better.

Retreating to the garden shed

Some people find that a desk in a shed at the bottom of the garden is the perfect location for writing. Famous shed-writers include Roald Dahl and Philip Pullman.

Your shed has to be warm, dry and not filled to the brim with stuff. Wedging yourself in between the lawnmower and an outgrown bicycle doesn't make you feel creative. Also, make your shed secure so you don't have to carry all your equipment down there every time you want to write. Anything that makes the process of sitting down to write harder is to be avoided at all costs.

Tucking away in a corner

Your workplace can have an important effect on your creativity. If you can, find a corner, perhaps by a window with a view or in a light spot in your living room or bedroom, to create a little place of your own.

All you need is a desk or table for your laptop or notebook. You can add a little vase of flowers or a candle to light when you're working or something else as a focal point when you're staring blankly into space!

Make a space dedicated to your creative writing alone. If you work at home or have a home office, that desk may be piled high with correspondence, bills, tax returns and so on, which offer too many distractions and may not be conducive to creativity.

Finding a place nearby

If you really can't find somewhere to work at home, consider some alternatives. Home is particularly difficult if you have a noisy and demanding family; going out of the house may be the only solution.

Sometimes your writing space can be just around the corner – a friend who works all day may loan you a room in her house – especially if you can be company for a cat or dog or wait in for a delivery in exchange.

I even know one woman who, when her children were small, had a study in the basement. If her children knew she was in the house, however, they'd evade the nanny and keep coming down on one pretext or another. Ultimately, she pretended to go to work, saying goodbye to the children and slamming the door as she went. Each day she'd wait a minute or two and then creep in through the basement door to her study.

Writers favouring cafés

Many well-known writers have written in cafés, including Ernest Hemingway, Jean-Paul Sartre and Simone de Beauvoir in Paris and Henry James in Venice. J. K. Rowling wrote the first Harry Potter novel in many different cafés in Edinburgh, apparently mainly because walking to one was the best way to get her baby to sleep!

The Austrian writer Alfred Polgar once described the literary café as 'a place where people want to be alone, but need company to do so'.

Writing in cafés and libraries

Cafés and libraries are the most obvious places in which to work. A library is quiet, warm, has all that reference material freely available and the staff are usually helpful and friendly. Many writers, however, prefer a café. You can sit and have a drink as you work, watch the world go by and even write about other customers if you feel lost for ideas.

Remember that you're taking up a table in the café – so don't make one coffee last all day and tip generously!

Unless you live in the back of beyond – in which case finding peace and quiet shouldn't be a problem – a café is bound to be nearby.

Assembling Your Writing Tools

As a writer, you need some basic necessities – pen and paper are the obvious! Here's a list:

- **A surface to write on:** Many writers don't have their own desks – they use whatever table's available in the house. Some writers find that their usual work stations are too cluttered with paperwork to be conducive to creativity so they take their laptops to another spot in the house – or even to the garden shed. If you decide to invest in a writing desk, make sure the height's right.

- **A comfortable chair:** If you're going to spend any time at your desk or work surface, you need to be comfortable. You need a chair that supports your back and is the correct height for the surface you're working at. You can buy special orthopaedic stools and chairs if you're prone to back problems.

- **A large supply of paper:** If you use a computer to write on, print out your work in order to read it properly – editing on-screen is difficult. Buying paper in bulk from specialist office suppliers is cheaper, and many deliver to your door.

- **A notebook:** Every writer should have one. Large or small, plain or lined, expensive or cheap, find a notepad that works for you. You'll probably need several of them, so buy a few at once; if you fall in love with a certain kind of notebook, you'll always have a supply. Use your notebook to jot down ideas, write in when you're away from your desk, sketch out your thoughts or even stick in newspaper cuttings, photos or pictures that will be useful for your writing.

- **Pens:** An ordinary biro is just fine, but some writers prefer the rollerball type of pen, which is smoother and glides more easily over the page. Select the colour of ink you prefer. If you enjoy the physical sensation of writing and like the look of the ink on the page, you'll be encouraged to write more. A red pen is useful for editing.

- **A desk lamp or good lighting:** Working by a window in daylight is best but not always possible, especially in the winter months. Use an Anglepoise-type desk lamp or strong-enough lighting to ensure you're not working in shadow. Some people think that neon lighting is bad for creativity and causes headaches, so use an alternative if you find it affects you.

- **Comfortable clothes:** You won't write well if you're physically uncomfortable. Wear loose, comfortable clothes that won't restrict or annoy you when you're trying to work.

- **A heater:** You sit still for long periods when you're writing and can become very cold. Keeping your writing space warm with a little heater makes a lot of difference to your creativity. Writing in a garret is all very well, but you don't have to suffer for your art in this way. Knowing you'll be too cold – or too hot – is a good way of avoiding sitting down to write.

- **Reference books:** Every writer should have:

  - A good dictionary

  - A thesaurus

And worthwhile extras are:

  - *Fowler's Modern English Usage*, which covers grammar, syntax and how to avoid common mistakes.

  - Lynne Truss's *Eats, Shoots and Leaves*, a useful guide to punctuation and why it matters.

  - A dictionary of quotations.

If sitting at your messy desk doesn't inspire you, take your laptop or notebook into the garden and write with the trees rustling and birds singing around you.

Avoiding Distractions

Deciding you'll write on Saturday and then, when the weekend comes, feeling you'd rather go to the park is part of the writer's lot. Possibly a friend rings and suggests a shopping trip. Even if you resist at first, when you sit at your desk and nothing happens, changing your mind and calling back is difficult to resist. Maybe Thursday's your writing night, and it just so happens that this Thursday is the only time you can make that film you really, really want to see; or a friend is passing through town and suggests a quick drink; or you're just too tired after a busy week and you really need a night off – and so on.

And then, what happens when you do sit down to write? First you check your emails just in case something urgent has popped up. Then you look at the weather forecast for tomorrow. Your desk is a mess – perhaps you ought to tidy it first. You're thirsty, so you make a quick cup of tea. Are there any biscuits? The tin's empty, so you make a piece of toast. You sit down again. You haven't vacuumed under the desk for ages and can't possibly concentrate on writing with all that dust lurking. The cleaner needs a new bag, which takes a few minutes to find and fix. Ping! Another email comes in. Now you just have to read it – and quickly respond to it. A whole hour has gone by, and you haven't written a thing.

Sometimes when you sit down to write, doing almost anything else seems preferable. Amazingly, even completing your tax return can seem more inviting. Every writer feels this way – you're not alone. Somehow you need to find a way to overcome these distractions.

Here are a few ideas:

- ✔ Take the phone off the hook or switch to answerphone.
- ✔ Put a 'do not disturb' notice on the door.
- ✔ Close down your email during your writing time.
- ✔ Delete those time-wasting games from your computer.
- ✔ Make a flask of tea or coffee so you don't keep nipping to the kitchen.
- ✔ Tell friends and family that you're never available between certain hours or on a particular day or evening.

Overcoming the Blank Page Syndrome

Something about the blank page or computer screen is terrifying. All potential and possibility is there. You're going to write a work of genius – or you're not going to write anything at all. All the ideas, excitement and images in your head, when they're finally written down in black and white, can fall far short of what you intended. You have an idea for a story; but where to begin? You write down a line and it seems banal. You cross it out. You take another clean page. Suddenly your writing is too real, too confronting.

If this scenario happens to you, take no notice; just write something. What you put down is irrelevant. As you write, things start to loosen up a bit. Musicians, before practising a piece of music, play scales to warm up their instruments, lips or fingers. Tennis players knock up to get their eye in and their muscles loosened before beginning a match. Just getting going is what's important!

Understanding the causes

Blank page syndrome occurs for several reasons:

- **Perfectionism:** When you start writing, you want it to be perfect – anything less and you're discouraged. You feel as though someone's sitting on your shoulder criticising every word you write.

  No one ever wrote a masterpiece straight off, with no editing, revising or rewriting. Even the great works of literature or bestselling books aren't perfect. Just concentrate on doing the best you can right now. As someone once said to me, 'In trying to write a great novel, the possibility always exists that you might write a good one.'

- **Self-consciousness:** Constantly thinking about what other people will think of your work is another problem. Worrying about your mother, partner or boss's opinion is likely to freeze you completely. You work best when you get in the flow and stop being aware of yourself, whether you're dancing, playing a sport or taking part in any artistic activity.

  When you're writing, just think about that. Forget about what other people will think. You're writing for you.

- **Procrastination:** Human beings are naturally lazy and would rather put off until tomorrow anything involving work or effort. Unlike with school or work, nobody's keeping you in line with your creative writing. Doing it is completely up to you.

  Give yourself a reward when you manage to get down to work. For example, don't allow yourself a coffee, glass of wine or piece of chocolate until you've actually completed some writing.

✔ **Fear of failure:** Many people are so afraid of failing that they never try anything. Don't set your sights too high. If you to write a prize-winning novel, you may well not succeed. But if your goal is writing to please yourself, failure isn't an issue.

Not telling anyone that you're writing is one way of dealing with fear of failure. Just get on with it, slowly and in secret. Then, if you decide to abandon the project, no one will know and you won't have to feel that you've failed.

✔ **Fear of yourself:** Sometimes others' opinions can actually be less scary than what may be lurking in your own unconscious mind. When writing, some people find that they experience powerful and unexpected emotions. If you're writing about lost love, for example, you may experience those raw and disturbing emotions all over again. Sometimes writers find they write things they never expected to – about horrific events such as murder or rape; so they censor themselves and focus on safer subjects.

Accept that experiencing strong emotions is part of the process of writing and don't try to block them. If you find yourself getting into scary territory, make sure you have someone to speak to when you end a writing session. Phone a friend or meet someone, or consider joining a writers' group for support.

Writing your way off the blank page

Set a timer for 10 to 15 minutes and do one of the following exercises to help you get started. Write without stopping, going back, crossing out or pausing, until the timer goes off.

✔ **Freewriting:** Just write the first thing that comes into your head, on any subject that occurs to you. Choose a season, or something you like or hate. Or think of an object – an old photo, a flower, an ornament – and write about that.

When you look back through this passage you may find a phrase or idea that is perfect for the beginning of a story, poem or other piece of writing.

✔ **Three random words:** Get a dictionary and pick three words at random. This exercise works best with three nouns – for example, ribbon, fork and buzzard. Then write a short piece connecting these three things.

✔ **Starting line:** Open a book or newspaper and take a line at random; use it as your opening sentence. Or think of a simple phrase:

- He opened the door and . . .
- She answered the phone and . . .
- We stepped out of the car and . . .

Carry on the story as your imagination dictates.

✔ **Chained to the desk:** If the easier exercises aren't working, try this one. Make an agreement with yourself that you'll sit at your desk for 20 minutes. Writing creatively is the only activity you're allowed to do. You're not permitted to get up from the desk, do any other activity on the computer or doodle in your notebook. Set the timer and begin. Sitting doing nothing is so boring that you'll almost certainly start writing.

If your writing difficulty persists even when you do this exercise every day, you may have some deep-seated resistance to writing. You may like to discuss this issue with a counsellor!

No one's forcing you to write. Sometimes people feel that they ought to be writing and create much stress and misery by forcing themselves to do so. Writing is difficult and challenging, without a doubt, but if you really aren't getting anywhere maybe you need to give yourself a break from it. Maybe too much is going on in your life for you to concentrate on writing or you're just not ready for it yet.

Be inspired by other writers – not intimidated

If you're experiencing problems writing, looking at the work of other writers can be helpful. Find a book you love – a really great book – and pick a sentence from it. For example, on page 80 of my copy of Graham Greene's *The Quiet American* is the sentence: *'A moment,' I said.* This line isn't especially eye-catching! Take a look at one of Shakespeare's less well-known plays, such as *King John*; or a mediocre line from a poem by one of your favourite poets. Realise that great writers can write indifferent works and that not every sentence has to be a work of genius.

Another useful exercise is reading a page or two from a book you think is terrible. Of course you could do better – get started right away!

Dealing with writer's block

An extended case of blank page syndrome is known as *writer's block*. Most writers experience this problem at some point – it can last for days, weeks or even years. Henry Roth's writer's block persisted for 60 years after the publication of his first highly acclaimed novel, *Call It Sleep*! Possibly his block was a combination of depression, political conflicts and an unwillingness to confront his past problems.

In most cases, though, overcoming a block is quite easy. Instead of sitting at your desk and berating yourself, try one of the following:

- ✔ **Go outdoors:** Take a walk, then come back and try again.
- ✔ **Go to an art exhibition:** Really study the exhibits, and then go to a nearby café and write.
- ✔ **Listen to music:** Write a piece connected with the music.
- ✔ **Meditate:** Empty your mind or do relaxation exercises to take the pressure off.
- ✔ **Have a change of scene:** Find somewhere else to write, perhaps a beautiful or inspiring location.
- ✔ **Find a writing buddy:** Make appointments to sit together and write. Don't talk to one another about what you're writing or share your work, just do the writing.

Separating Drafting and Editing

Two completely different processes are at work when you write – drafting and editing. *Drafting* is the process of simply getting the words down on the page and creating something to work with. *Editing* means going back over your work and improving on it. See Chapter 10 for more information on rewriting and editing.

When drafting, just getting the material down on the page or computer screen is what matters. Don't judge, criticise or think about it. Just write, and keep on writing.

Thinking about whether what you're writing is good or bad, works or doesn't work is pointless. Later on, you can go back, read through it and discard what you don't need. If your writing doesn't work to begin with, have confidence that you can make it do so later on.

Don't get hung up on what doesn't work. Writing is a bit like building a house. First, you have to dig the foundations – similar to the process of incubating a project, thinking about what you want to write. Second, you put up the scaffolding, which resembles drafting. Third, you build your house. Fourth, you remove your scaffolding. View the material you don't use as scaffolding – you needed it to get your real work written, but then you had to take it away. Regarding material you delete as scaffolding rather than rubbish is more positive!

Developing a Routine and Sticking to It

Be regular and orderly in your life so that you may be violent and original in your work.

Gustave Flaubert

A general idea exists that creative types must be disorganised and chaotic. In fact, writers and artists are as varied in this regard as any other people. Some are tidiness freaks, others thrive in a mess. Recognising your ideal writing environment is all that matters.

Generally, though, some kind of routine and order in your life is helpful if you want to be creative. Sticking to a structure can protect you from the onslaughts of your unconscious and the chaos of your project – especially at the beginning.

On the other hand, cleaning and tidying can be a real distraction from getting writing done. Unfortunately, keeping on top of housework resembles painting the Forth Bridge – an endless process. You don't want to live in total chaos, but sometimes lowering your standards is necessary to give yourself more time for writing.

Organising your writing, though, is crucial for motivation. You need to know where your notes are and which version of a piece of writing is the most recent. Hunting through computer files and piles of paper when you're ready to start writing can be demoralising. You can employ various techniques for controlling the chaos in your writing life.

Using a notebook

Notebooks are wonderful things for writers. I have a whole collection of them, for different projects and ideas, in different colours, shapes and sizes. Nothing makes me want to write more than a new notebook.

Carry a notebook around with you wherever you go. Sometimes an idea comes to you when you're relaxed and far away from home – on a train, on the top of a bus, sitting in a friend's garden. Keep one on your bedside table – often an idea occurs to you in the night, and you may forget it by morning.

Also consider using your notebook to write during dead bits of time – waiting at the dentist, in your lunch hour, on the commute to and from work. Jot down ideas or sections of work for which you don't yet have a real place. Note down pieces of information you need, bits of research and inspiring quotes. Stick in photos or cuttings.

Beware the thief. If you carry your notebook around with you wherever you go, the possibility always exists that you'll lose it or have it stolen! Losing your work is a heartbreaking experience, which has happened to me and many well-known writers.

Remember to put your name, address and telephone number in your notebook in case it falls into the hands of the police or an honest person. Consider photocopying important pages so you have them safe at home. Or use a ring-bound notebook and take the pages out as they get written on. Many a writing project has been abandoned because of a stolen notebook.

Storing and filing ideas

If you tend to work on loose paper rather than in a notebook, getting a ring-binder or box-file into which you can put anything related to your writing is a good idea. Keeping everything in the same place is very helpful. Newspaper cuttings relating to your story, scribbled notes on the backs of envelopes, loose sheets of writing – you'll know where they all are.

A scrapbook for your project is another possibility. Use it to store ideas, sketches, photos, cuttings and so on.

Keeping track on your computer

Computers are wonderful tools, but many writers complain of chaos in their filing, especially when they have several versions of a piece of writing. Save your work regularly and label different versions with a number or the date. Create a separate folder for your project and regularly back it up. You can set your back-up system to automatically save Word or other word-processing programs regularly – mine is set to save every ten minutes.

Forgetting to change the title of a file when you work on a revised version is the most common way of losing material. Change the title of the file as soon as you start work on a new version. Also avoid creating parallel files – working on two different versions at the same time is a nightmare.

Whether you keep all versions of your story is up to you. I usually hold on to them until I've finished the work and am satisfied with it. Other people keep every version indefinitely, thinking that the different drafts may be of interest to posterity!

Once a week or so, back up all your documents onto a CD or external drive to avoid the horror of losing work when a computer crashes or gets corrupted.

If you're really worried about losing data, print out a hard copy of your work as you go along and keep it somewhere safe. You can also save data by emailing it to someone you trust.

Learning to Live with a Degree of Chaos

Any writing project, even a short poem, takes time to complete. Not knowing how your work will turn out is one of the difficult things about creative writing, especially in the beginning. This not knowing is sometimes hard to live with.

People writing a novel often feel that they have to know the ending before they begin, or have at least some idea of how things are going to turn out. In truth, many writers don't have the slightest idea. Writing is taking a great step into the unknown.

Realising the importance of not knowing

Admitting that you really don't have a clue where you're going or what you're doing with your writing can be difficult. Just saying 'I don't know' can actually be quite useful, though. Knowing that you don't know is the first step to finding something out. Not knowing leaves you open to many possibilities; you can explore, try out different ideas and enjoy a journey of discovery. Lack of knowledge can very liberating.

Medieval Christian mystics called the process of relinquishing all images and preconceptions of God in order to get closer to what He really is, the 'Cloud of Unknowing'. This process involves letting go of everyday rational modes of thought and accepting how much you don't know and don't understand. Writing creatively is a bit like the Cloud of Unknowing. The process involves delving into your imagination and unconscious mind, tapping into areas you don't usually access.

Realising that you don't know is the first vital stage in every act of problem-solving. By moving forward into that space of not knowing, accepting that your mind is a blank and you really don't know where to go next, you'll feel free to try out different approaches and see where they take you.

Taking time to develop your ideas

New writers sometimes rush at the task and think that they can dash it off reasonably quickly and easily. When this scenario doesn't actually happen, they then get discouraged. In fact, the writing of most books, poems or stories is far more chaotic than sitting down, starting at the beginning and working through to the end. Ideas come at you, and you can't keep track of them. The narrative splinters off in different directions, and you don't know which to choose. A character you thought was unimportant suddenly starts taking over your narrative and the hero unexpectedly turns out to be up to no good. A poem you thought would be short runs on for pages and you don't know what to do with it. A piece of research makes you completely re-evaluate the book you're working on or see things in a completely new light. When writing, always expect the unexpected.

Writing is a process that takes time to germinate, grow and develop. A story, novel or poem won't come to you complete; it'll emerge gradually, revealing itself only over time. Relaxing and enjoying the journey is thus important. Pressurising yourself to get everything finished quickly doesn't usually help creativity and won't produce your best work.

Real-world examples of writing chaos

Even novels regarded as masterpieces have led their authors astray, for example:

✔ Fyodor Dostoevsky's *The Idiot* is a fine example of how chaotic the composition of a work of fiction can be. According to the introduction to the Penguin edition by the translator David Magarshack, Dostoevsky started with the idea of writing a book about 'the perfect man'. He wrote eight versions of the first draft, in which the hero belonged to different families and underwent many melodramatic adventures. As Dostoevsky's notes and correspondence have survived, you can see that in some versions the protagonist marries one of the two women he loves, in the others he doesn't. Feeling he was getting nowhere, Dostoevsky then scrapped this entire opening of the novel and started again. At one stage he was tearing up pages as quickly as he could write them. As he had to write the novel in instalments for publication, he had to complete and send off sections without knowing how the novel was going to turn out. After the publication of the second part, he completely changed his plan and, before sitting down to write the third part, confessed to his editor that he was 'disgusted with it'. At one stage he despaired of ever being able to finish the novel and debated delaying the publication of the fourth and final part.

✔ Philip Pullman, author of the bestselling His Dark Materials trilogy, has written about the process of starting on the first book, *Northern Lights.* He said that what came to him first was a feeling: 'Just a sense. Not a picture, not a character, not a theme.' Initially he couldn't even begin writing: 'I just sat there at my desk for days and days, for weeks, actually, in what would have looked, if anyone had been there to see, like a sort of stupor, a day-dream.' He tried out names, scribbled a word here or there, drafted the first chapter and rewrote it over and over again, aware that something wasn't right.

Then eventually the solution came, and he was able to get going and keep writing – for another 1,300 pages. But, as he says, 'It took weeks of sitting there just idly waiting and writing the same thing over and over again' before the breakthrough came.

✔ The First World War poet Wilfred Owen developed shell-shock and was sent to Craiglockhart War Hospital, where, in October 1917, he wrote the first known draft of *Dulce et Decorum Est.* After the first draft, Owen revised the poem continuously. All the drafts are in the English Faculty Library at Oxford University and seeing how the poet worked on his original idea is fascinating. The passage dealing with shelling and poison gas was originally much longer. Owen deleted some *onomatopoeic* language (words sounding like the type of thing they're describing) – 'fup, fop, fup' – because it failed to evoke the true horror of the bombardment for him. He tried several 'g' words – 'gargling', 'gurgling', 'goggling' – before settling on 'guttering'.

Chapter 3

Finding Material to Work With

*M*ost fiction comes from your own experience and your own emotions. The poet William Wordsworth once famously said that poetry was 'emotion recollected in tranquillity'. Both aspects – emotion and calm recollection – are equally important in creative writing. Your emotions are what drive you, what make you want to express whatever it is that you want to express. Even if your aim is to articulate an idea, that idea resonates with powerful emotions for you.

You need to develop a certain distance from your emotions, however, in order to write about them effectively and communicate them to others. And you need to develop a story, situation or scenario to enable those emotions to build up and be released in a way that makes sense of the experience to yourself and to your readers.

Writing from Experience

In one sense, everything that you write about is connected intimately with your own experience because that's what connects you to the world. Everything you see, feel, think or imagine comes from you, or is filtered through you.

Philosophers through the ages have struggled with the fact that humans can never be sure that one individual's experience is the same as anyone else's. For example, no one can prove that my subjective experience of the colour red is actually the same as yours.

Realising your own wide experience

People read fiction and autobiography, watch films and read poems to discover other people's experience of the world. Reading about a character in a story reacting in a certain way or hearing a poem and thinking, 'Yes! I've felt just like that', is wonderful. And coming across a new image in a poem or piece of writing that causes you to see things in a fresh and different light is amazing. Readers also love to experience, through other people, situations they've never encountered themselves, such as what it would be like to be stranded on a desert island or involved in a major disaster.

Your individual experience is multi-faceted and involves many elements, such as:

- Your memories, which often stretch back much further than you think, to early childhood.
- Your relationships with other people and their effects on you.
- The information and knowledge you've gathered from your schooling and beyond.
- The music you've listened to.
- The books you've read.
- The films you've seen.
- The places you've visited, countries you've travelled to and the people you've met along the way.

Your experience also includes your dreams, hopes and fears, your sorrows and joys, the people you've loved and those you've lost, the people you've hated, envied, fought with or betrayed.

Mining memories

Your life and thus your story is made of memories; without these recollections, you wouldn't be who you are. Recalling memories and writing about them is a really helpful way to get started in creative writing. You'll probably be amazed at how much you can remember.

As you grow older, you start to forget things that happened when you were younger. Even if 'younger' is only a couple of years ago, you can bring back memories by:

✔ Re-reading old diaries or journals. An old diary is a great tool for when you come to write later on in life.

✔ Going through old photographs can trigger memories and provide forgotten visual details.

✔ Talking to grandparents, old family friends, your siblings and others to find out information about the past that you may have forgotten or remember only vaguely.

✔ Heading up to the attic. Most people hoard things, and an afternoon spent going through a box in the attic can help bring back the past. Objects have a useful way of reminding you of things that happened, and of scents, sounds and colours.

The more you find out about your family and your past, the more you may discover that you don't know. Every family has its secrets, and subjects that people don't talk about. Exploring these murky areas can be fun – and sometimes frightening, too. Make a list of all the things you don't know about your family. Then start to find them out!

Ask elderly relatives to write down important things they remember or talk to them and record the conversation.

You can write up these memories, using as many details and as much of your relative's voice as possible, as the basis for a memoir or short story.

Try the following exercises. Write even if you think you can't remember; just make things up. Some of these exercises may not work for you, but you may be amazed at how much comes back from early childhood when you put your mind to recalling and writing about it.

✔ You're a baby lying in your cot. Describe this scene, concentrating especially on your sensations.

✔ Write about the first thing you remember about your nursery or school. Recall a teacher, the classroom or playground, or another child.

✔ Write about your first best friend.

✔ Write about a pet, or a friend's pet if you didn't have one.

✔ Write about a favourite item of clothing, when you wore it and how you felt.

The malleability of memory

Scientists studying how memories are formed are coming to the conclusion that much memory is created. Every time you recall a memory to consciousness, you change it. You're also highly influenced by what others say about your memories. For example, an oft-repeated family memory – 'Do you remember when we . . .' – tends to influence how you recall it.

Research into the 'false memory' syndrome also backs up the way in which people elaborate memories and then take them to be real. False memory syndrome is the belief that you remember events, especially traumatic ones, that haven't actually occurred.

So when you're using a memory in a piece of writing, feel free to make changes to it – that memory probably isn't exactly what happened in the first place.

Making use of other people's experiences

Your own experience is ultimately the basis for all your writing, but you can also benefit from other people's knowledge and deeds. If you only write about what you know, or only write about yourself, other people may find it difficult to connect with your work.

You can find out about other people and their experiences by talking to them, observing how they behave and listening to their conversations with others. As a writer, you need to be curious about other people and what makes them tick. Watching other people is fascinating and can provide you with lots of material to utilise in your writing.

However, be careful of the pitfalls of including other's experiences in your writing:

- ✔ **Hurting others.** If you write about other people and they recognise themselves, they can be upset and angry.

- ✔ **Appropriating experience.** You run the risk of stealing other people's stories if you relate things that happened to others directly in your own work. Using other people's experience is only acceptable if you transform it in some way.

- ✔ **Getting blocked.** You may find that you struggle to write about people you know because you wonder what they will think after reading your work or worry about creating bad feeling.

- ✔ **Running the risk of libel.** If you use real people in your writing, giving them different names doesn't help in law if they're still recognisable. See the nearby sidebar on staying on the right side of the law.

A note on libel

UK libel laws are notoriously unpredictable and costly to address. If someone identifies herself as a character in a book, even if it is fictional, and can argue that the way she has been described is defamatory, she can sue for libel. *Defamed* means that a person is exposed to hatred or ridicule, is shunned, lowered in the estimation of 'right-thinking' people, or disparaged in his or her work.

As a sued author, if you can prove that what you wrote is true, you can take that line in defence – but this can be hard to do.

Libel actions can be incredibly costly, often running into hundreds of thousands of pounds. The loser almost always has to pay the costs of the winner, as well as damages.

Writing 'This is a work of fiction and any resemblance to actual persons is purely coincidental' in the preface doesn't protect you from accusations of libel. Most publishing companies now put the onus on authors to make sure their work contains no libellous statements, whether fictional or not.

Writing what you – and other people – know

One of the most true and simultaneously untrue statements ever made about creative writing is that you should write what you know. This approach is fine as far as it goes, but is ultimately rather limiting. If authors wrote only from experience, no historical, science fiction or fantasy novels would ever be written. Authors wouldn't describe characters they've never met or places they've never visited.

If you don't know something, you can always explore ways to find out about it. If you need information about a medical condition, for example, you can talk to someone who suffers from it, read a medical book or visit a website to research symptoms and treatments.

Many successful writers are successful because they research the world they are writing about so thoroughly. Patricia Cornwell, for example, took a job as a data programmer at a morgue that was run by a female medical examiner. Cornwell even became a volunteer police officer and worked every weekend for three years in order to attend an autopsy.

Engaging Emotions

Emotion is vital in any form of creative writing. Other kinds of writing may be about facts, but creativity trades in feeling. Many people write precisely because they want to communicate powerful emotions that have stirred them deeply, or because they want to explain how much something hurt or how beautiful it was.

Be careful when conveying emotions. If they're too raw or too personal, they don't communicate well to others. Too much emotion can seem sentimental or overwhelming, or make the reader uncomfortable. Emotions need to be the driving force behind your writing but don't let them intrude too obviously into it.

Not only the reader may find too much emotion off-putting, but also your own fear of your emotions can hold you back from writing, or even block you altogether. Writing about immediate personal experience or even a fantasy or something you've made up can make old fears and anxieties resurface – as well as joys, of course. Sometimes these emotions are very powerful, and can be disturbing, so you stop writing to protect yourself.

You may need to let some time elapse before you can write properly about things that are very close to you. You can go ahead and write out whatever you want in the white heat of your rage or grief. But go back to what you've written in a calmer frame of mind. You'll almost certainly find that it needs editing and pruning before you make it suitable for showing to others. On the other hand, getting something down in that first rush of feeling is extremely valuable – you can draw on it later and something of that raw energy may come across.

Try this exercise to harness your emotions on paper.

1. **Write down a variety of emotions – rage, jealousy, joy, anxiety, confusion, gratitude and so on – on separate pieces of paper.**

2. **Shuffle the papers and then pick one.**

3. **Write about a situation in which you felt this emotion.**

4. **Concentrate on the physical sensations.**

5. **Describe the emotion as a colour and a sound.**

Read through what you've written and then work this into a story or short piece of writing.

Writing as therapy

Writing has been used as a form of therapy in hospitals and prisons, and for people who've suffered traumatic experiences. Some people say that writing down what happened to them helps them to come to terms with the experience and then put it to one side. By recording what happened in black and white, the person can feel he no longer needs to hold on to his thoughts and memories, but can let go of them. However, don't forget that writing as therapy and writing to communicate to others are two different things.

Taking a Step Back

As a writer, distancing yourself from your own experience, at least to some degree, is important. In order to communicate what's in your mind to others, you need to be able to step back and observe what happened, not just see it from within. If you write just from within your own experience, you're so close to what you're writing that seeing it clearly is impossible. You can't create a picture that makes sense to others.

What you want to communicate to others is often a feeling, mood or situation that caused you to change or to see things in a new light. You may describe a moment of realisation, an insight or a shift into a new phase of life. In order to write about such details, you don't have to describe them exactly as they happened, or even as they happened to you. You can choose to change things in a way that is true to the emotions and feelings behind what you're describing, though not a literal truth.

These exercises may help you take a step back from writing about your experiences exactly as they happened and enable you to write more freely about the feelings involved:

- ✔ **Shifting into third-person voice.** Come up with a memory, something that happened to you before the age of, say, nine or ten. Write what you remember. Now change point of view. Give the child a name – any name – and write out the memory again, in the third-person voice.

- ✔ **Changing gender.** Take a memory and this time write about it happening to someone of the opposite sex. See how much this changes the story.

- ✔ **Finding the kernel.** Think about the core of the memory. Was it feeling lonely, losing something, receiving a gift? Take this kernel and write about it happening to someone else, in another time, another place, to a character of a different age, background or gender.

✔ **Altering the details.** How much do the details matter? Try changing the small things – the colour of a dress, the name of a house, the type of dog. What happens? Does it change things, and if so, why?

✔ **Finding an observer.** Write about a memory of you doing something, perhaps performing in a school play, running down a street, having an argument with someone. Now think of someone observing you and write what happens from the point of view of the observer.

When trying out these exercises, you may find some surprising things come up. People usually find that as the story moves away from themselves, it changes slightly, and often becomes more interesting. You want to communicate what's interesting about a situation, what is learned from it and what emotions are felt.

Trying Techniques to Transform Your Experiences

You put your experiences and emotions to use in your writing by shuffling them up and looking at them from different perspectives. The following sections talk about some of the lenses you can use to view your writing.

Making use of myth and reality

A myth tells a story that isn't true, that never happened in reality, but that reflects the inner truth of how people feel and relate to the world. A myth often helps people make sense of their lives and reveals things about human psychology that are hard to access in other ways. Myth is explained as what 'never was but always is'. The myths and fairy stories of the past can reveal the fact that human nature hasn't changed very much in hundreds or even thousands of years.

When you talk or write about yourself, you create myths and stories as a way of giving shape to your life and defining who you are. You may be the 'Ugly Duckling', the 'Cinderella' or the 'Beast tamed by his Beauty'. You might be the hero who does battle with monsters or the redeemer of your world. The outer monsters and demons who appear in fairy stories and mythology can easily be read as inner aspects of your personality. An ugly sister can be an aspect of your own jealousy and a hideous beast can be your own repressed anger and rage.

When you're writing creatively, in a sense your experience is always exaggerated, multiplied and made bigger, partly as a result of convention. For example, when actors appear on stage they wear thick make-up and rich costumes, and make exaggerated gestures to communicate to the audience. If someone with stage make-up walked down your local high street, he'd look completely wrong. Similarly, if someone in ordinary dress and speaking normally went on stage, he'd look wrong there too. He'd seem dull, out of place and a very poor actor. In the same way, when writing fiction you often use more poetic language, make characters larger than life, and tell more compact and exciting stories, than real life. Doing so doesn't actually make these stories 'untrue' – in fact, by decorating and enlarging the scale, we help the truth within the story to communicate better to others.

If you're having trouble writing, take a fairy story that you know and like and read the original. Then rework it, fitting your own life to the story and giving it a modern twist. For inspiration, look at the work of such writers as Angela Carter and Sara Maitland.

Being selective

Film director Alfred Hitchcock said, 'Drama is life with the dull bits cut out.' Never was a truer statement made! One of the main problems with writing from your own experience is the tendency to put in everything that happened, simply *because it happened!* Because it happened doesn't automatically mean that something's interesting.

Curb your self-indulgence. When writing about yourself or your own experiences, you sometimes forget that, while of course you're the most fascinating person on the planet, your readers probably don't feel the same way.

When writing for others, thinking about which aspects of your experience are interesting to others is vital. Everyone wants to find something of universal significance when they read – something that touches them and connects with their own life. At the same time, the material needs to be something different, to show readers something that they didn't know before.

Taking the periods or moments in life when something really significant happened – when your life took a turn for the better or for the worse, when an important choice had to be made, when you had to cope with a crisis or make a dramatic change in your life – is a helpful approach.

Linking turning points together can help you to clarify the significant moments in your life, which might make a good basis for a story. Try the following exercise:

1. **Plot your life as a series of six major turning points.**

2. **Take each turning point and write a story around it, restricting yourself to the time leading up to it and immediately afterwards.**

3. **See if you can link the stories together.**

Jumping in time

When writing narrative, watch out for creating a paragraph like this:

> For the next few days, nothing much happened. Jim got up every morning at about the same time and went through his usual routine, getting dressed, going to work, slaving away in front of his computer, coming home, eating his dinner, watching TV and going to bed.

Now, how entertaining is that? Just jumping to the next moment when something interesting happens is the best approach. The reader can imagine the missing details.

You realise that you can tell a story with snapshots from a timeline in this exercise:

1. **Imagine a couple cast away on a desert island after a boat wreck or plane crash.**

2. **Describe what is happening, spending five minutes on each time period:**

   - **An hour after they're washed ashore**

   - **A day later**

   - **A week later**

   - **A month later**

   - **A year later**

You can tell the whole story just by writing about these five periods of time – the readers' imaginations can fill in the gaps. They don't need to know about the days and weeks and months of unimaginable boredom in between!

Transforming fact into fiction

Because of the difficulties inherent in writing directly from and about life, many people decide to transform their life stories into fiction. Many novels, especially first novels, are disguised autobiographies – sometimes quite thinly disguised.

Simultaneously, you could argue that all autobiographical writing is in fact fictional, in the sense that:

- ✔ You select only part of the story.
- ✔ You're limited by your own knowledge and can't see things from another point of view.
- ✔ You may not remember the past accurately.
- ✔ You may consciously or unconsciously repress material you don't want to acknowledge.
- ✔ You may change or colour things that happened in order to protect people.

Accepting that, as you've already parted from 'the truth' (insofar as an ultimate or absolute truth about your experience can ever exist), you may as well go a step further and acknowledge that you're writing fiction makes sense. The fiction may be based on your life, or your own character or personality. But instead of sticking to what actually happened, you can let your imagination run free.

You may develop a wish-fulfilment fantasy (getting the right man or murdering your wife's lover) or a morality tale (warning others of the dangers of drug addiction). As you change the characters, they may take on a life of their own. In a poem, you might change the season when a bereavement took place to winter because it suits your mood, or change a colour from red to blue because it rhymes better. Or you may change the era or the place where you lived or where an event occurred to make a piece of writing more interesting. Whatever happens, and wherever your journey takes you, you may find that writing fiction is more fun.

Part II
Introducing the Elements of Creative Writing

'It's not been 20 wasted years on that desert island, oh no – Written on palm leaves, I've got a great story about a middle aged cheese-loving inventor called Horace & his clever dog, Comet – Horace & Comet battle against giant rabbits & evil penguins – There'll be a TV series, feature films, books, merchandising....'

In this part . . .

Writers, like all artists, use certain techniques to convey what they want to say. These techniques include revealing and conveying character, telling a story from a certain point of view, writing dialogue, using metaphors, similes and symbols, and structuring your story, play or poem.

This part explains all those techniques in detail and inspires you to try them out.

Chapter 4

Creating Characters

. . . .

. . . .

Character is fundamental to writing any kind of autobiography, biography or fiction. A piece of writing can be in the voice of a character, it can be about a character, it can be one character writing about another character. The voice of the character can dictate the style and subject matter of the poem, story or book, and the reader can be so close as to actually 'inhabit' the character. At other times, the characters are mysterious, kept at a distance, their inner lives unknown.

You create major characters, heroes and heroines, villains and flawed anti-heroes, as well as vividly portray minor characters who play small, specific roles in your story.

All your characters need to seem real; they need to have both depth and surface if they're to be convincing to the reader. In this chapter, I cover how to create lifelike characters.

Defining Different Kinds of Characters

You may come across some technical terms about different kinds of characters, especially in fiction. The main character, the hero or the heroine, is called the *protagonist*. The main opponent, or the villain of the story, is the *antagonist*.

An *anti-hero* is the protagonist, but one who has weaknesses and doesn't fit the usual stereotype of the hero. In traditional drama or fiction, the hero – or heroine – is undoubtedly morally good. The anti-hero is bad, flawed or morally ambiguous.

Minor characters can be important characters, highly significant to the main character, or they can be brief walk-on parts. They can be helpers, who support the main character in achieving his goals, or they can be hinderers, who actively oppose the main character or who, by having different aims, get in his way.

To make fiction more interesting, some characters who appear to be helpers turn out to be hinderers, and the other way round.

Discovering Where Characters Come From

You can create characters in one of three main ways:

- ✔ **You borrow from life.** If you're writing autobiography, you draw on yourself; in biography, you write about another person. Although these people are real, you still often need to use fictional techniques to convey them to the reader.

  In writing fiction, you often use a real-life person as a basis for a character, and then change and adapt his characteristics for the story you're writing.

- ✔ **You find a character comes to you.** In writing fiction, a character may spring to your mind, unbidden, and take on vivid shape. Sometimes writers say a character just comes to them, fully-formed, and they feel they know this character inside-out, without having to think about him or consciously 'create' him at all.

  A character may come into your mind fully formed because you're tapping into some of the unknown aspects of your own personality.

- ✔ **You create a character from scratch.** You may need a particular character to fill a role in your story and find that he stubbornly refuses to come to life; you may have to create him through a conscious process, sitting down to decide what he looks like, his background and how he behaves.

Detailing Clues about Your Characters

When creating fictional characters or portraying real people, making a list of their characteristics is helpful. Even if you don't tell your readers about every quirk, your characters come across as more fully fleshed if you write about them from a position of knowledge. Aspects to think about include:

- ✔ **Personal details:** Gender, age, ethnicity, sexual orientation, marital status, parental status, height, weight.

- ✔ **Social details:** Social class, level of education, job, how much money they earn, how much their partners or families earn, religion, how they vote.

- ✔ **Family details:** Family background, what jobs their parents did, if they have brothers and sisters, what position they occupy in the birth order of their families.

You can also create a history for your characters – or at least your main characters. The English poet Gerard Manley Hopkins wrote, 'The child is father to the man'. This famous paradox is certainly true. What happens to someone in childhood can determine her character and personality and what happens to her throughout her life.

A child who's abused often grows up to be a victim or an abuser. A child who's unloved may spend her whole life searching for an unconditional love that she can never find or accept. Unless the abuse or lack of love is extremely severe, however, most people can, with help, overcome their difficulties. This struggle to overcome the problems in their personalities often creates the drive and motivation for characters.

So thinking about your character's childhood, and what happened to her when she was young, is important. You can refer to her background through memories and flashbacks, or have the character reveal details bit by bit.

Try this exercise to really pin down your characters:

1. **Write down three significant events that happened to a character in her childhood.**

2. **Put them in order of importance.**

3. **Write about these events.**

4. **Think about what influence these events have on the character in adulthood.** For example, one of the events might be that a woman's father left when she was six. This fact explains why, in adult life, she can't trust a man to stay with her.

Making use of birth order characteristics

The psychiatrist Alfred Adler first came up with the theory that a child's position in the family strongly influences his personality. Since then, many other psychologists have agreed with him.

Generally, a first child is a natural leader, a high achiever, who's organised, responsible and tends to obey the rules. His faults tend to be bossiness and being a know-it-all.

A middle child is more flexible, easy-going and sociable. He tends to be a peacemaker and negotiator, is independent and generous. On the flipside, middle children can be secretive and feel that everything is unfair.

The youngest child tends to be a risk-taker, is outgoing and creative, likes to be made a fuss of and has a sense of humour. He can be very competitive, is easily bored and can be irresponsible.

Only children tend to be close to their parents, self-controlled and often mature for their age, and are usually dependable and sensitive. They can, however, be demanding and unforgiving, and want to be the centre of attention.

Twins can have identity problems, especially if they're identical and are made to wear the same clothes. Often, the older twin takes on the characteristics of the older child while the second-born the role of the younger.

Pick a person to observe – someone on the bus or Tube, someone you see in the street – and then write about her. Think about who this person is – how old she is, what kind of job she does, what her hobbies might be. Consider the clothes she wears, her style, the expression on her face, the book or newspaper she's reading. Think about whether anything about her seems odd or doesn't fit with the rest. Speculate about the reason for any anomalies.

Now invent a character and write about her in the same way. Describe the clothes she wears, her mannerisms, the kind of book she's reading, the music she likes to listen to. Write about where she likes to go on holiday, what kind of car she drives. Describe her bedroom, think about the kind of food she likes to eat, and what she enjoys doing in her spare time.

By describing these details, you're telling your reader a great deal about the character.

Portraying Personality

The four main methods you can use to reveal character are pretty intuitive as they're the same you use to learn about people you meet in real life. How people look, what they think and feel, what they do and how they speak reveal their personalities. The next sections cover each of these aspects.

Fleshing out your character's . . . well, flesh

Describing what a character looks like is a fairly easy and straightforward way to tell your readers something about her.

Inhabiting a body

When creating or writing about a character, make sure that she inhabits a real body, if only in your mind. Whether a character is conventionally beautiful or ugly, tall or short, fat or slim informs not just the reader's image of her, but the character's personality too. A tall person sees the world quite differently from someone who's very short. A young person is often self-conscious about her appearance, and thinks a lot about how she looks. An old person may be restricted in her movements, have to walk slowly or may suffer from some illness or complaint. Think about the effect physical appearance has on your characters.

In describing the shape of a character's face, her expression and whether she looks after herself or is unkempt, you reveal her personality and explain some of her traits and behaviours.

Find a photograph or portrait of an interesting-looking person. Describe the person in minute detail. Then go back, selecting the most important features, and write a shorter description.

Write about a character who's dissatisfied with her body. Why is this so? Think about how her self-image affects the choices this character makes in your story.

Leaving room for imperfection

Nothing's as boring as describing characters as incredibly good-looking or ravishingly beautiful and leaving it at that. You need to be more specific. What is it exactly that makes them so attractive? Do they have any flaws and, if so, what are they? Often the flaws are what make a person interesting or endearing. Remember that your character must be an individual, not a stereotype, to be believable. Nobody's perfect.

When writing minor characters, you can make them memorable by giving them physical characteristics that a reader can latch on to. A shock of white-blonde hair, unusually coloured eyes, a small scar, a limp, poor hearing in one ear – these little quirks help you get a grip on the characters and help make them interesting to the reader.

Sharing a character's thoughts and feelings

If you're writing through the eyes of a character, you can reveal her inner thoughts and feelings through how she expresses herself, her preoccupations, hopes and fears. Whether a character is obsessive or cool and rational, emotionally needy or focused on helping others helps your readers relate to her.

Imagine your character keeps a diary. Write down a diary entry for a random day, writing in her voice, as you think she would write. Look at what style the character wrote in. Is she wordy or terse? Does she write about herself or about other people or events? Does she reveal her thoughts and feelings, or is she hiding from herself? Is she angry, happy, jealous, sad? You can then use what the diary entry reveals to portray that character more completely.

Letting actions speak for your characters

A character can be revealed through his actions. If you're writing about a character from the outside, this device is the main way that you can show what a character might be thinking or feeling. Is he a 'doer', or does he hang back? What does he like to do when he's alone? How does he move – quickly and confidently, slowly and hesitantly? Is he cautious or impulsive?

Think about how a character would react if given bad news or on meeting a person he's attracted to. Remember that people often behave in surprising and unexpected ways – for example, people responding to bad news with hysterical laughter, not tears, isn't unheard of.

Write about your character doing an ordinary, everyday activity, such as making a cup of tea, combing his hair or going for a walk. Describe his actions in detail. Does he chuck a teabag into an old mug and bang it on the table? Does he serve lapsang souchong in a silver teapot? Does he quickly run his fingers through his hair or does he spend hours in front of the mirror? Does he stroll along looking at the scenery or scurry, eyes fixed on the ground or talking on his mobile phone?

Listening to how your characters talk

Dialogue is one of the main ways you can directly reveal character, especially if you're writing about someone from the outside rather than the inside. If you're writing from the inside, however, you can also show the gap between what a person says and what he thinks. Chapter 5 deals specifically with dialogue, so here I offer just a brief introduction to the subject.

Imagine that your character meets another character and write a conversation between them. Consider how your character speaks and what accent he has, if any. Does he gabble about himself or ask questions of the other? Is he secretive or up-front?

Think about your character's choice of words. Use vocabulary that's appropriate to him. Some characters have verbal mannerisms or tics – words or phrases they use repeatedly. Don't overdo this feature, though.

Revealing Character Indirectly

How a character dresses, where she lives, who she associates with, who she avoids, the objects she possesses, the things she carries around with her – even her name – all divulge some aspect of her personality. By describing these details, you can reveal a lot about the character indirectly.

Write a list of six objects your character may have in her pocket, handbag or briefcase that help reveal her character. Adding something odd or unexpected helps you to avoid stereotypes. Randomly choose an object and then try to work out why your character owns it. Then consider how this object can help suggest the character's personality.

The art of Holmesian deduction

Sherlock Holmes could famously deduce a vast amount of information about people from a quick glance at them or by inspecting objects they possessed. For example, on their first meeting, in *A Study in Scarlet,* Holmes tells Dr Watson, 'You have been in Afghanistan, I perceive.' His chain of reasoning, later revealed, is that Watson is of military bearing, has a tanned face but pale wrists, is haggard from hardship and sickness, and has been injured. In the first chapter of *The Sign of Four,* Holmes deduces from a watch Watson hands him that it belonged to his elder brother, who was untidy and careless, and that,

after several periods of relative prosperity followed by poverty, he died of drink. Holmes works these facts out from the initials on the case, the fact that the watch is dented and worn, from the tiny scratches around the keyhole made by someone not sober, and from the tiny pawnbroker's marks on the inside of the case.

When writing about characters, give clues about them and let the readers use their powers of observation and deduction to come to a conclusion. Readers find seeing that a character is careless from her actions far more satisfying than simply being told so.

For example, in a woman's handbag you may find all the usual things – a diary, a lipstick, a travel card, a purse, keys – and then a little statuette of a Buddha. Think about why she carries it – was it a gift, does it remind her of travelling to the Far East, is it carried for luck, does she meditate, and so on. This is definitely the most interesting and revealing object in her bag.

Describe a room in your character's home – her bedroom, study or living room. What objects are in it? What colours predominate? Is it messy or tidy? How does her private space relate to her public face? Think about how the room reflects who she is and how you can use this information to tell the reader a great deal about your character.

Gathering friends and enemies

You tend to identify with people you feel strongly about for one reason or another. The people who remain in your memory longest are those you love or hate. If you're indifferent to a person, not only are you likely to forget him, but you're also unlikely to engage with him.

If you hate a person, you're usually tied to him for one reason or another. Obviously, you'd probably choose not to spend any time with such people unless you had to! So people you hate tend to be those in your family, that you work with or are linked to in some way – perhaps you rely on them for your livelihood or owe them money.

Of course, many relationships involve an element of both love and hate. An ambivalent relationship is much more interesting, so you can make good use of this device to add depth, subtlety and complexity to your work.

Try alternating paragraphs, sections and scenes in which your character feels positive towards someone with ones in which he feels negative. This approach can help build tension in a story and often is much closer to real life.

Also realise that everyone feels more comfortable with some people than others and tends to like or dislike them accordingly. These people aren't necessarily good or bad – others just don't see eye to eye with them. Resist black and white stereotypes. Try the following exercise.

Write about a character from the point of view of someone who:

 ✔ Likes or loves him

 ✔ Dislikes or hates him

Realising that someone out there doesn't like your lovely hero or heroine can be quite a shock!

Choosing a name

Names are hugely important for characters and can simultaneously reveal something about them and create an impression on the reader.

Putting first names first

Usually authors choose first names that they like or which are fashionable for their heroes and heroines, and names they dislike for their villains. You might, however, find it fun to reverse this convention and see what happens!

Sometimes people choose an ordinary name for a character who's a kind of Everyman or Everywoman – someone everyone can identify with. If your character is unusual, however, and you want to underline this fact, pick a really singular name.

You may also like to think about whether your character likes her name or hates it. Does she shorten it or have a nickname?

Most first names have a meaning; consider looking them up and making sure they fit your characters.

Think about why a character has her name. Was she named after a relative or a loved friend, after a character in a famous play or novel or a real-life hero? This detail tells the reader something about the parents and the expectations they had of the child.

Considering some famous fictional names

Fictional characters with unusual names include: Hannibal Lector in *Silence of the Lambs*, Atticus Finch in *To Kill a Mockingbird*, Keyser Söze in *The Usual Suspects*, Forrest Gump and Sherlock Holmes.

Common names in film and fiction include: James Bond, Annie Hall, Sam Spade in *The Maltese Falcon*, Agent Smith in *The Matrix* and Mr Jones in Joseph Conrad's *Victory*.

Sometimes a common name is mixed with an unusual one: Indiana Jones, John Rambo and Scarlett O'Hara.

Adding surnames and family names

Some writers choose very common surnames – Graham Greene called all his unpleasant characters names like Brown and Smith after being sued because J. B. Priestly thought the self-satisfied novelist in *Stamboul Train* called Q. T. Savory was based on him. Part of the libel action was based on the similar sound of the names.

Dickens was adept at using names suggesting character. Consider Uriah Heep (in *David Copperfield*), Ebenezer Scrooge (*A Christmas Carol*), Wackford Squeers (*Nicholas Nickleby*) and Lady Dedlock (*Bleak House*). Mervyn Peake does much the same in his *Gormenghast* trilogy, with Steerpike, Fuschia, Swelter the cook and the Prunesquallors. On television we have Basil Fawlty, Inspector Morse and Captain Mainwaring in *Dad's Army*.

Assigning a name that implies the personality of a character is common, for example Armstrong for a physically active hero, Tweed for a country type, Gore for a surgeon, Eatwell for someone who loves food.

Taking care in choosing foreign names

Take care choosing foreign names, especially if you're not familiar with the culture. Picking a name you just like the sound of can be a mistake. Some cultures have rules on naming, in law or tradition, such as that you can only use the names of relatives when they're no longer living, or that you must choose from a list of acceptable names. In France, for instance, you can't register a made-up name.

Also check the meaning of foreign names; for example, in Japanese the name Ichiro means *first son* and so wouldn't be appropriate for a youngest child.

Some cultures put the given name first and the family name second; others, like the Chinese and Hungarians, reverse this tradition. In some cultures, the family name comes from the father's side and in others the mother's is used. Both are used in Spain, so people have a double surname (consider the poet Federico García Lorca – García is his father's surname and Lorca his mother's). Russian names are notoriously difficult, as you'll know if you've read *War and Peace*!

Uncovering hidden aspects of yourself through your writing

Psychologists believe, and research tends to show, that people inherit many characteristics that they don't ultimately express due to their upbringing. They may be stifled by attitudes in their society in general or their families in particular. For example, a child may inherit a lively and curious personality but have it drummed out of him by a very strict upbringing. The social conditioning of men and women is a case in point. In western society, men are meant to be more physically active, aggressive and competitive, less skilled at interpersonal relationships and more rational. Women, in contrast, are meant to be more passive, gentle, interested in other people and emotional. While some differences are likely to be biological, society tends to reinforce them.

As a result, men tend to repress their more sensitive side so they can be 'real men', while women damp down their more aggressive and competitive instincts. Psychologists have shown that these repressed instincts reside in people's subconscious and can build up until finally released. For this reason, someone who appears to be very controlled can suddenly erupt in a fury, or a normally extremely shy person can become the life and soul of the party, especially after a few drinks!

When you're writing, sometimes hidden parts of yourself come to the fore, and the results can be quite surprising or shocking, especially when you find your character wants to kill someone or engage in some pretty bad behaviour! Don't worry if this happens in your writing – everyone has fantasies; they only become dangerous when you act on them.

Avoiding Stereotypes and Tapping into Archetypes

Avoid *stereotypes*, or clichéd or predictable characters, as a general rule. Stereotypes are one-dimensional short-cuts and therefore not very interesting. They have limited potential.

Archetypes, on the other hand, are symbolic representations of aspects of our psyche. Archetypal characters are very powerful and can be used to great effect in a story.

The next sections look at the pitfalls of using stereotypical characters and examine what an archetype is and why it can be so important in a poem or narrative.

Diversifying stereotypes

Stereotypes are often used in fiction as a kind of shorthand to identify *stock characters*.

Stock characters go back to ancient Greek drama and appear in the plays of writers such as Aristophanes. They include such characters as the Flatterer, the Buffoon, the Miser, the Faultfinder, the Show-Off and so on. Stock types often show up in Hollywood movies; the Tart with the Heart of Gold, the Absent-minded Professor, the Femme Fatale, the Wise Old Man, the Strong and Silent Hero, the Romantic Heroine, the Trickster or the Holy Fool.

These characters are actually closer to archetypes than stereotypes, though they're usually less well-developed. They can be useful – for example, they can be very funny when used in comedy and can be a very quick way of connecting an audience with a character as they're so familiar. They're often used in minor roles when a writer doesn't want to spend time establishing a character, and where any real character development is a distraction from the main story.

Uncovering archetypes

The psychoanalyst Carl Jung suggested the existence of archetypes. He believed that people actually inherit certain instincts, behaviour patterns, images and symbols that form part of what he called the *collective unconscious.* The images and symbols surface spontaneously in all religions, in art, dreams and creative processes.

Jung thought that in men lies a hidden female personality, the *anima,* and in women, a hidden male one, the *animus.* You're always looking for this other half, and when you fall in love you feel that you've met it. You can thus fall in love at first sight, immediately and unconsciously recognising this hidden aspect of yourself in someone else.

Usually, you find someone close enough in personality to your animus or anima for the relationship to work. However, some people project this animus or anima figure onto someone who's quite unsuitable or unavailable. Then, when the truth finally dawns and they withdraw the projection, the relationship abruptly comes to an end.

Avoiding stereotype traps

Many stereotypes, especially in films, are demeaning to particular ethnic groups, gay people or people with disabilities. Examples are the crazed effeminate gay psychopath, the sinister predatory lesbian, the 'magic' black man or the black sidekick who helps the white guy out, and the Latina maid. Also, people with disabilities are very seldom portrayed in mainstream roles.

Consider diversity and stereotypes when creating characters and try to create characters from all backgrounds to more accurately reflect the society in which you live.

Jung also thought that people have:

✔ An *ego*, the conscious part of their personalities.

✔ A *shadow*, the repressed, unknown part.

Often, you project the shadow side of yourself onto other people and then criticise them instead of looking more deeply at yourself. For this reason, you may often find profoundly irritating in other people characteristics that you also possess. Jung also developed the concept of the archetype of the *Self* – the complete personality that brings together a person's ego and shadow side.

Jung also talked about the *Persona*, the mask of personality with which you face the world. This persona is often influenced by your work or profession; a doctor behaves like your conception of a doctor, an artist as you expect an artist to behave. However, this public persona involves a repression of other aspects of your personality, which are often acted out in private. A contrast exists between someone's public face and private life; someone who's organised at work may be messy at home, someone who seems sweet and kind to outsiders may be a tyrant domestically. Because of this contrast, people love stories of politicians who present themselves as family men but are secretly having torrid affairs, vicars who consort with prostitutes, celebrities who are secret drug abusers and successful-seeming bankers who are gambling away or embezzling money.

Understanding the concepts of Jungian personality theory can make a big difference to the way that you write about character. Readers are always interested in getting beneath the skin of the main character. They want to know what's going on underneath the surface cool manner, competent exterior or superficial charm. Thinking in terms of surface appearance and hidden reality can help you to create or communicate powerful, deep and realistic characters who disturb, charm and fascinate your readers.

Chapter 5

Discovering Dialogue

. . . .

In This Chapter

▶ Developing an ear for dialogue

▶ Creating tension and conflict

▶ Revealing hidden messages

▶ Displaying dialogue on the page

. . . .

Dialogue is the conversational element of literary or dramatic writing. Strictly speaking, dialogue involves two people. Although a two-way conversation is the most common form of dialogue, you can of course write one involving more people.

Dialogue is one of the most important elements in all creative writing. Realistic conversation is the essence of a good play, screenplay or radio script. Dialogue brings characters to life in novels, autobiography, biography and narrative non-fiction. It can also be important in poetry, which is often written to be spoken aloud.

Writing dialogue sounds easy, but is actually extremely difficult. How do you convey the impression of real-life speech, yet make every word count? How do you capture the way that individual characters speak, and yet still make it intelligible? How do you create the sparkle and tension that makes good dialogue compelling? In this chapter, I tell you.

Remembering that Dialogue is a Two-Way Street

Crucial to writing dialogue is remembering that each character involved must have his or her own agenda. Each person has his own way of speaking, his own hopes, fears and motivation, and each wants something different out of the conversation.

If you eavesdrop on real-life conversation, people really listen to one another amazingly seldom. Often, each person is simply waiting to get back to what *he* wants to talk about; no real exchange of ideas, thoughts or feelings occurs.

Note that in real dialogue people:

- ✔ Often don't really listen to one another; they're thinking about what they're going to say next.
- ✔ Often seize every opportunity to turn the conversation back to themselves.
- ✔ Interrupt, fidget or think of something else.
- ✔ Make statements unrelated to what the other person has just said.
- ✔ Are oblique – they say something that really means something else.

Whether writing dialogue in a fictional or factual work, writers usually select only that part of the dialogue where something significant is happening between two people.

Conflict is essential to good dialogue. Consider the following exchange: 'It's a nice day.' 'Isn't it.' 'It's really lovely.' 'Yes, it is.' If two characters agree with each other like this, the reader is immediately thinking: what are they not talking about or why am I reading this?

Before starting to write dialogue, consider for a moment what each character wants to get out of the conversation. Do they both want the same thing – in which case, it won't be very interesting to read – or do they each want something different? Does one, for example, want to find something out, while the other wants to conceal it? Does one want the other to admit to something, which the other has no intention of doing?

Distinguishing Voices

Listening to how people actually speak and trying to copy them is the best way to work on your dialogue-writing skills. Eavesdrop on conversations wherever you go. Jot down phrases you overhear so that you can use them in your own writing. Listen to the words people use, the expressions they repeat. Think about what's going on behind the conversation.

Mobile phones are great for capturing at least one side of a conversation. And, if people are going to inflict their private conversations on you in a public place, you may as well make use of them!

Creating natural rhythm

If you look at any direct transcript of an interview or record everything really said, you'll know that people rarely speak with any degree of clarity. Real conversations are made up of hesitation, repetition, incomplete sentences, grammatical mistakes and so on. After an American professor of psychiatry claimed that men spoke only 7,000 words a day while women spoke 20,000, *The Guardian* newspaper wired up a woman and a man – both writers – to see if this was true. They found, in fact, that very little difference existed in how much they spoke. What was fascinating, however, were some of the transcripts of what was actually said. For example, the man, in an office setting, said:

> 'Well, I was just thinking, well I mean maybe if we, uh, 'cos, I mean if you look at some, taking a survey of lots of different blogs, and they're all kind of laid out in a way that kind of, I guess the object is to put the comment . . .'

Dialogue on the page bears little relation to real-life conversation. What you're used to reading, or hearing spoken in films and plays, is a compressed and often highly stylised version of the real thing. In a play, dialogue can be poetic and stirring, or commonplace. In film, it can be amazingly compressed – just a few words can say volumes. In fiction, it often has a rhythm, a cadence, to it. But for dialogue to work, it must sound natural.

How do you write realistic dialogue? The short answer is, read as much dialogue as you can in books to see how it works. And practise as much as you can. You need to aim for speech that sounds natural – not too formal or stilted – and yet which makes sense when you read it. So, for the man above, you might write:

> 'Well, I was just thinking, if we made a survey of lots of different blogs, we could see how they're laid out.'

Here, you're using the phrases that he used, but missing out the bits that don't make sense to form a coherent sentence.

Constructing a voice

Keep in mind that different characters use diverse vocabularies and rhythms of speech. Some characters are talkative, others taciturn. In theory, a reader ought to be able to identify which character is speaking simply from the way she talks. Mannerisms and catch-phrases can help too.

The way a character speaks can be a powerful way of revealing her character. You can immediately tell the difference between a character who writes:

- ✔ This morning, as I purchased my groceries in the shop, I observed a small child emerging from the doorway on the opposite side of the street.

- ✔ This morning, when I was doing some shopping, I saw a girl coming out of the door on the other side of the road.

- ✔ I was out shoppin' this mornin', I was, when I saw this wee gel come out of yonder door across the street.

- ✔ Yeah, well, I was just buying a couple of things in the shop when I saw this, kind of, girl come out of that door over there.

Considering the degree of formality in spoken language is also useful. In some situations people use more formal language – a barrister in court, a politician making a speech or an advertising executive impressing a client. On other occasions, people talk in a casual manner – in the privacy of their homes or out drinking in the pub. Characters who spend a lot of their lives in a more formal setting often use a more formal language all the time, while others never do.

Consider all the gradations in this simple phrase:

- ✔ Excuse me, would you mind leaving the room?
- ✔ Could you leave the room?
- ✔ Please go.
- ✔ Get out of here!
- ✔ Shove off!

Talking in Varied Situations

When writing dialogue, think about some of the specific ways that you can reveal who's speaking, how he's speaking and what may lie beneath his spoken words.

Getting into he said, she said

In prose writing, using 'he said' or 'she said' is sometimes the only way to make it obvious who's speaking.

Many writers find indicating tone of voice with an adverb helpful. On the whole, I disagree. Dialogue works far better if you can make the character's tone of voice and feelings obvious through the words he uses, as you'd do in a play. Far better to write:

> 'For God's sake, get out!'

Than

> 'Get out,' he said angrily.

Nothing's worse than reading pages of fiction full of 'he said loudly', 'she said softly', 'he murmured sadly', 'she shouted angrily'. Such description just sounds feeble, as if the writer can't trust the dialogue to speak for itself.

Whenever possible, keep your dialogue simple: just use 'said'. Ultimately, 'said' becomes invisible; the reader doesn't really notice it. 'Asked' for a question is fine and 'replied' and 'responded' are just about allowable but nowadays sound mannered. Otherwise avoid using words other than 'said', as these draw attention to themselves and distract from the flow of the dialogue.

Some writers seem to feel that using any alternative to 'said' more than once is a mistake, so their dialogue is peppered with: pleaded, cajoled, demanded, interrupted, wheedled and so on. These phrases don't add to the quality of the writing and can just annoy readers. In the past, writers have taken avoiding 'said' to a completely ludicrous degree. My favourite is Sir Arthur Conan Doyle's *'Holmes!' I ejaculated.* A cheap Western has *'Draw!' Slim grated.* I've even read *'Go to your kennel!' George barked*, and *'I don't like that high-pitched noise,' she whined.* Avoid!

Speaking face to face

When people are physically together and can see one another, a writer can rely on descriptions of body language and other props to indicate to the reader what people are thinking or feeling. Characters who avoid looking at the person they're talking to may be lying or trying to avoid conflict or intimacy, awkward or nervous fiddling with objects can reveal nerves, characters who are insecure may be constantly aware of their appearance and adjust their hair or clothes or glance in a mirror, while those who are confident look people straight in the eye, shake hands and may lean forwards towards the other person.

According to numerous surveys, only about 20 per cent of the meaning in a dialogue is transferred through the words themselves. The rest of the information is conveyed through tone of voice, gesture and body language. To write dialogue that says more than appears on the surface, bear this fact in mind.

Talking on the telephone

People can misunderstand one another so much more easily when speaking over the phone, partly because words can be mistaken, but mainly because no clues are offered by gestures or a person's facial expressions. People can also lie or mislead one another over the phone more easily. Evelyn Waugh, a master at dialogue, made great use of this fact in his novels, when the telephone was a very new device.

Today we also have mobile phones to complicate the picture. We also have text messages and emails, which are an intermediate form of communication, even more liable to lead to misunderstandings as even the tone of voice is missing. As many people have found to their cost, knowing whether a text or email is ironic, humorous or just plain rude is quite hard!

When writing telephone dialogue, always remember that the characters can't see each other. Try writing the dialogue with nothing in between the character's words and see how it sounds. Remember that people can be doing something else while talking on the phone, which the other person can't see, so it's much easier to misunderstand things or miss things when talking on the phone.

Containing a crowd

Although, strictly speaking, a dialogue is a conversation between just two people, sometimes you need to write conversations when three, four or even more characters are present. Doing so can present quite a challenge.

When more than two people are present, you have to work quite hard to make it clear who's speaking. One useful way is for the characters to use one another's names. This technique is quite realistic, because you often say the name of the person you're addressing specifically when several people are present.

 Beware of overdoing the use of names or the conversation can sound false and contrived.

Particular mannerisms of speech can also be used to identify a speaker, such as a stutter or repeating certain words. Writing 'said Mark' or 'Isla said' is fine if no other way of doing it is obvious. In this instance, clarity can be more important than style!

People use someone's name repeatedly in conversation when they're trying to be intimate with them or curry favour.

Creating a Dynamic

When writing dialogue, making sure that the conversation's going somewhere is crucial. Don't let your dialogue resemble a game of ping-pong, with the characters simply trying to keep the ball in play with no tension and no point, just endless conversation.

Common faults in written dialogue include:

- ✔ **Conversation going nowhere.** People just talk to one another, with no particular aim or agenda. This dialogue is boring and frustrating to read.

- ✔ **One person feeding lines to another so the other character can say exactly what you, the author, wants him to say.** This form of conversation seldom happens in real life – except in an interview – and sounds stilted and contrived.

- ✔ **Dialogue goes on too long.** Don't let your conversations meander on for pages – keep them short and make every line count.

Have a dialogue-writing session with another writer. Agree on a situation and two characters. Then, write lines of dialogue for your character and pass it to your writing partner. Your partner writes her character's lines and passes it back. Immediately you lose control of what the other character is saying, and the dialogue comes alive – much more like real speech.

Keeping it short

Many beginner writers make their characters too wordy. Most people don't make speeches. New writers often make their dialogue too obvious and literal; the characters are made to say too much. For example:

'Hello Jack, good to see you. Are you enjoying your cup of coffee?'

is better as:

'Hi Jack. Coffee okay?'

Write a dialogue between two people. Don't allow them to use sentences of more than four words. See how much you can convey and how natural it sounds.

Paying attention to place

Where a conversation takes place makes a huge difference to the dynamic, and what people do and don't say. A huge gulf exists between what people say in the privacy of their home and in a public place. Conversations in a crowded place are different to those in spacious venues and between places where people can easily get away from one another and where they feel trapped.

Think of a conversation between two people who are thinking of splitting up. Imagine them having the conversation alone at home, then in a car travelling somewhere, then in a crowded pub.

Write an argument between two people. First, set it in their living room, then when they're walking on a deserted heath, then when they've been trapped together in a locked room.

Revealing the Subtext

One of the most intriguing things about writing dialogue is that as much is conveyed by what people don't say as by what they do. People seldom talk about what they're really thinking, and social conventions mean lots of lies get told. If you think this notion is far-fetched, just consider the following questions and responses:

- ✔ 'Do you like my new dress?'

  'Oh, it's nice . . . I like the colour.'
- ✔ 'Do you want me to come?'

  'Of course I do.'
- ✔ 'Are you sure you're not disappointed?'

  'No . . . not at all.'
- ✔ 'You don't mind, do you?'

  'No, not really.'

Try reading each question and response several times, using a different tone of voice each time. Do the characters really mean what they say or are they just trying not to hurt or offend the other person or admit to their own hurt feelings?

Most people talk about one thing while thinking about something else. Psychoanalysts make great use of this fact in therapy sessions. Consider the following exchange:

'It's cold.'

'Not really. I think it'll get warmer later.'

'The forecast said it was going to rain.'

'It really doesn't look like rain. Look, there's a blue patch over there.'

What are these characters really talking about? The weather is unlikely to be the genuine subject. Possibly one of them wants to go for a walk while the other doesn't. Or maybe one's depressed and the other is trying to cheer her up. Or one of them hates the other and can't bear to agree with her about anything. Or maybe one of them desperately wants to talk about something with the other but she can't bear to bring it up. Something else is going on, under the surface, and the reader knows it and wants to read on to find out what it is.

Harold Pinter is a master of dialogue with layers of subtext. Part of the fun of reading or watching his plays is trying to work out what the characters are really trying to communicate beneath the banal surface conversation. When Pinter was awarded his Nobel Prize for Literature, the citation said that he 'uncovers the precipice under everyday prattle'.

Very often, people talk about their work or everyday tasks and issues they're engaged with on the surface. Yet bubbling beneath these conversations are hidden other issues. Take a conversation in a magazine publisher's office:

'I've done the cover. What do you think?'

'I don't like that typeface. We need something plainer.'

'I chose it to reflect the period. Look, it goes with this image, and these on page 91. It shows the influence of the seventeenth-century costume . . .'

'It's too flashy. Let's try something else.'

'I've worked really hard on this design. I think it works as it is. A plain typeface would just be too boring.'

'No, we're a modern magazine.'

Now, are they really talking about a magazine cover? Or does the plain-speaking editor think his new designer is too flashy and the new designer think her boss is boring? Is the boss trying to establish his superiority and that he's not as old as the young designer thinks?

People often talk while doing something; they don't speak in a vacuum. They talk when walking, driving in a car, dressing to go out in the evening, cooking, fishing, at business meetings or fixing the car. Use the topic at hand to reveal the thoughts and conflicts of the characters.

Using Accents and Dialect

When writing dialogue, you need to convey the direct voice of the character. Doing so can be challenging, as it means you may sometimes need to write dialogue spoken by people with regional or foreign accents, in local dialects, or in the vernacular of different historical periods.

Some writers lay on accents so thickly that reading them is almost impossible. For example, in Mark Twain's *Pudd'nhead Wilson*, Roxy tells fellow slave Jasper:

> ''Clah to goodness if dat conceit o' yo'n strikes in, Jasper, it gwine to kill you sho'. If you b'longed to me I'd sell you down de river 'fo' you git too fur gone.'

And in the first chapter of *Trainspotting*, Irvine Welsh imitates the Scottish accent of his characters:

> -How should ah go n see her? It's goat nowt tae dae wi me, ah sais defensively.
>
> -Yir her friend, ur ye no?

Both writers have been hugely successful, but their books aren't easy to read! A more subtle approach is often best – use a few words and phrases, but don't try to render every word phonetically. Andrea Levy's *Small Island* is a good example – her characters speak with a West Indian lilt, but the dialogue's easy to read and understand.

Rendering foreign accents

You can convey a foreign accent in two ways. You can note differences in pronunciation of individual words and sounds or change the rhythm or word order to reflect the cadence of the speaker's native language.

In order to make changes in pronunciation or sentence structure convincing, you need to know a bit about the language concerned.

Highlight the sounds in English that aren't present in another language. French doesn't have the *th* sound in *the* and *this*, so French speakers are often depicted saying *ze* and *zis*. In German, *w* is pronounced as *v*. Be careful writing a German accent, though; it can sound condescending or funny: 'Vee have vays of making you tok!'

Use the sentence structure common to the foreign language. In German, for example, the verb comes at the end of a sentence. A German person may thus say, 'I to the shops am going.' In Russian, *a* and *the* aren't used, so a character may say, 'I will catch bus.'

Using foreign words is another approach to signifying the origin of your characters; Germans in war novels are always saying '*Nicht wahr*' or '*Nein*' or '*Gott in Himmel!*' Again, don't overdo this tactic; use foreign words sparingly, where their meaning is obvious, just to remind the reader now and again.

John le Carré has an excellent ear for the way people speak: In *The Russia House* Katya's English is formal and stiff, conveying the fact that it isn't her native language; when congratulated on her English, she replies: 'Thank you. I have a natural comprehension of foreign languages.' Her conversation is full of sentences like: 'It is not convenient. It is not relevant.' The foreign accent comes through loud and clear without a single change in the spelling of the words.

Remembering historical voices

If you want to convey language from an earlier time, no substitute exists for simply reading books written at the time you're writing about. Read novels, plays, factual books or newspapers. Try to internalise the rhythms of the prose. Make a list of unusual words or expressions so that you can use them.

In particular, avoid modern-day phrases. Nothing's worse than coming across an eighteenth-century character saying things such as 'In your dreams' or 'Make my day'.

Sarah Waters provides an excellent example of creating historical speech. In her novels *Affinity* and *Fingersmith*, she beautifully recaptures the way Victorian people spoke in a way that sounds accurate but unforced.

Laying Out Dialogue

Many people are confused about how to lay out dialogue on the page. Dialogue is usually contained within punctuation marks called *inverted commas* or *quote marks*. In the UK, you use single inverted commas for dialogue, and if you quote dialogue within dialogue, you use double inverted commas (the opposite is true in the US). Sometimes this convention means you use both together, as below:

'Mother said, "You mustn't go out",' said Siri.

Each character's dialogue is usually set on a new line. If you're putting in a character's actions or other information about him in between the dialogue, try to keep it on the same line as that character's lines, or things can get confusing, especially when you use 'he' or 'she' rather than the character's name.

> 'What are you doing here?' asked Jack.
>
> Jim looked at the floor. 'Nothing.'

Not:

> 'What are you doing here?' asked Jack. Jim looked at the floor.
>
> 'Nothing.'

If you put 'he' rather than the names, you obviously create a problem – in the second version, the reader doesn't know who's looking at the floor. In the first version the meaning is clear, even without the names.

Rarely, other conventions for laying out dialogue are used. On the continent, putting a dash in front of the speech and omitting the quote marks is the usual way to indicate that someone's speaking. Some British writers also use this convention, such as Roddy Doyle in *Paddy Clarke Ha Ha Ha*. So the dialogue looks like this:

> - What are you doing here? asked Jack.
>
> Jim looked at the floor.
>
> - Nothing.

In a play, the dialogue is simply prefaced with the character's name and a colon:

> Jack: What are you doing here?
>
> Jim: [Looking at the floor] Nothing.

And in a film script, the dialogue comes under the character's name:

```
        JACK:

What are you doing here?

        JIM:

 [Looking at the floor]

Nothing.
```

Chapter 6

Choosing a Narrator

*O*ne of the fundamental issues in writing any fiction, narrative non-fiction or poetry is finding the right point of view for your story. Autobiography naturally makes use of the first-person viewpoint, but using this perspective is a common technique in fiction and poetry too. The third-person voice is extremely flexible and includes a range of options that enable your reader to close in on the thoughts and feelings of the main characters – a common device in fiction – or to step back and listen to a more distant, authoritative voice, as is the case with much biography and non-fiction.

Being consistent about the point of view is one of the main elements in creative writing that enables your narrative to be clear and to connect to the reader. Inconsistency in the point of view, rapid shifts from one character's consciousness to another, being too distant or being too close are all common problems for the beginner writer.

Defining Voices

The main voices you can use when writing are first person, *I*, and third person, *he, she* and *they*. However, within third person you have two main techniques; the limited point of view, where only one character's perspective, thoughts and feelings are used, and the omniscient viewpoint, where the narrator knows the thoughts and feelings of all the characters.

Focusing on first and third person

Try writing in the first- and third-person voices to see how different they are and to find out from first-hand experience what you can and can't do using these different techniques.

Following are examples of these three techniques, using the same scene, involving two characters, Sarah and Jenan.

- ✔ **First person:** Here, you write as yourself or as if you were the character, using pronouns such as *I, me* and *my*.

  > I opened the door and walked out into the garden. It was very cold. I noticed the frost lying on the lawn and the crisp puddles of ice on the drive, and felt myself begin to shiver. The milkman had not come – what a nuisance, there was none left in the fridge. I went back into the kitchen, slamming the door, and drew my dressing-gown around me.

  > Jenan came down the stairs. He had dark circles under his eyes and looked as if he had hardly slept. As soon as I saw him, all my anxiety returned. What should I say to him? How could I break the news?

  > 'Coffee?' he asked me.

  > 'I've boiled the kettle, but I'm really sorry, there's no milk.'

- ✔ **Third person, limited:** Here, you use *he*, *she* or *they*, and pronouns like *his, hers* or *theirs*. You limit the narrative to the thoughts, feelings and consciousness of only one of the characters – the *viewpoint character*.

  The passage is written from Sarah's point of view:

  > Sarah opened the door and walked into the garden. It was very cold. She noticed the frost lying on the lawn and the crisp puddles of ice on the drive, and felt herself begin to shiver. She saw that the milkman hadn't come, and felt annoyed, as there was no milk left in the fridge. She went back into the kitchen, slamming the door, and drew her dressing-gown around her.

  > Jenan came down the stairs. Sarah noticed that he had dark circles under his eyes, as if he had hardly slept. As soon as Sarah saw him, all her anxiety returned. What should she say to him? How could she break the news?

  > 'Coffee?' he asked.

  > 'I've boiled the kettle, but I'm really sorry, there's no milk.'

- ✔ **Third person, omniscient:** This voice is that of an all-knowing narrator. The sample passage shows both Jenan's and Sarah's viewpoints:

> While Jenan was waking upstairs, Sarah opened the door and walked into the garden. The frost was lying on the lawn, and there were crisp puddles of ice on the drive; Sarah began to shiver. The milkman had not come. She felt annoyed, knowing there was no milk left in the fridge.
>
> She went back into the kitchen, slamming the door, and drew her dressing-gown around her.
>
> Jenan came down the stairs. He had hardly slept, and there were heavy, dark circles under his eyes. As soon as Sarah saw this, all her anxiety returned. What should she say to him? How could she break the news?
>
> Jenan stared back at Sarah, wondering why she was looking at him so nervously. He hoped that nothing was wrong.
>
> 'Coffee?' he asked, thinking this might help him to wake up.
>
> Sarah was apologetic. 'I've boiled the kettle, but I'm really sorry, there's no milk.'

Even in such a short passage, some of the advantages and disadvantages of these techniques show. The first-person voice clearly limits the reader to only one perspective. You get just one person's sensations and feelings – and anxieties, in the case of Sarah.

Switching to the third-person voice, but still from a single point of view, changes the voice slightly. In the sample passage, although most of the text is exactly the same, the added phrases 'Sarah saw' and 'Sarah noticed that' remind you, as the reader, that you're filtering everything through Sarah's consciousness.

The third-person perspective creates a slight distance between the character and the reader.

More importantly, because you're in one character's mind, that character – and therefore you, the reader – can't know what any other characters are thinking or what their experiences are. Sarah notices the dark shadows under Jenan's eyes and deduces that he hasn't slept well, but she can't *know* this. Sarah has some bad news to break to Jenan, which she is anxious about, but he can't *know* what this is, even though he may suspect something.

When you're writing using the third-person limited, never change point of view in the middle of a scene. Shifting from one character's viewpoint just for a sentence or two to say something interesting about what a different character is thinking is a common beginner's mistake. Don't do it; changing perspective is confusing and distracting for the reader and loses the clear focus on the viewpoint character. You can find some other way around the problem – have the viewpoint character deduce what another person is thinking from his actions or the way he looks at her, for example.

In the omniscient voice, the narrator knows what's happening to every character and what everyone's thinking. This voice has the effect of removing the close focus from one character and opening up to all the characters in a scene. The writer – and the reader – thus need to switch from one character to another.

Within these three distinct techniques are still more differences in voice and tone. Because the first-person voice *is* the character talking or narrating the story, when writing from this perspective you need to capture the direct voice of the character, using the words and phrases that the character would use. In the Sarah and Jenan example, Sarah's voice is not so different from the voice of the author. But imagine that Sarah has a particular way of speaking or being – that she's a young child, for example. The passage may be written very differently:

> I opened the door. It was very cold in the garden. There was a bit of white snow lying on the lawn and shiny ice puddles. I started to shiver. No milk. I went back into the kitchen, banging the door, and pulled my dressing-gown tight.
>
> Jenan came down the stairs. He looked sleepy. I was scared. What should I say to him? Would he be angry?
>
> 'Coffee?' he asked me.
>
> 'There's no milk.'

The vocabulary changes to that of a young child. A child might think thick frost was snow and wouldn't use the more sophisticated words and expressions that seemed suitable for an adult Sarah.

Think about the voice your character might use. An old person might ramble, an uneducated person use simpler vocabulary, a poet be lyrical and a scientist be absorbed in her inner world. If you have a character who can't express herself clearly – if you're writing from the point of view of someone with learning difficulties, for example, or someone who's insane – choosing the third-person limited voice may be more appropriate.

Examples of books with unusual first-person narrators include Mark Haddon's *The Curious Incident of the Dog in the Night-time* (told from the point of view of a 15-year-old autistic boy) and *A Concise Chinese-English Dictionary for Lovers* by Xiaolu Guo (told from the perspective of a Chinese woman who speaks poor English).

The first-person voice is the direct, unmediated voice of the character. The third-person limited voice is the point of view of the character mediated through the voice of the author.

Table 6-1 summarises the advantages and drawbacks of the various voices.

Table 6-1	Pros and Cons of Different Techniques	
	Advantages	*Disadvantages*
First person	Direct voice of the character.	Limited to one voice.
	Immediate connection with the character's inner world.	You can only let the reader know what the character knows.
	Easy to handle – you may be used to writing this way in diaries and letters.	Can be claustrophobic, especially if you don't like the character.
	Perspective is always clear.	Hard to bring in other perspectives or swap to other characters' viewpoints in other chapters.
Third-person limited	The author's voice interpreting the character.	Still limited to one person's viewpoint.
	Can still identify with the character's thoughts and feelings.	You can still only let the reader know what this one character knows.
	Can be more descriptive, and easier to shift to other characters' viewpoints in different scenes, without a complete change of voice and tone.	More distance from the character, not so immediate.
		Easier to swap viewpoint without being aware of it.
Omniscient	Very flexible.	Can feel too distant.
	Can connect with a larger number of characters.	Hard to handle all the different characters.
	Easier to handle plot and story.	Can seem old-fashioned or contrived.
	Enables you to move around in time, space and from one character's thoughts to another's.	Can be difficult to know which character's viewpoint to enter and when.

Surprising with the second-person voice

You can use the second-person voice – *you* – for effect. This technique is very common in poetry, especially love poetry, which addresses the beloved, but it can also be used in a narrative. The second-person voice always implies the *I* who's addressing the *you* and so is really a form of the first-person narrative. It can be intimate, poetic and surprising, as in the next passage:

> You opened the door and walked out into the garden. It was very cold. You noticed the frost lying on the lawn and the crisp puddles of ice on the drive, and felt yourself begin to shiver. The milkman had not come – what a nuisance, you knew there was none left in the fridge. You went back into the kitchen, slamming the door, and drew your dressing-gown around you.

Some writers use this perspective for short periods, especially in a first-person narrative, when the 'I' character is thinking about someone. It can also be used as an introduction to draw you into a piece of writing, before switching to a more conventional viewpoint.

Finding the Right Point of View

The next sections talk about the different voices and how to use them, pointing out all their advantages and disadvantages.

Going personal with first person

The first-person voice is popular because it's easy to use, connects the reader straight away with the character and encourages a spontaneity of voice and style. This voice is clearly appropriate for autobiography and the autobiographical novel, in which it helps create a feeling of authenticity.

Within the first-person voice, though, a variety of style and tone is still available. The next sections cover some commonly used techniques.

Becoming a traditional storyteller

Here, the character tells the story in a straight line, from beginning to end, perhaps with some flashbacks and memories woven in. The events unfold as they're happening to the narrator, and the reader therefore can only know what the narrator knows.

The narrative voice is fairly simple and uncomplicated, with the voice of the character generally being not too different from yours.

Riding a stream of consciousness

This form of narration lets the reader right into the mind of the character, telling the character's thoughts and feelings exactly as they occur to give an impression of the character's inner consciousness.

In practice, writing in stream-of-consciousness style is hard to achieve and sustain for any length of time, so most writers tend to use it for effect now and again.

The stream-of-consciousness technique is more usually used in first-person narratives, though it can be used in the third-person limited viewpoint, too (read the opening of Virginia Woolf's *Mrs Dalloway* for an example).

Sarah's story may look something like the following in stream of consciousness:

> The door opened with a little creak. How cold, the garden! Frost lying like icing on the lawn and crisp little puddles of ice on the drive, and myself shivering. The bare step – the milkman had not come – what a nuisance! None left in the fridge. Back into the kitchen, slamming the door, my dressing-gown warm and scratchy. Itching.
>
> Jenan's feet banging on the stairs. Heavy dark circles under his eyes – he can't have slept, tossing and turning all night, how miserable! Nasty feeling in the pit of my stomach. What should I say to him? How to break the news?
>
> His voice, booming loudly. 'Coffee?'
>
> No milk. Serve him right.

Conniving with the unreliable narrator

Generally, the reader makes the assumption that the narrator is telling the truth. Of course, this isn't always the case. The narrator of a story may be lying deliberately or be deluded. Sometimes the narrator's lies are revealed at the very end of a story, which tends to be really irritating to readers. Slipping in clues to make readers begin to suspect that all may not be as it seems works far better. Such stories tend to shock readers into examining their assumptions and thinking more deeply about the question the writer is addressing.

Kazuo Ishiguro's *The Remains of the Day* provides a good example of an unreliable narrator. Here, the main character is blind to things the reader gradually becomes aware of. The reader sees everything through the narrator's eyes but makes interpretations of what people say and do that the narrator cannot as a result of the limitations of his personality. Another example is Dostoevsky's *Notes from the Underground*, in which the narrator plays around with the reader: 'When I said I was a spiteful man just now I was lying. I was lying out of spite.'

Revealing a journal format

A journal is a frequently used first-person format. The narrator of the story uses the conceit of writing a journal, enabling him to comment on the story as it happens. Some journals also address the reader. Some are written as the story unfolds; others after the ending of the story, which enables the narrator to drop clues about what's going to happen. (See the 'Recording past history' section later in this chapter.)

Writing letters

Many of the earliest novels were written as an exchange of letters, and this format is still in use today, especially in historical fiction. Sometimes letters or journals are worked into a traditional narrative to convey another voice, point of view or information hidden from the narrator.

If you use a letter format, remember to make each writer's voice different. In order to keep the format lively, you need to get your letter-writer to describe things in more detail than is usual in real life and perhaps to reproduce whole conversations in dialogue, so that the letters aren't merely the writer 'telling' the story.

Representing one character's view

Third-person limited is probably the most common technique used today. This approach is also known as *first-third* voice as it shares some characteristics with first-person voice because the viewpoint is restricted to what's seen by one character. The difference is in distance; one writer described first person as looking out through the eyes of the character and third-person limited as sitting on the character's shoulder. You see things from the character's point of view, but you're not actually the person.

This technique combines some of the immediacy of a first-person narrative and its subjectivity with a more detached authorial voice. In the third-person voice, you get the voice of the author, sometimes tinged with the voice of the character.

Free indirect style is the technical term for a very common technique in which, in a third-person narrative, the writer temporarily goes into the character's consciousness and provides thoughts and feelings directly as the character would have expressed them. This tactic is also sometimes known as *going into character* or *close writing*.

Jane Austen's free use of this technique is one of the secrets of her success – moving from a traditional third-person narrative to the thoughts, feelings and expressions of her characters.

When writing in first person, writers very seldom have problems with handling the point of view. Whose eyes the story is being seen through is obvious – the 'I' character. However, as soon as you shift into third person, the point of view becomes more tricky. Shifting point of view to another character, which effectively means making your reader jump out of one character's head and into another, can be jarring.

Also, if you allow readers to know one or two things a character is thinking, they may start to wonder why they aren't being given more information about that otherwise undeveloped character – another frustration.

Never change point of view in the middle of a scene!

You can tell a whole story in third-person limited from the point of view of just one character. However, in a third-person story, bringing in the viewpoint of other characters, perhaps in different chapters or different scenes, is easier (see the 'Handling multiple narrators' section later in this chapter). On the whole, though, having a more or less equal balance between the different viewpoint characters is important, so they can be more or less equally developed as characters and have evenly proportioned parts in the story. A novel in which 90 per cent of the chapters are from one character's point of view and only 10 per cent from another's would be odd.

Switching perspectives

A story is very different when told by another character. Suppose that, instead of seeing the story from Sarah's point of view, you see it from Jenan's. The sample passage may look like this:

> Jenan woke up. He heard the door bang downstairs and got up to look out of the window. He had hardly slept, wondering why Sarah had summoned him to come and then refused to talk to him last night. He hoped there wasn't something serious the matter.
>
> He looked in the mirror and grimaced at himself; he looked dreadful, with dark circles under his eyes. He quickly pulled on his clothes and went downstairs.
>
> Sarah was standing in the kitchen with her dressing-gown pulled tightly around her. She looked up nervously as he came down but said nothing.
>
> 'Coffee?' he asked her, hoping this might wake him up.
>
> 'I'm really sorry, but there's no milk.'

Whether this story is Sarah's or Jenan's of course changes it completely. Suppose the news that Sarah wants to break to Jenan is that his wife, Amanda, has left him for another man. If Sarah is the narrator, it could be a story about her unfulfilled love for Jenan, who, though he is now free, refuses to marry her. If Jenan tells the story, it could be about his attempts to free himself from this woman who won't take no for an answer.

Choosing which character's viewpoint to narrate the story from is one of the most important choices you make. Sometimes the obvious viewpoint is actually the least interesting.

Write a piece about a character doing something while someone is watching. Now swap and write from the point of view of the watcher. See which perspective interests you most, and why.

Being the all-seeing and all-knowing narrator

Third-person omniscient, although seemingly the simplest technique, is actually the most difficult one to make work. This difficulty is partly the result of taste and fashion. The omniscient voice is that of the great nineteenth-century novelists like Leo Tolstoy and George Eliot, who wrote in an era when people generally believed that there was one truth and that it could be known. The omniscient narrator was like God, looking down on everyone and knowing everything about them, even their most secret thoughts. Further, the omniscient narrator could comment on the characters and their choices, and even further, knew the past and future, and could recall what had happened to the characters in the past and foretell what would happen in the future.

In the twentieth century, however, belief in God waned and science and literature both explored the idea of *subjectivity* – that what you observed depended on, and was affected by, you as an observer. Henry James began to explore the idea of an interior consciousness, which was then developed further by writers such as James Joyce and Virginia Woolf, who were both famous for pioneering the technique known as stream of consciousness. This technique aims to reflect exactly how people think and feel (see the 'Riding a stream of consciousness' section earlier in this chapter).

As a result of the increasing problems inherent in using an omniscient narrator, writers started to find other ways to fulfil that role, using the two main methods I cover in the next sections.

Observing from a distance

The *detached observer* is a character outside the main action but connected to it. The narrator, Nick, in Anthony Powell's *A Dance to the Music of Time*, is a good example. Nick knows the characters, sees them from time to time, talks to them, finds out about what they've been doing from others, and thus puts their story together. Another excellent example of this approach is the narrator in Somerset Maugham's *The Razor's Edge*.

This technique can help to create a mystique about the main characters who are being observed, as the writer never enters into their viewpoint; consider F. Scott Fitzgerald's *The Great Gatsby*. The narrator can tie up different stories, move from one place to another and perform many of the functions of the omniscient narrator – although you have to make sure the effect doesn't seem too contrived.

Staying on the surface

In the late twentieth century, some writers played around with the idea of the omniscient narrator by having a completely detached observer who had no access to the thoughts and feelings of the characters. Malcolm Bradbury's *The History Man* provides a classic example. The reader has to deduce from the characters' speech and actions what they're thinking; this technique can reflect the superficiality and lack of depth of people in the modern age.

The report of a detached observer in the story of Sarah and Jenan may look something like this:

> Niall was reading the paper while Jenan was still upstairs. Sarah opened the door and walked into the garden. Through the open door Niall could see the frost lying on the lawn and the crisp puddles of ice on the drive. He saw Sarah begin to shiver.
>
> Niall put down the paper as Sarah came back into the kitchen, slammed the door, and drew her dressing-gown around her.
>
> Just as Niall was about to ask her what was wrong, Jenan came down the stairs. He looked as if he had hardly slept and there were dark circles under his eyes. As soon as Sarah saw this, it seemed that all her anxiety returned. Niall imagined she must be wondering what she should say to him, and how she could break the news. He felt awkward sitting there and wondered if he should leave. He wasn't sure he wanted to be around when Sarah broke the news.
>
> Jenan stared back at Sarah; clearly, he had no idea that anything was wrong.
>
> 'Coffee?' Jenan asked.
>
> Sarah was apologetic. 'I've boiled the kettle, but I'm really sorry, there's no milk.'

Recording past history

You can tell the story with hindsight, relating events from the viewpoint of any of the characters, with the narrator looking back at what happened in the light of knowledge and interpreting the story as she goes along.

Sarah and Jenan's story may go like this:

> Sarah remembered that day when Jenan had come all the way down to her cottage, not yet knowing that Amanda had run off with Sam. It was still etched in her mind as if it were yesterday.

It was so cold that morning. While Jenan was still lying in bed upstairs, Sarah opened the door and walked into the garden. The frost was lying on the lawn and there were crisp puddles of ice on the drive. Sarah began to shiver. The milkman had not come. She felt annoyed, knowing there was no milk left in the fridge.

She went back into the kitchen, slamming the door, and drew her dressing-gown around her. Soon she was going to have to tell him; nothing would ever be the same again.

Jenan came down the stairs. He had hardly slept, he had told her later, and there were dark circles under his eyes. As soon as Sarah saw this, all her anxiety returned. What should she say to him? How could she break the news?

Jenan had stared back at Sarah. At the time she had thought he was angry at having been called all the way down to the cottage, but now she knew that he had suspected all along and was afraid.

'Coffee?' he asked.

Sarah had, she remembered, been apologetic. 'I've boiled the kettle, but I'm really sorry, there's no milk.'

Deciding How Close to Be to the Character

Thinking about the writer's – and therefore the reader's – distance from the character is a helpful way of considering voice and perspective. You can write from five main degrees of closeness with your main character:

- ✔ Being totally inside a character's head, seeing everything from her point of view and hearing her thoughts as they happen. This degree of closeness can create an intense, almost claustrophobic effect.

- ✔ Writing from the point of view of a character, reflecting her thoughts and feelings, but also describing what's going on outside her so that the readers can see some things directly for themselves.

- ✔ Portraying the point of view of a character or characters, but also stepping outside the action, which allows you to comment on or interpret the story as it happens.

- ✔ Being omniscient, describing the world of the story in an objective, detached way.

- ✔ Being totally outside the story, not knowing what's going on inside the characters' heads, but simply describing what they do from the outside. This approach runs the risk of being disengaging and uninvolving.

The first technique gets you right into a character, but can be claustrophobic if used for long periods, especially if the main character isn't very likeable; the last technique is very uninvolving for the reader. In practice, therefore, these techniques aren't often used. Most writers nowadays actually use the second and third techniques.

Handling Multiple Narrators

No rule says that you have to restrict yourself to a single voice when telling a story. Many stories are told from the point of view of two, three or four different characters, although as you expand the number of narrators you also expand the likelihood of confusing your readers.

If you're using different points of view, you need to think of how you're going to alternate them and whether some points of view are more important than others.

You can divide up a multiple narrative in the following ways:

- ✔ Divide the story into two, three or four parts, one for each narrator.
- ✔ Alternate chapter by chapter.
- ✔ Offer a different point of view in each separate scene.

If you're using the third-person perspective, you can use the same authorial voice throughout the work. If, however, you're using the first-person perspective, you need to capture a different voice for each character. This approach can be really interesting, but also very risky, as readers may like some voices but struggle with others.

When using multiple narrators, you can have each narrator tell a different part of the story so the reader can put them all together to make a whole, or you can tell the same story from several alternative points of view. If you choose the second option, be very careful to tell the story differently enough to be interesting to the reader. Repeating the same story with slight variations is dull. Let characters lie, or omit or add details that the other characters left out. Your aim is to make your readers feel that they've solved a puzzle and have worked out what really happened.

Try writing about a car accident from the point of view of

- ✔ The driver
- ✔ The passenger
- ✔ A witness
- ✔ A police officer

Rashomon is a classic film by the Japanese film-maker Akira Kurosawa. In the story, two men shelter from a rainstorm in a temple. As they wait for the rain to stop, one of the men tells the other the story of a warrior, his wife and a bandit, from their three different points of view. Each one tells a different story, in which the character who's narrating justifies his or her own actions and comes out best. Ultimately the man reveals that he witnessed the whole thing and tells a completely different version of the story. In the end, the viewer is left not knowing what to believe.

Chapter 7

Describing Your World

Descriptive writing is one of the fundamentals of all creative writing. Whether you're describing nature in a poem, a place in a piece of travel writing, objects you remember in an autobiography or creating a setting in a novel, you need to find ways of communicating what things look and feel like, so that the reader can see and feel things as you intend.

Yet describing things effectively isn't easy. You may fall into the trap of using clichés that fail to awaken the reader's imagination, putting down clunky metaphors and similes that fail to communicate meaning or writing long passages of description that just slow down the plot. You need to fight any tendency to be lazy so that you look at and describe things clearly and in a fresh way.

Used well, descriptive writing can transform a narrative, make a poem sing, add to the reader's sense of realism and authenticity, and make both real and imaginary characters and settings vivid and compelling. In this chapter, I show you how.

Recognising the Power of Description

One of the most astonishing things about creative writing is that, as a writer, you can see something in your own head – a place, a person, an object from your childhood – and write about it in such a way that the place, character or object springs to life in the reader's mind almost exactly as you saw it. How can this happen? Just by writing a few words on a page, what's in your mind leaps into someone else's. Creative writing's really a form of telepathy!

Acknowledging what objects can do

Objects are incredibly useful in fiction. When you describe an object in detail, it becomes significant and important – the reader will remember it. Objects can be made to accomplish many things, including to:

✔ **Be a clue:** A bell cord in the wrong place in Arthur Conan Doyle's Sherlock Holmes short story 'The Adventure of the Speckled Band'.

✔ **Represent the person it belongs to:** Piggy's glasses in William Golding's *Lord of the Flies*.

✔ **Trigger a flashback or a memory:** The *petite madeleine* in Marcel Proust's *In Remembrance of Times Past*.

✔ **Act as a plot device, be the thing that everyone is after:** The One Ring in J. R. R. Tolkien's *The Lord of the Rings*.

✔ **Serve as a symbol, standing for something bigger than itself:** The golden bowl in Henry James's novel of the same name.

✔ **Be a character in its own right or link separate narratives together:** The violin in François Girard's 1998 film *The Red Violin*.

Signposting importance

Describing something in a story or piece of writing means you're signalling its importance. The more detail you use, the more important that place, character or object is.

The amount of description you use is a handy way of signposting to the reader what's important and what isn't. If you describe something specific, make sure that you do so for a reason; if it doesn't have a role to play, don't mention it. To paraphrase Chekhov on writing plays, 'If there's a gun hanging on the wall in Act One, it must be fired by the end of Act Three.'

If you want to hide a clue in a story, common practice is to bury it in a wealth of detail. If you hide the key object in a group of other objects, the reader won't notice its importance, but will remember it was there later when it becomes significant. If, however, you want to draw attention to one object among a group, describe the important object last and in more detail than the others.

In fiction, as in life, a tiny detail can mean life or death. Even the colour of a coat can be vital. Suppose a character goes climbing in a dangerous place wearing a green jacket. She falls. When the rescue helicopter looks for her, she can't be found; her green jacket renders her invisible in the landscape. Suppose, however, that she's wearing a red jacket; the helicopter pilot sees her easily, and she's saved. You may not even notice when you're busy writing that such tiny details, which you may not even think about at the time, can change the whole story.

Noting the details

When you look back you remember the details of things, and the details you include in your writing are what helps the reader to picture a scene.

A character is drinking tea from a cup. How do readers imagine 'a cup'? They can't – the description's too vague. But put in the details and they can see it perfectly. Is it a thin blue porcelain cup with a gold rim, an old chipped pottery cup with a brown glaze or a seventies style retro cup with an orange zigzag pattern?

A 'house' could be anything, but you can picture a red-brick thirties semi-detached house, a Victorian Gothic mansion or a country cottage with roses climbing up the door. You can't taste a 'cake', but if described specifically – a heavy fruitcake, a lemon sponge or a brownie – you can imagine the taste and texture of each of these vividly.

Never use a general word when a specific one works better. Rather than 'animal', use 'horse', 'cow' or 'pig'; rather than 'building', use 'office block', 'mansion flats' or 'warehouse'. Sometimes just a detail or two can give you the whole scene. 'The hotel room was dowdy with a faded orange candlewick bedspread and a tattered sentimental print of the Virgin and Child on the wall by the window.' That's enough. You don't need to know the colour of the carpet or the walls or the shape of the lamp-stand, the exact dimensions of the room or the height of the ceiling, or that the wardrobe, chest of drawers and bedside table don't match.

Too much detail can be oppressive, can clutter the imagination and actually make you less able to see the scene in your mind's eye. How much is too much? Well, some writers are wordier than others, and style and taste partly influence the decision. To judge how much detail to use in your own writing, read works by really great writers or those of people writing in the genre that you prefer, see how they do it and copy them.

The same less-is-more approach applies when describing people. Don't give a blow-by-blow description: *Yuri was exactly six foot one tall, with grey-blue eyes and dark hair. His face was square-shaped with high cheekbones and he had a slightly lop-sided smile. He was broad in stature, with . . .* and so on. You don't want to read any more and may stop taking the details in. In life, you don't see people in detail at first meeting. You don't have time to look at them for hours because that would be staring and anyway, you have to talk to them and interact. You form an impression – that a person is tall, short, attractive or plain – and as you see more of them, you notice the details. You can feed little details to readers bit by bit as they get to know a character, just as happens in real life.

Details matter. They matter because they're what make things precious to us. A child who loses her teddy won't be happy with a new one that's much the same. She wants her old one, with the tattered left ear, the mend on the elbow, the lopsided nose and the stain on its back where she dropped it in a puddle.

Good poets have a remarkable capacity for writing about small, individual details, which make an object concrete and appear almost miraculously vividly in the reader's inner eye. Consider this line from Stephen Spender's poem, 'The Pylons': 'There runs the quick perspective of the future.' From this handful of words I can see a row of pylons, the cables dipping and rising, going on and on towards the horizon, the wires crackling with energy. When reading Matthew Arnold's poem, 'Dover Beach', I can hear the sound of the sea:

> . . . the grating roar
> Of pebbles which the waves draw back, and fling,
> . . . But now I only hear
> Its melancholy, long, withdrawing roar

Small, vivid details can tell a lot about both characters and their relationships. In *Anna Karenina*, when Anna returns home having met her future lover, Vronsky, at a ball, the first thing she sees is her husband. '"Oh my God! Why do his ears stick out like that!" she thought, looking at his frigid and distinguished figure, and especially the ears that struck her at that moment as propping up the brim of his round hat.' This detail signals the new way in which Anna perceives her husband after falling in love with Vronsky.

Look out for details and images and record them. Notice objects, sounds, textures and impressions as you go about your daily business, and then write them down.

Being authentic

Details are important in a piece of writing because they create a sense of authenticity. They make the reader think that this character, this writer, knows; she's been there; he's seen it himself. Therefore I trust what this writer is saying; even though I know this character's experience is in a work of fiction, I believe in it. Often you need to research the little details to get them right. Some of your readers will be experts on the subject you're writing about and they'll notice if you get things wrong; spotting mistakes can ruin their whole experience of your story.

Trust is very important when you're describing something technical, a specific job or a legal or medical procedure. For example, if you're writing about a character involved in an accident who needs medical treatment, you need to be able to describe such details as the exact injuries, the procedure that takes over when the character reaches the hospital, what treatment the doctor administers and how long the injuries take to heal. These details need to be right or readers won't believe them.

In Michael Ondaatje's *The English Patient*, the character Kip has to defuse a bomb. The procedure is described in exact detail. Ondaatje cannot have been at the defusing of a war-time bomb, but reading about it, you know that he has spoken to someone who was there or has read an accurate account of it. No one could invent such detail. It has to be true.

Similarly, in his novel *Saturday*, Ian McEwan describes an operation in perfect detail. You know that he has witnessed an actual operation and therefore knows that the antiseptic solution used to clean the patient's skin before surgery is yellow; he's heard the hiss of the oxygen and smelt the 'sharp odour of singed flesh'.

There's no substitute for getting the details right. Observe an unfamiliar procedure or talk to someone who knows what it entails before committing a description to paper.

Using All the Senses

Beginning writers often write very visually, describing how things look. This information is important, but people also hear, smell, touch, taste and sense, and these forms of awareness often work at a deeper, more visceral level. Making use of the full range of senses can really hook readers into a story and make them experience that world as if they were actually there themselves.

Utilise the senses in turn:

- ✔ **Sight:** Write about colour, shape and texture. Consider the way light falls on an object. Does an object look like something else, and if so, what? (See the 'Comparing with similes and metaphors' section later in this chapter for ideas.)

- ✔ **Sound:** Stretch your vocabulary: describe the sound of a plane in the distance without using the word 'rumble', wind in the trees without 'sighing' and a piano without 'tinkle'.

- ✔ **Smell:** Smell is the most evocative of the senses and can recall a memory like nothing else. Think of words you could use to describe the smell of freshly roasted coffee, a cake baking or manure freshly dug in the fields.

✔ **Taste:** Flavours can also evoke strong emotions. *Bitter, sweet* and *sour* are powerful words that can link to deep-felt emotions.

✔ **Touch:** Describing how an object feels gives it a solidity and presence in a piece of writing. Is an object hard or soft, rough or smooth, heavy or light? What does it feel like in the palm of your hand? Imagine stroking it with your eyes closed, rubbing it against your cheek or finding it in a dark place.

Beware of using too many adjectives in your descriptions. Many writers use double or even triple adjectives a great deal. Too often you read of the thin attractive woman lifting the fine green porcelain cup to her red pursed strawberry-shaped lips with her soft white hand and taking a small, tentative gulp before setting the cup down on the hard, smooth surface of the mahogany table.

Try to resist crowding your writing with adjectives – the reader finds it repetitive and tiresome. Using too many adjectives sounds over-written, and the reader becomes aware of the writing itself, rather than the picture you're trying to create.

At its best, writing that utilises the full range of senses can tap into a reader's full emotional range, as demonstrated in the following examples and my reaction to them:

✔ **'Out of the abandoned garden came the forlorn cry of a bird.'** Jorge Luis Borges, *Death and the Compass.*

I can hear that bird. All the loneliness and melancholy of the world is in its call.

✔ **'Ada [. . .] scooped berries into her mouth. The preserves had been made with little sweetening and tasted fresh and sharp.'** Charles Frazier, *Cold Mountain.*

When I read these words the saliva pours into my mouth as if I'm tasting blackberries.

✔ **'The second man's rifle was suddenly reduced to a tiny black hole no bigger than a ten-kopeck piece.'** Mikhail Bulgakov, *The White Guard.*

This terrifying image of a man pointing a gun straight at someone makes my heart pound.

Defamiliarisation is a technique whereby a writer describes an object in such a way that it takes the reader some time to realise what it is. This device can have the effect of making the reader see something in a new light. Defamiliarisation can also show that the character has never seen anything like this before – useful for someone who's travelled in time or is visiting a country he's never been to before.

Describe an object as if a character has never seen it before. Describe a familiar object from the point of view of an alien from another planet.

Employing the Tools of Description

When you describe the world you want to convey in your writing, you'll most likely employ similes and metaphors, and perhaps even symbols.

Comparing with similes and metaphors

If you've forgotten what you learnt in school about similes and metaphors, don't worry. Just to clarify:

✔ A *simile* is a form of comparison which uses 'like' or 'as':

- The sea is transparent, like glass.

- The room was as dark as a cave.

✔ A *metaphor* does the same thing, but omits the 'like' or 'as':

- The sea is glass.

- The room was a dark cave.

Similes and metaphors, then, do much the same thing. However, a metaphor is stronger, more poetic and can be more surprising. A metaphor offers a curious paradox: a statement that is technically untrue (the sea is *not* glass) creates an image of surprising truthfulness. A commonly accepted definition of metaphor is the practice of finding the similarity in dissimilarity.

You use metaphors all the time, without even realising it, when you talk about an old flame, things going smoothly, feeling rough, a glowing review, a shady character, dog tired, the sweet smell of success.

 Overused metaphors, known as *dead metaphors*, have become a form of cliché. They don't surprise you or make you see things anew. Phrases like 'he was flogging a dead horse' or 'she lost her head' no longer actually conjure up those images.

Using metaphor is much more difficult than it seems. First, you need to avoid the dead ones. Second, you need to make sure that they feel right. A metaphor should make you agree with the comparison instinctively: 'yes, a calm sea does look like a sheet of glass' or 'yes, a dark room is a bit like a cave'. A really good metaphor makes you sit up and feel that you can see something in a fresh and new way.

According to Graham Greene, in a footnote to his *Congo Journal*: 'Memories are a form of simile; when we say something is "like", we are remembering.' You can use similes to provide readers with information about your characters without obviously telling them. If you write, 'The diamond shimmered like the icebergs in the Arctic she had seen as a small girl', the reader knows she went to the far north as a child.

Metaphors and similes that draw attention to themselves or don't really work can ruin a piece of writing even more than using hackneyed ones. 'When he woke his mouth was as dry as sandpaper' is hardly original but at least you know how the character feels. 'When he woke up he felt as if a thousand snakes covered in grains of desert sand were writhing and blasting hot air around inside his mouth' may be original but is completely distracting.

You can write really good, clear, imaginative description without ever using a simile or metaphor. These devices are best used sparingly, for effect now and again. Peppering your story, novel or poem with metaphor upon metaphor can seem pretentious, cluttered and contrived. Metaphors and similes are powerful tools, so respect them and handle them with care.

Exploring symbols

In his book *Man and His Symbols*, Carl Jung wrote: 'We constantly use symbolic terms to represent concepts that we cannot define or fully understand.' They 'imply something vague, unknown, or hidden from us.'

Symbols often come into poetry, prose or a script without your conscious thought because they tend to work at a subconscious level. They slip in from some deep place in your mind while you're writing, and you only recognise them later.

Symbols often have a number of different meanings and are powerful partly for this reason. Consider some common symbols and their meanings:

- **Scales or a balance:** Justice, truth or judgement
- **Heart:** Love or passion, also courage
- **Dove:** Peace, hope or spirituality
- **Ring:** Oneness, unity or bondage
- **Owl:** Wisdom, but also occult powers
- **Skull:** Death or danger

Psychoanalysts make use of dream symbolism to see what might be troubling the dreamer. Knowledge of some common symbols can be helpful if you want to create dreams and fantasies for your characters. Jung's *Man and His Symbols* and a dictionary of symbols may be useful.

Some writers, artists and film-makers rely heavily on symbolism in their work. You feel that something powerful is running beneath the image or writing, which you want to reach but can't quite understand. This use of symbolism gives the poem, story or film real depth. On the other hand, putting in symbols too obviously and deliberately can kill a piece of writing. Letting symbols emerge naturally and then shaping them is a better approach than shoe-horning them in.

Symbols often appear in dreams and fantasies. Because some thoughts are too scary to be acknowledged, you tend to repress them until they appear in symbolic form in your dreams – and sometimes in your writing too.

Creating a Sense of Place

A story's setting is all-important, so describe a place in such a way that you bring it vividly to life. Doing so doesn't mean that you have to describe everything about a location. The small details of everyday life that are specific to one place rather than another are what's important. Remember to think about the smells, sounds and feel of a place, as well as visual details.

Place can be vital in a piece of fiction, so much so that it becomes almost a character in itself. Each place has a different language and codes of behaviour, its own difficulties, hardships and pleasures. A story set in London is very different to the same story told in New York, Paris or Calcutta, or in the middle of the outback, on another planet or in the distant past. Nineteenth-century novels commonly opened with long descriptions of the setting. Consider the description of Egdon Heath at the opening of Thomas Hardy's *The Return of the Native* or London in Charles Dickens's *Bleak House*. Nowadays such descriptions aren't enough to hook the reader. You probably need to focus much more on a character in a landscape, or on the feelings that the setting arouses in the character, or the character's response to the location. The opening of Graham Greene's *Brighton Rock* provides a classic example. Brighton is described in some detail, but only after Greene grabs you with a character's life being in peril.

Having a map or guide to the place where your story is set can be helpful, so that you can use actual place names and refer to buildings and landmarks. If you travel to that place, take a notebook with you and note the details you'll need later, such as the colour of the banknotes, the cost of the train tickets or the name of a particular shop or restaurant.

Tantalising with exotic places

One of the great pleasures of reading, whether a poem, novel or historical account, is the ability to travel to a distant land or culture from the comfort and safety of your own armchair.

Many of the novels and travelogues of the nineteenth century are heavy with description of places, with details of the landscape, the weather, the people, the clothes they wear, the food they eat and the houses they live in. These details were important because people travelled so much less then and had limited access to images, photographs and illustrations of exotic places.

Nowadays, people are so used to seeing television documentaries, films and photographs that describing places in great detail isn't necessary. People can imagine a lot for themselves; they may be more interested in the details that a photograph can't offer – the feelings a place evokes, the smell, the tiny details of people's lives.

Imagining fantasy places

The popularity of science fiction and fantasy in the twentieth century encouraged many writers to invent their own worlds of the future or historical fantasy. Doing so isn't as easy as it sounds. Creating an imaginary world, working out what it looks like, what laws govern it, what language the people speak and its history involves a great deal of thought. If you're writing science fiction, you also need to decide whether the same laws of nature apply in the world of your story. For example, a cubical planet would conflict with the laws of science in our universe, and you'd need to create a universe with very different scientific laws to make it plausible.

Inventing a world that bears some similarity to your own is easiest – otherwise you'll end up spending more time on describing the world you've created than telling your story. Remember that the setting is only the *background* to your story and shouldn't take centre stage.

Some authors have created worlds so vivid that they exist like a real place in the imagination of the reader. *Solaris* by Stanislaw Lem (made into a film of genius by Andrei Tarkovsky – give the modern remake a miss) and *The Lord of the Rings* by J. R. R. Tolkien are two examples. These novelists created worlds with their own histories, maps, languages, laws of physics and internal logic. The details are so well described that the reader utterly believes in them.

Creating Mood and Suspense

You use description to set the mood or tone of a story. The way you describe a place, the time of day, weather or season can set up what's going to happen; it is a bright landscape on a sunny day in early summer or a brooding, dark place in autumn when the sun is about to set.

Using the weather to reflect the mood of the character is a device called the *pathetic fallacy*. Jane Austen's *Emma* provides an example: Emma goes to the shrubbery to confront Mr Knightley in the pouring rain, but the sun comes out after he's proposed to her. You can also reverse this expectation to good effect; a character going to her child's funeral on a bright spring morning when the daffodils are in bloom provides a contrast that makes the death seem even starker.

Describe a place familiar to a character in a story. Look carefully at the adjectives you used. How does changing them affect the mood of the piece?

Creating a mood can in itself lead to suspense. It can foreshadow something that you know is waiting to happen. A storm brewing may not only mean physical danger for the characters, but also that an explosive confrontation is coming.

Suspense comes from knowing that something will happen but having to wait, and often description can be used to fill the gap. (See Chapter 8 for more on creating suspense.)

A letter arrives on the mat. Have the character pick it up, turn it over and describe it in great detail. Don't let the character open it for ten minutes! The longer you describe the letter, the greater the reader's impatience to find out what's in it (but don't allow the tension to become so unbearable that the reader skips ahead).

Description on its own, without narrative tension, can be dull. The reader tends to skip it or start thinking about something else. Keep your description for those points where a character is threatened or where something dramatic is expected to happen; it creates a gap between the threat and the action and acts to increase the suspense.

Chapter 8

Plotting Your Way

*P*lotting is both the easiest and most difficult aspect of storytelling. Easy in the sense that you're familiar with stories from fairy stories in childhood to the novels, films and newspaper articles that you read or watch, and so know a thing or two about how to tell a story; but difficult in that the plot holds the whole structure of your writing together, and is actually much more challenging than expected.

How do you write a story where the outcome isn't completely obvious from the start, but not so confusing that the reader gets lost? How do you keep the reader engrossed? How do you create that 'ah-ha!' sense of satisfaction at the end when everything comes together and all is revealed?

Plot is most easy to follow in straightforward genre novels where the author's only intention is to keep the reader turning the page. Even if these novels aren't your kind of fiction, studying them to see how the plot works is well worthwhile. After all, you can't begin to do clever things with narrative until you've learned the simple rules.

Listing the Seven Basic Plots

Film producer David O. Selznick once said that only one plot exists: boy meets girl, boy loses girl, boy finds girl again. Christopher Booker, in his excellent book entitled *The Seven Basic Plots: Why We Tell Stories*, says that writers can use (you guessed it!) seven basic plots; others have come up with six, twelve and twenty-one. Personally, I think there are six basic plots, and one reversal of them all.

The basic plots are found in myths, fairy tales, novels, plays, films and almost every kind of story you can imagine. They are:

- **Overcoming the monster or the battle between good and evil.** The traditional tale of triumph over an opponent or obstacle. In myth, the stories of Hercules and Beowulf serve as examples; in modern cinema James Bond films or *Jaws*. In modern fiction, the monster is more likely to be something internal – the monster of alcoholism, greed or paedophilia.

- **The quest.** An adventure story, in which the protagonist goes off in pursuit of some goal. Examples are Jason looking for the Golden Fleece, the Knights of the Round Table searching for the Holy Grail and Indiana Jones seeking archaeological treasures. The quest can be for something physical, a real object, or for something spiritual; it can also be for a piece of information or a person – the classic detective story, for example, is the quest to find the murderer. It can also be the quest for Mr Right, as in Helen Fielding's *Bridget Jones's Diary*.

- **Voyage and return or coming of age.** Here, the protagonist sets out on a journey (this can be an internal journey, though most often is an actual one) and eventually returns home older, wiser and in some way changed. Many road movies also follow this pattern, with the outer journey reflecting the inner growth of the character. Examples are *Le Grand Meaulnes* by Alain-Fournier, *The Catcher in the Rye* by J. D. Salinger and *The Bluest Eye* by Toni Morrison.

- **Rags to riches.** This is the Cinderella story, or any story in which the main character starts out poor and humble and, through his own efforts or aided by others, comes into wealth and riches. Sometimes these can be inner riches as well as, or rather than, outer ones. Examples include Charlotte Brontë's *Jane Eyre* and *Great Expectations* by Charles Dickens.

- **The romance or classical comedy.** The romantic plot has been unchanged for generations, from Jane Austen's *Pride and Prejudice* to Audrey Niffenegger's *The Time Traveler's Wife*. In a romance, the two potential lovers meet but are kept apart by a series of misunderstandings and circumstances. In the end, all is clear, and the couple are free to marry. The Shakespearean comedies are also all romances. Here, the term *comedy* isn't used in the sense of humour or satire but refers to a dramatic work that has a happy ending.

- **Death and rebirth or redemption.** The great mythic story is told in many religions around the world, from that practised in ancient Egypt to Christianity. The God dies, often as a result of jealousy and treachery, descends into hell, but is then resurrected. In the process, this character or others are redeemed.

In modern fiction, the death and rebirth are usually spiritual not physical. For example, in A. J. Cronin's *The Citadel*, the main character becomes a successful doctor to the rich and is then arrogant and out of touch. He operates on a friend's child, and the child dies. He then undergoes a crisis before reforming himself and going on to serve as a doctor to the very poor, seeking no material reward. Dostoevsky's *Crime and Punishment* is also a redemption narrative.

✔ **The tragedy.** The tragedy is really the inversion of all these plots. Tragedy involves the character who fails to overcome the monster, never ends the quest, goes from riches to rags, embarks on a voyage from which he doesn't return, ends up apart from his lover and dies with no hope of rebirth.

In classical tragedy, the hero or heroine fails because of a fatal flaw; an element in his personality prevents him from achieving what he should. The thirst for revenge, too, usually ends in a tragic outcome for all concerned.

If you're struggling to find a structure for your story, consider taking one of these classic plots and re-telling it in a modern context.

Seeing the classic plots in everyday life

Even in non-fiction, the classic plots apply. Newspapers, magazines and television chat shows are full of real-life stories:

✔ The politician who starts out poor, climbs to the giddy heights of fame and then is undone by a financial or sexual impropriety (rags to riches, riches to rags).

✔ Lovers from rival communities who come together despite the odds (romance).

✔ A mountaineer who ascends an unclimbed peak, surmounting tremendous obstacles (overcoming the monster).

✔ A person with a fatal disease who, against all the odds, goes into remission and has a child (death and rebirth).

Managing main plots and sub-plots

If your story follows a complex narrative, taking one thread as the main plot and the others as sub-plots can be helpful. Sub-plots can be used for:

✔ Telling the main story in reverse; so if the main story ends in tragedy, the sub-plot can end happily, providing light relief.

✔ Adding complexity to character; so in a gripping thriller, for example, a romantic sub-plot develops the characters' inner lives.

✔ Providing a different mood or tone; in a comedy you can develop a much darker sub-plot, or vice versa.

✔ Developing layers within the story, creating greater realism and depth; real life is complex and doesn't simply follow a single narrative.

Plotting Consciously and Unconsciously

Some people are conscious plotters; they like to have all the details worked out, they draw up a synopsis and a plan, and then they write. Others could never work that way. They have an idea of a character in a situation, and they want to find out what happens next. They don't know, and if they did, they wouldn't want to write the story. They are unconscious plotters.

These techniques have their own strengths and weaknesses, and most writers combine a bit of each. The next sections consider both approaches.

Thinking things through ahead of time

Conscious plotters like to know where they are before they start. You have a clear idea of the outline of the story and may even know what happens at the end. You may draw plans, graphs, storylines and chapter-by-chapter breakdowns, and have everything pretty much worked out by the time you start the real writing.

This method has three main problems:

✔ The characters, after they come to life, may turn out not to want to do what you've planned for them to do. You may realise that, while you thought George was a coward, in fact he has reserves of courage that come to the fore in a certain situation. Now what do you do?

✔ If you know what's going to happen at the end, the writing process itself isn't very interesting. You have nothing to discover, and the writing can thus become a bit dull and formulaic, resembling joining the dots or painting by numbers.

   ✔ Because you know what's going to happen, conveying any real doubts to the reader is difficult. The story can turn out flat and conventional, with no surprises.

Screenplays and plays tend to be more tightly structured than prose fiction. In films and plays, particularly, the script is agreed before filming or rehearsals start, although actors quite often make changes ('My character would never say that!'), and the writer can be asked to make changes and rewrites on the set.

Writing off the cuff

Some writers just start writing without a plan. A voice comes to you, a character, a situation. You start writing to explore it, and some great ideas come up. Characters sometimes reveal themselves to have intriguing secrets. You write a scene between two characters who are meant to dislike one another and to your delight find that they're starting to fall in love.

As you keep writing, problems often appear:

   ✔ The story goes down side-tracks and peters out. You haven't got a clue what a certain scene is there for. You don't know what's going to happen or why you're writing. Then you give up.

   ✔ You throw away an awful lot of writing. As your story becomes clearer, many scenes don't fit in and have to be discarded or rewritten altogether.

   ✔ The story ends up unfocused, baggy, disconnected and hard to read.

Merging conscious and unconscious plotting

Most writers use a mixture of conscious and unconscious plotting, though you probably lean towards one or the other. Keep your mind fixed on the central dramatic question of your story. In doing so, you won't go too far wrong, however you approach your writing.

Ultimately, maintaining a balance between these two extremes is best. Conscious plotters may need to loosen up a bit, be prepared to tear up their plans from time to time and allow their unconscious minds to tell the story. Unconscious plotters may need to spend a little bit of time thinking about their stories and becoming more aware of plotting issues, especially when they come to revise and edit their stories.

Keeping focused

Keeping the story focused on the main issue at hand is one of the hardest aspects of plotting. First-time novelists, especially, tend to get carried away with trying to fit in too many characters and too many issues. The plot becomes increasingly baggy and finally runs out of steam.

In your first novel, concentrate on telling a simple story really well. After mastering this one, you can go on to more complex narratives.

If, however, what you want to write really demands a large cast of characters and a complex narrative, try to break it down into separate strands and think about plotting them separately. In particular, focus on the fact that every main character must have his own narrative. Then you can braid the strands together at the end.

Asking the Central Question and Including the Essential Elements

At its most simple, a narrative asks a question at the outset and answers it at the end. Even something as short as a five-line poem follows this rule. In between, the story twists and turns, for a few lines or for hundreds (even thousands) of pages, keeping the reader in suspense about the outcome, how the question is answered, whether things turn out well or badly.

Plot includes the following essential elements:

- ✔ **A character:** In order for a plot to exist, so must a character – the narrator or someone the narrator writes about – and about whom the reader cares enough or is sufficiently interested in to want to know what happens to her.

- ✔ **Motivation:** That character, the protagonist, must want something – your character must have a motivation. The question often then simply becomes whether the protagonist triumphs.

- ✔ **Conflict:** To create doubt about the outcome, a reason must exist why the character can't easily achieve her aim. Perhaps an antagonist works against her, or some inner conflict in the protagonist – a fear or character trait she needs to overcome – prevents her from doing so. Sometimes both apply. Whichever is the case, you need to include a conflict or difficulty.

> ✔ **Connection:** A good plot gives readers a sense that all the events in the story are interconnected – that one thing leads to another, that what one character does affects others, that what others do affects the protagonist.
>
> ✔ **Climax:** A point at which the outcome is decided, and after which the story naturally comes to an end.

Including all these elements isn't easy. The next sections offer tips on making the task manageable.

Seeing character as plot

Some say that 'character is plot'. The character's actions drive the story. Plot also focuses on the choices a character has to make.

A story resembles a garden of forking paths – the title of a famous story by the Argentine writer Jorge Luis Borges. Every time your character faces a choice, the plot potentially splits. Marking the moments when importance choices happen is important in fiction. Should your character go to the party (where she might meet Mr Right) or stay at home (where a stranger might come to the house and propel her into an adventure)? Should your character take the money or refuse it, answer the challenge or dismiss it, commit the crime or resist it?

Thinking about the characters' backgrounds is very important. You need to understand why they make the choices they do and the reasons behind them. Why are they acting in character or going out on a limb, or behaving in a surprising or contradictory way – as people often do? Chapter 4 offers tips on developing your characters.

Try this exercise to help you think about the importance of the choices a character makes in the development of a story.

1. **Write the beginning of a scene in which a character has to make a choice** – she's invited to a dinner, for example.

2. **Write the scene with her choosing one path.**

3. **Now write the scene with her choosing another path.**

4. **Now think of a third possible outcome** (perhaps she decides to go to the dinner but is prevented for some reason).

5. **Consider which version is the most interesting, and why.**

Thinking about choices in this way is really important for fiction, and can also be very useful if you get stalled. If your story runs out of steam, track back to the last moment when the character made a choice and take a different fork in the path. Doing so often gets the story rolling along again.

Make sure that the choices your character has to make are significant; that they're issues of life or death – at least to her. Readers aren't likely to become deeply engaged with a character whose sole choice in life is whether to make a pot of English Breakfast or Earl Grey tea.

Balancing plot and character

A tension always exists between the dictates of the plot – the story – and the characters who carry it. This conflict can often cause problems, whether you write more consciously and create plot-driven narratives or prefer to let the story be dictated by the characters.

If a story is too plot-driven, you risk reducing the character to a cardboard cut-out – someone who simply exists to do the things the plot dictates he does.

In many high-tech thrillers, the main character seems devoid of inner life. Many of these stories don't really go into the interior consciousness of the characters at all, but describe their heroic deeds solely from the outside. Occasionally some internal motivation is revealed – the hero's father was killed by the Russians, so he wishes to avenge himself – but this is covered only at the most superficial level. Such stories can often have great plot twists, but the secrets and surprises revealed to the reader are often things the hero knew all along – and which the readers would have known had they been given any insight into the character's thoughts and feelings.

Character-based fiction, however, can often lack drive and drama because creating surprises is harder if you know everything the character is thinking and feeling. Avoid situations in which most of the action is inside the character's head and very little happens in the physical world. In a narrative, the inner conflict becomes externalised into action. If a character has an abstract motivation – for example, to achieve fame or fortune – translate that into a more specific goal.

For example, compare two methods of dealing with the story of a woman coming to terms with the death of her husband. In one version, the husband died of a heart attack. The woman spends a lot of time washing up, staring out of the window, remembering happy times they had together and not knowing what to do with her life. Finally she decides to get a job. In the second version, the woman's husband died trying to climb a mountain. She decides to help herself come to terms with his death by climbing the mountain herself. The difficulties she faces in the journey up the mountain mirror the internal stages of her grief.

Of course, you could make the first version of the story more interesting by re-working the story as the woman's search for a job (the quest!). Perhaps she breaks down in the first interview and can't stop crying when she's asked if she's married. Perhaps she turns down another job because it entails being based in another city, and she realises she's not ready to leave the house she and her husband shared. Your character needs to have a goal and to face plenty of obstacles along the way.

 All great fiction has an inner and outer aspect. Consider Hamlet. Hamlet's motivation is to find out if his uncle killed his father and, if so, to avenge his father's death. When he discovers that his uncle did murder his father, Hamlet has a choice to make – to kill his uncle or not to. But his conscience troubles him. Hamlet spends time in reflection – to be or not to be – but he acts too, often impulsively. If the story was just about the action without the reflection, or if Hamlet simply dripped around the stage for hours wondering what to do, the play wouldn't be the great work it is. Its genius lies in the way that Hamlet's interior battle with his conscience is externalised into the action of the play.

Revealing motivation

The engine behind every plot is the motivation of the central characters: what they hope or fear, what they want to achieve.

People's motivations often stem from their early lives and their childhood experiences (Chapter 4 covers creating characters). In adult life, people often try to make up for things they feel they missed out on as children or to put right wrongs they think they suffered. A person brought up in dire poverty may want to make money to avoid suffering privation again. Someone who was unloved as a child has a great need to be loved as an adult. A refugee seeks security, and someone who suffered a great injustice seeks to put it right.

Frequently, however, people tend to re-enact the patterns of the past and their search for what they lack thus backfires: in trying to earn that bit more cash, a banker overreaches his capabilities and loses everything; the person who desperately seeks love can't offer it himself and so can't find anyone to love him; and the person who seeks security can never trust anyone and therefore find rest.

By trying to hang on to things, you often lose them, and sometimes, when you seem to reach your goal, you sabotage yourself because you can't bear to end the search. Out of these tensions a great story can emerge.

Writing on big themes

Some writers put pen to paper because they want to write about a big theme – corruption, politics, financial greed, religion, sexual identity, persecution or exploitation. Some write about clashes between cultures, globalisation or the consequences of global warming.

If you're writing a fictional book based around a theme, you need to find a way of translating it to readers through characters they can identify with and really care about. Make the big theme matter to the characters in a very real and concrete way.

Tom Wolfe's hugely successful novel, later filmed, *The Bonfire of the Vanities* provides a great example. The novel concerns ambition, racism, class politics and greed in 1980s New York City. Wolfe explicitly set out to write a 'great American novel' about these themes. He wanted to show the greed of Wall Street, corruption in the legal and criminal justice system and the division between rich and poor and black and white, but he doesn't do so in the abstract. Wolfe covers these themes through the story of bond trader Sherman McCoy, who runs over a young black man in the Bronx after taking a wrong turning when picking up his mistress. A journalist, Peter Fallow, investigates and gets caught up with a local religious and political leader, Reverend Bacon, who's using the case to improve his own political standing, and Sherman is accused of manslaughter. Through the unfolding of his story, you see how all the issues Wolfe wanted to write about affect individual people.

Handling connection and coincidence

Coincidence is absolutely essential to fiction. You tend to think of it as being a bad thing, when in fact coincidence is a standard narrative convention. Stories happen, after all, because something coincides. If the two lovers didn't happen to bump into one another in the supermarket, the romance would never take place. If the woman didn't happen to miss her train and end up walking home alone late on a particular night, so that her path crossed with the criminal, the murder wouldn't have taken place. If the man on the train had never met the woman with a scheming mind, he wouldn't have been enticed into breaking up his marriage and embarking on the path that led to his downfall.

An initial coincidence that provides the spark for the plot is very different to a narrative that piles one coincidence on top of another. These rapidly cease to be believable. Coincidence clumsily used is such an obvious device that it alienates the reader from the narrative.

Coincidences matter because you take them to have a meaning. A piece of writing tends to connect events and people, to show that a structure, purpose and meaning are evident in the chaos of everyone's lives. People like coincidences because they tend to make them think that perhaps life isn't just a random chain of events.

Because a work of fiction *is* planned, it always has coincidences. Everything in a work of fiction exists for a reason. In life, a character may go jogging late in the evening and notice that a light is shining in Mr Brown's house. That observation would be the end of it. In a novel, though, if a character noticed this detail it would show that Mr Brown was at home that night, or perhaps that he was not but wanted to make it look as if he was, which would be significant for an alibi to a murder or to hint at adultery, for instance.

You can sometimes get away with a coincidence if the characters acknowledge it openly. 'What a coincidence, meeting you here!' – well, these things do happen. What would be odd is if the characters didn't realise it themselves.

If you use coincidence, try to find a reason for what happens. 'Oh, I always shop here on Mondays', 'I came to the village because my aunt lives here' or 'I stopped here because my car broke down'. What the reason is doesn't matter; it just needs to make sense within your story. Consider making what happened accidentally happen deliberately. For example, instead of having the hero accidentally overhearing an important conversation, have him eavesdrop because he's suspicious. Instead of characters meeting accidentally, have a third person set up the meeting, for reasons of her own.

If you've written the phrases 'at the same time', 'accidentally', 'luckily' or 'unfortunately', these can be a tip-off that you have events happening by sheer coincidence. Search for a better alternative.

Write a story in which a character finds or receives something that later turns out to be connected to another character. Explore the impact of this incident.

Delivering a punch

Every narrative is working its way inevitably towards its conclusion. In a story or novel, the number of pages left makes clear how much of the story remains. Thus the tension needs to rise as the story approaches its climax and draws to its conclusion.

You can achieve a climax by increasing the stakes as the story progresses. A journey becomes ever more difficult and dangerous. As a character gets closer and closer to uncovering the truth, the harder her opponent tries to stop her. The more deeply in love a character becomes, the more dreadful the consequences of losing her lover.

Conflict, climax and resolution is the classic narrative structure. The next sections look at these in a little more depth.

A real-life coincidence

In a real twist of fate, the actor Anthony Hopkins was offered a leading role in a film based on the book *The Girl from Petrovka* by George Feifer. After signing the contract, Hopkins travelled to London. He visited several bookshops, hoping to buy the book, but none had it in stock.

Waiting for the Tube at Leicester Square station, Hopkins saw a book discarded on a bench. When he picked it up, he saw it was *The*

Girl from Petrovka, with some notes scribbled in the margins.

Two years later, filming in Vienna, Hopkins was visited by Feifer, who mentioned that he'd lent a copy of the book with his notes in it to a friend who'd then lost it somewhere in London. Hopkins handed the copy he'd found to Feifer. It was the same book.

Including conflict

Without conflict, there's no story. A character wants something, reaches out and gets it – the story's over. A story only comes to life when the character is blocked from getting what she wants and has to overcome obstacles and difficulties along the way.

You can use four main kinds of conflict:

- **Inner conflict.** The character has a personal dilemma – she wants something, but perhaps feels she doesn't deserve it, or she's been told from childhood that what she wants is bad, or she's afraid of the responsibilities it brings.

- **Personal conflict.** The character comes into conflict with people she's close to and emotionally involved with – parents, partners, lovers, friends. Fear of conflict or explicit arguments and fights with these people may hold your character back.

- **Social conflict.** The character experiences conflict with society more widely – at work, with the law, with religion, with people in the street.

- **Cosmic conflict.** The character's situation involves the fate of the human race, the world or even the whole universe.

Although including conflict in a story is absolutely essential, that doesn't mean that characters have to be continually screaming at one another or that your narrative is an endless series of battles. For most of the narrative, you need to create suspense by holding on to the conflict and not always acting it out straight away (see the 'Creating suspense' section later in this chapter). You can create a great deal of tension through dialogue in which something's bubbling away beneath the surface but doesn't come out, or a character wants to hit someone but manages to restrain herself.

Concluding with the climax

Sooner or later, when the pressure has become unbearable, the conflict needs to come out into the open at the climax of your story. At this moment, the truth is finally revealed, a confrontation that's been brewing for the whole book finally occurs, the big battle or the duel takes place or the lovers finally get together or agree to part.

Writing a climactic scene is difficult because:

✔ It requires all your skill as a writer to set the scene, make the dialogue crackle, describe the action and make it really work.

✔ Many writers are so afraid of being melodramatic that they do the opposite and hold back too much, creating a scene that falls flat.

✔ The success or failure of your whole story ultimately depends on this moment – your readers have been waiting for it, and you can't disappoint them.

No magic approach to writing such scenes exists – and no excuses. You just have to jump in, do your best and rewrite and polish, until your conclusion is as good as you can possibly make it.

Resolving the question

Whatever your main narrative question is, by the end of your story it must be answered. The conflict, whether emotional, personal, social or cosmic, must be resolved.

Dotting all the *i*'s and crossing all the *t*'s isn't necessary, though – some things can be left open for the reader to think about. But essentially your story ends here, and you have to be able to let go of it.

Hooking Your Reader

A story works simply by making the reader want to find out what happens next. Creating this situation sounds easy, but isn't. A narrative isn't simply a succession of one thing following another, a series of 'and thens'. The story needs to provide a motivation for the character, an important goal to aim for, so readers can experience a sense of suspense and tension and enjoy setbacks, surprises and undercurrents as they wait to see what happens.

Consider these two stories:

> Carlo sets out to go to the park. Then he goes to the playground. Then he sees his friend Fred. Then they talk. Carlo invites Fred to dinner. Then Carlo goes to the shop. Then he buys some supper. Fred comes round and they eat and talk. Fred goes home, Carlo watches TV and goes to bed.

Aaarghhh! This narrative provides no tension or dramatic interest.

With a bit of rewriting, this story becomes:

> Carlo sets out to go to the park because he wants to meet his friend and invite him back to dinner to make a business proposal (motivation!).

> Will his friend be there? As he approaches the park, there is no sign of him. Disappointment (setback). He is about to leave when Fred arrives (surprise!). They talk. Will Fred accept the invitation to dinner (question)?

> Fred agrees to come, and Carlo goes shopping. What should he cook to make a good impression (question)? What kind of food will Fred like? Carlo is anxious as he is not the world's best cook (undercurrents).

> Fred arrives for dinner. Carlo is running late and has forgotten a vital ingredient (setback). Will the dinner be a success? Will Fred accept the deal (question)?

> At first Fred is reluctant (setback). Then he says he will – but with several conditions (complications). Can Carlo meet them (question)?

Now the plot is rolling.

At every stage of the story, you need to raise questions in the reader's mind. Sometimes a narrative involves an over-arching question right from the beginning – who carried out the murder? Often a narrative proceeds with a series of questions; a new one is posed as each earlier one is answered.

Creating suspense

Suspense is created when you set up an expectation of what's going to happen, and then hold off from revealing whether it actually does. With no expectation of what might happen, the reader can't follow a narrative thread, and there's no suspense.

Readers must always be looking ahead, so that they can interpret the events that happen now in the light of whether they make the outcome the main character wants more or less likely.

In an adventure narrative, for example, the narrative question may first be: will the character reach the treasure? And, second, will she die in the attempt? Something may go well, and the reader thinks the character's more likely to find the loot. Then something goes really badly, and the reader starts to doubt whether the character succeeds. A suspenseful narrative alternates the good things and the bad things, keeping the reader well and truly hooked.

In a romance, the narrative question is: will she get her man? A secondary question might be, will he be the right man for her?

Study the construction of Jane Austen's *Pride and Prejudice* to see how the plot works. Austen establishes right away that the Bennet daughters need to marry rich men, as their house is entailed to a male relative. Elizabeth, the main character, meets Mr Darcy at a dance and finds him cold and arrogant. She also meets Mr Wickham, who seems dashing and kind. But as the story goes on, you begin to suspect that Lizzie and Mr Darcy are attracted to one another, though when he proposes, he does so in such a way that her pride makes her reject him. Later, you discover that Mr Wickham is up to no good, and Mr Darcy's good character is slowly revealed. Just at the point where it seems Darcy and Lizzie will marry, Mr Wickham runs off with Lizzie's youngest sister, Lydia, thus disgracing the family and making the outcome now look hopeless. I won't give away the ending of the novel, in case you haven't read it, but Jane Austen tells such a skilful tale that you can't see how events can possibly turn out well.

Readers need signposts – pointers to the direction in which your story is going. Don't leave them in a thick fog so they can't see where they're headed.

Foreshadowing

Foreshadowing the future is a great way to build suspense. You hint at what's going to happen so that the reader knows what they're waiting for. 'Little did he know' is the simplest form of foreshadowing. Little did he know that Sue was going to be waiting for him, little did he know that a giant lorry was about to pull out round the corner, little did he know that the share price was just about to fall. . . .

The problem with 'little did he know', apart from its obviousness, is that only an omniscient narrator can know these things. If you're writing from the perspective of a character, he won't know what's about to happen. So, you need to foreshadow an event in a different way. Maybe the character has an uneasy feeling when he wakes up in the morning, or his horoscope tells him to be extra careful that day; he sees a dead cat on the path as he leaves the house, or he saw an accident at the same place earlier in the story.

Future events can also be foreshadowed through dreams. Your unconscious mind can warn you of things that are dangerous that you don't want to bring into your conscious thoughts. So your character could dream of an accident, and not know why. Maybe, in fact, his mind (perhaps dwelling on the car accident he saw there earlier) is warning him that he doesn't drive carefully enough around that corner.

A classic example of foreshadowing occurs in Leo Tolstoy's masterpiece, *Anna Karenina*. When Anna meets the man who'll be her lover, Count Vronsky, at the railway station, a man falls under a train and is killed. Later, when she meets Vronsky at a railway station in a storm, she sees a shadowy figure checking the couplings between the carriages. At intervals throughout the story, Anna has a bad dream about this crouched figure, and on one occasion Vronsky does too. Ultimately, Anna commits suicide by throwing herself between the carriages on a train; when this happens, you realise how carefully Tolstoy prepared for this ending all along, and the story seems somehow complete.

Another way of using foreshadowing, common in films, is to run two story-lines simultaneously, so that you follow the progress of the man driving the lorry, for example, with that of the woman who's going to crash into it. You can watch their paths converge and wait for the inevitable collision – or the nick-of-time escape.

Write about a character going to an important meeting, perhaps to tell a partner or lover that the relationship is over. Don't write about the meeting; instead, describe the character's journey to it – what he sees.

Springing surprises

One of the obvious dangers of foreshadowing is that it can make the events of the story seem too obvious or perhaps too contrived. Sometimes foreshadowing makes it seem as if only one outcome of the story was ever possible from the beginning. If readers can predict everything that's going to happen, they're unlikely to find a story gripping.

Any story can benefit from a sudden surprise, which twists the plot and makes the reader see things in a new light. Such a reversal usually comes about through a character discovering something that he didn't know before. However, the twist must be believable when it happens.

The two surprises below are taken from nineteenth-century novels serialised in magazines. Just like today's soap operas, each episode had to end with a twist or surprise to keep the reader hooked till the next instalment:

✔ In Thackeray's *Vanity Fair*, readers are meant to spend a great deal of time wondering which rich man the gold-digger heroine Becky Sharp, a penniless orphan working as a governess, is going to marry. Finally, when she receives a proposal from the rich and elderly Sir Pitt, you discover that she can't marry him – she's married already!

✔ In Charles Dickens's *Great Expectations*, readers are led to believe that the hero Pip inherited his money from Miss Havisham. Halfway through the novel, the revelation of the real provider of the legacy gives the reader a shock and turns the story in a whole new direction.

Chapter 9

Creating a Structure

. . . .

In This Chapter

▶ Making breaks in your work

▶ Starting at the beginning, going through the middle and reaching the end

▶ Presenting your work in time

. . . .

Some writers structure their piece of fiction, play or book before they even begin to write, while others apply a form only after they complete a first draft. But any piece of writing, whether a short poem or massive novel, needs a structure: plays are divided into acts, poems into verses and novels into chapters. Any piece of writing needs a beginning, a middle and an end – and it must start and end somewhere.

However, where to make your divisions isn't always clear when you first start writing. In this chapter, I help you make structural decisions for your work.

Dividing Your Work into Chapters and Parts

Pick a book – any book – off your shelf. Look at how the author has structured it. Maybe the text is divided into parts. Count the chapters and see if each part contains the same number. Check if all the chapters are roughly the same length, and if the book has lots of short chapters or a smaller number of long ones.

In a long poem, look at how the verses are arranged. In a play, count the acts.

Now look in more detail at chapters and parts to work out why they're structured as they are. For instance, the chapters or sections may be divided by subject matter. In a biography or autobiography, they may be divided according to different periods of the subject's life – for example, childhood, teenage years, young adulthood, mature adulthood and old age. In a novel, often the different parts focus on individual characters. In a short story collection, the stories may be grouped according to length, theme or when they were written.

Can you see any obvious patterns?

Charles Palliser's novel *The Quincunx* concerns five generations of five branches of a family; each branch is covered by a part, divided into five books, containing five chapters. *An Instance of the Fingerpost* by Iain Pears is divided into four books, each one telling the story from a different character's perspective. Carol Shields's ingenious novel *Happenstance*, about a week in which the wife goes to a convention while her husband remains at home, is in two parts. The novel is presented so that you choose which half to read first – the wife's or the husband's story. Whichever one you read first completely changes the way you read the other half.

Some writers like to plan out a template or structure for their stories before they begin, dividing the novel or play into a number of parts, chapters, scenes and acts, and keeping each section roughly the same length. Others prefer to just write and structure the story after they've got a complete draft. This decision is just a matter of personal choice; either approach is fine.

Sometimes, making decisions about the book's structure before you begin can be liberating, because it gives you a template to work within. Curiously, when you pick a structure or place some limits on your story you have more freedom to play around within it than if you're free to do anything at all.

Creating chapters and scenes

Each chapter or scene within a longer piece of prose or fiction should act as a complete story in itself, except that its ending doesn't resolve the conflict but opens up into more possibilities for the future. So, if you're writing fiction, try to create clear, well-defined scenes, each of which moves the story on but is also satisfying in itself. Each scene may be a chapter in itself, or a longer chapter can be divided into several shorter scenes marked with a line space or asterisks to indicate the break.

Each chapter usually revolves around a single event or takes place within a single setting, and is told from one point of view (Chapter 6 talks about narrators). Events in a chapter should be linked together in some way.

Ideally, a chapter should end at a crucial moment, finishing with a question that won't be answered until a following chapter. A chapter that ends at a critical point is called a *cliffhanger*.

Using acts and scenes in plays and screenplays

Most traditional plays are divided into three or five acts, with a number of scenes in each act. Today, many plays are performed in just one act, but still with a number of scenes. Playwrights commonly arrange a play with the same number of scenes per act, though this isn't always the case.

Screenplays still often use the three-act structure, although the acts aren't always spelt out in the way they are in the theatre, because a film runs continuously, without breaks. Films still proceed through a number of different scenes, though. Television dramas are often divided into a number of different sections, especially if they're to be broadcast on independent television, to allow for commercial breaks.

Making verses and stanzas

In longer poetry, the text is often divided into verses – groups of lines with a space in between. Even free verse, one of the least structured forms of poetry, is divided this way. Poetry also can contain *stanzas* – groups of lines in a poem having a definite pattern. Many different structures or templates for writing poetry exist, some of which are familiar – such as a sonnet or haiku – and others that are much less well known, like a villanelle. Chapter 16 has lots more information about structuring poetry.

Following the Three-Act Structure

For most plays and screenplays, but also in many novels, the three-act structure is the most commonly used. This narrative structure involves:

  ✔ **The beginning**

- Introduces the *characters* – the people who are involved in the story.

- Establishes the *situation* – when and where the story takes place.

- States the *conflict* – the issue at stake between the characters.

- Poses the *story question* – the central narrative hook that the audience wants answered.

✔ **The middle**

- A progression of events, each one influencing the next, in which the conflict escalates.

- Each event must intensify the conflict but also lead toward its resolution.

- Each event must reveal more about the characters.

✔ **The end**

- The *climax,* the pivotal event which resolves the conflict.

- The *resolution* answers the story question and reveals what happens to the characters.

Making a good beginning

Every story has to begin somewhere. According to Graham Greene, however, at the beginning of his novel *The End of the Affair:* 'A story has no beginning and no end: arbitrarily one chooses that moment of experience from which to look back or from which to look ahead.'

When you write a story, you're creating a world in the minds of your readers, and they need to know at least the basics of this world so that they can orient themselves within it. Remember to be clear and to help the readers into your story. You need to establish who the main character is, where the story's taking place and what the main issue at stake is.

Ideally, you hook your readers in with the very first line, and then continue to hold their rapt attention by moving the story forwards. This approach is most important in books, where so much competition exists. Modern readers are usually not prepared to wait several pages to get into a story – if they don't like the opening, they'll pick another book. Most films and plays also aim to grab the audience straight away.

Setting the scene

The beginning of a story has to do a lot of things:

✔ Introduce the characters who tell the story or are involved in it, and especially the main character or protagonist.

✔ Introduce the time and setting of the story.

✔ Have some kind of narrative hook that makes the reader want to continue reading.

✔ Introduce the theme or the dramatic question of the story.

Remember, when your readers start to read your story, watch your play or film, or read your poem, they know absolutely nothing about it. They don't know the characters, where they are, what's going on, what's at stake or why they're reading it. A factual book is slightly different; people are reading it for information. But, as the writer, you still need to make the structure clear and convey to the reader how you're imparting the information.

Choose a character, a place and a feeling. Write about that character, in that place, experiencing that feeling. Consider why he's feeling it and what he's going to do about it.

Actually, all you need to start a story is a particular person in a particular place experiencing a particular emotion.

Crafting an alluring opening line

Reading as many opening lines of stories, novels and other books as you can to see what makes you want to read on can be helpful. If you're writing plays or screenplays, look at the openings of plays or films, and how they set the scene.

In prose, and most importantly in the novel, the opening line is all-important. This line sets the whole tone of the story and should provide a sense of the author or the main character's voice, an idea of her dilemma and pose a question – something that the reader wants to find out.

An opening line's purpose is simply to make you want to read the next line.

The three main kinds of openings are:

- ✔ **A philosophical statement that introduces the theme of the book.**

  'The past is a foreign country; they do things differently there.' L. P. Hartley, *The Go-Between* (1953)

- ✔ **A character caught in a particular and often perilous situation.**

  'Hale knew, before he had been in Brighton three hours, that they meant to murder him.' Graham Greene, *Brighton Rock* (1938)

- ✔ **The individual voice of a character.**

  'If you really want to hear about it, the first thing you'll probably want to know is where I was born, and what my lousy childhood was like, and how my parents were occupied and all before they had me, and all that David Copperfield kind of crap, but I don't feel like going into it, if you want to know the truth.' J. D. Salinger, *The Catcher in the Rye* (1951)

Each of these lines is intriguing in a different way. In the first, you want to know why the writer has made this statement. You know that this story will reveal how someone's past affected him, and how he can't go back and change it. In the second, you want to know who wants to kill Hale, and why, and whether or not they'll succeed. In the third, you want to know who this character is and what's troubling him.

Of course, when you're writing, you don't start with a great and wonderful opening line. For starters, you may wait a very long time for one to suggest itself. In truth, many great opening lines occurred to the authors only after they'd finished their books. Some may have taken a long time to find; others may have been hidden away in the depths of the story somewhere. Don't wait for the perfect opening line to come to you before you start writing; get started and trust that you'll eventually find one.

Starting in the middle with an inciting incident

Curiously, much fiction starts *in medias res* – that is, in the middle of things. Nowadays very few readers want to read long introductions about a place, a character's early life or her philosophy. Jumping in and starting at the point where a story really becomes interesting is usual. Many great works of fiction follow this pattern. Shakespeare's *Hamlet*, for example, instead of starting with Hamlet's birth, his schooldays or even his father's death or mother's remarriage, opens with the appearance of his father's ghost on the battlements, telling Hamlet he was murdered.

Especially in film, where stories are usually much more tightly structured than in any other narrative form, the story often starts with the *inciting incident*, the event that kicks off the story; the thing that happened without which there would be no story. The inciting incident is, for example, the lovers meeting in a romance. If no meeting occurred, neither would the romance, adultery or drama. Consider the murder, without which the detective would have no crime to investigate; the natural disaster, without which the characters would have nothing to overcome or the life-changing event that takes the main character out of her comfortable existence into a world of adventure. The inciting incident could be somebody dying and leaving the main character with a dilemma, winning the lottery, the temptation to commit a crime, deciding to adopt a child or to climb a mountain.

You can use an inciting incident as the start to almost any form of creative writing.

Keeping the tension going in the middle

The beginning isn't always the hardest part to write. In fact, it may be the easiest: the idea comes to you, and you start writing. But, as you go on, the writing begins to get more difficult. The longer your story or novel, the more complicated the task becomes. The middle starts to sag, and suddenly all the steam seems to go out of your project.

Often this lack of direction happens because you haven't thought enough about ways to delay the ending. In the middle of a story, you need to introduce more and more conflicts and complications. You need to keep new things happening, adding twists and turns that the reader or audience hasn't anticipated.

To keep the narrative interesting, try some time-honoured ways of increasing dramatic tension:

- ✔ **Add time pressure:** Putting your character under severe time restraints increases narrative tension hugely. A character has seven days to sort out his life, four hours to defuse the bomb, ten minutes to rescue the child from the flood. Give your hero or heroine a window of good weather to climb the mountain or a few days to close the crucial business deal. Make it clear that the oxygen in the spaceship will only last for two more days or that the wedding is in three days' time.

- ✔ **Increase the obstacles:** Increase the number and severity of the obstacles as the protagonist gets closer to the goal. The weather worsens, the character's illness becomes more critical, the characters have fallen more deeply in love or the antagonist has decided to stop at nothing to prevent the main character from achieving her goal.

- ✔ **Introduce new dramas or dilemmas:** If your story is running out of steam, try introducing a new character who can open up fresh possibilities or a surprising or unexpected event. Throw in something completely unexpected and see what happens.

  The Victorian novelist Edgar Wallace was reputed to have invented a device called a plot wheel, which he used to help create his stories. Whenever he didn't know what to write next, he'd spin the plot wheel for suggestions such as 'a telegram arrives' or 'an unexpected visitor calls' or 'a murder is committed'. Adding this detail to the plot soon got his story rolling again!

- ✔ **Create complications:** The middle of a narrative can be complex to handle if you have more than one main character or a variety of subplots. Keeping track of what's happening or finding ways to connect the different strands of the story can be difficult.

  Make sure that all the separate strands of your story interconnect. Ideally, what happens in one part of the narrative should directly affect what happens in the other strands.

Ending well

The ending of a story has a great deal of work to do. It must answer the main question posed by the beginning, satisfy the reader's curiosity about the characters and their dilemmas, and create some emotional response. Finally, the ending must provide a sense of completion, that the wheel has come full circle.

Building to the climax and resolution

The last section of any piece of structured writing consists of the climax and the resolution, as well as the actual ending.

At the *climax* of a story, all the narrative threads come together. Someone once said that the novel charts the progress from innocence to experience, and often the climax of a narrative is the moment of revelation, where all is revealed and the main character is changed forever.

Below are two examples of a well-delivered climax:

✔ Jane Austen's *Emma*, in which all the misunderstandings are laid bare and it goes through Emma 'with the speed of an arrow, that Mr Knightley must marry no one but herself!' This point isn't the ending of the novel – you still have to discover whether or not Emma will marry Mr Knightley – but this is the moment when Emma understands her own heart and, however the story ends, she'll never behave in the same way again.

✔ In J. R. R. Tolkien's much imitated climax in *The Lord of the Rings* trilogy, Frodo reaches his goal against all the odds, but refuses to destroy the Ring and claims it as his own. When Gollum bites the Ring from Frodo's finger only to stumble and fall into the Crack of Doom, Gollum's role in the story and why his life had to be spared over and over is finally made clear.

This climax also shows how drawing on the dark side, the shadow self, to overcome evil is sometimes necessary.

This scene, with its double twist, demonstrates how a good writer can work out an ending you expect but bring it about in an unexpected way.

The *resolution* is the result of the climactic scene – for example, that Emma will marry Knightley, and that because the Ring has been destroyed the Dark Lord is vanquished. At the resolution all the narrative threads come together, and if many exist, as in *The Lord of the Rings*, they're all interwoven.

If you can't find an ending to your story, go back to your first paragraph. Make sure the beginning and ending connect, perhaps picking up images or phrases from the start to echo at the end.

Examining types of endings

Three main kinds of endings exist:

✔ **A happy ending:** Here, the couple get married, the murderer is revealed, the mountaineer makes the ascent and returns safely, the asteroid doesn't hit Earth. Loose ends are tied up, and everyone lives happily ever after.

Happy endings are great – except that they can seem contrived, sentimental and trite. You know that life isn't really so neatly wrapped up. So sometimes happy endings work best when a seed of doubt is sown in them; the couple marry, but you can see that all kinds of difficulties lie ahead; the murderer is found, yes, but the death was still tragic; the quest has been fulfilled but perhaps the victory has been achieved at a great cost.

✔ **A tragic ending:** Tragic endings can be satisfying in a way, if you feel that the character deserves what he gets. But sometimes tragic endings can be a real downer, especially if you suspected that things would end this way. Also, if you've followed a character through hundreds of pages of a novel fervently hoping that he'll return home safely to his lover who's waiting for him, only to find that he dies just a few miles from home, you may feel like throwing the book out of the window (I have a real novel in mind here, but I'm not going to tell you what it is).

Many tragic endings contain a seed of hope, though. The main character dies, but his child lives. The lovers separate, but a chance exists that they'll find happiness with others. The hero dies, but he's saved the whole community.

✔ **An open ending:** When a piece of fiction isn't finally and completely resolved, the ending can resonate much longer with the reader. You're left wondering what ultimately happens, and may perhaps think about it for hours or days, weeks or years after finishing the story. However, sometimes an open ending is just too unfinished and the reader is left unsatisfied.

In an open ending, the climactic scene is very important. Readers need to have the main question answered and see that the protagonist has changed forever. Conveying the resolution, or what happens as a result of the climax, isn't as important.

In the past, a tendency existed for tragic endings to be made more ambiguous or even happy. Shakespeare was often the victim of this process; the far more popular version of *King Lear* for centuries had a happy ending in which Edgar and Cordelia marry.

Some more recent novelists have explored the idea of multiple endings. In *The French Lieutenant's Woman*, John Fowles provides three different endings, each of them slightly ambiguous. Other fiction, like Peter Howitt's 1998 film *Sliding Doors*, explores the idea that a small event or a different choice can transform a character's entire life. The writer wants to explore the way these different choices could have affected the story – what might have happened as well as what did.

Occasionally the writer reveals a twist at the very end of the story that changes the way you view it. This approach is common in the short story but less so in a novel. Whatever happens, you need to beware of the 'but it was all a dream' scenario or of revealing that the main character is actually a dog.

Both ideas have been used too often before, and readers really don't like being tricked in this way or having the rug pulled out from under them after they've invested their time in reading the story.

Avoid the following:

- ✓ **Irrelevant endings.** Don't introduce a new concept or character right at the end of your story, something or someone with no or little connection with what went before.

- ✓ **Fizzle-out endings.** Don't just let your story fizzle out with no real climax or resolution – end with a bang, not a whimper.

- ✓ **Endings that go on and on.** Some authors can't bear to leave their stories and let them drift on after the main story has finished.

Here are some of my favourite endings:

- ✓ **'Yes, she thought, laying down her brush in extreme fatigue, I have had my vision.'** Virginia Woolf, *To the Lighthouse* (1927)

  Here, the character completes her painting just as the author completes her own work. Woolf uses a perfect conceit.

- ✓ **'After all, tomorrow is another day.'** Margaret Mitchell, *Gone with the Wind* (1936)

  Though you feel that the story has been played out for now, Scarlett isn't defeated, and her life will go on.

- ✓ **'He loved Big Brother.'** George Orwell, *1984* (1949)

  Orwell provides a diabolically cruel twist, which is completely unexpected and yet makes perfect sense within the world of this novel.

- ✓ **'His soul swooned slowly as he heard the snow falling faintly through the universe and faintly falling, like the descent of their last end, upon all the living and the dead.'** James Joyce, 'The Dead', from *Dubliners* (1914)

  The beautiful rhythm in this prose is what makes it so satisfying; Joyce borrows the 'dying fall' from Shakespeare's *Twelfth Night.*

- ✓ **'"Well, I'm back," he said.'** J. R. R. Tolkien, *The Lord of the Rings* (1954)

  This simple, mundane ending to a huge adventure leads us gently down and back into our own world.

- ✓ **'But she turned to the door, and her headshake was now the end. "We shall never be again as we were!"'** Henry James, *The Wings of the Dove* (1902)

  Here, James brilliantly encapsulates the whole point of a story – that the characters will be changed by its events forever.

Writing within a Timeframe

A major element determining the structure of a piece of fiction is the time period involved and how you handle it. The length of a written story doesn't necessarily correspond with the length of the story being told; some short stories may describe a whole lifetime, while a whole novel can tell the story of a single day, such as James Joyce's *Ulysses* or Virginia Woolf's *Mrs Dalloway*. Of course, flashbacks and memories of the past are used to make what Virginia Woolf called 'a whole life in a single day'.

Many biographies and memoirs cover a whole life, but to make them readable and compelling, authors tend to concentrate on the most interesting periods and often also use the technique of flashback. Plays and films more usually use a tighter timeframe than narrative prose; some plays take place in 'real time', covering just an hour or two of a life. Below are some common time structures used in narratives, plays and films.

Lining up a linear narrative

A *linear narrative*, starting with an event and moving forwards in time to the end result of this event, is the easiest way to tell a story. This classic structure is used in many nineteenth-century novels, for example Charles Dickens's *David Copperfield* and Charlotte Brontë's *Jane Eyre*, and is usual in autobiography and mainstream genres such as crime fiction, which starts with the murder and ends with the discovery of the killer. Most films and plays also use this type of narrative structure.

Going linear with flashbacks

The main narrative moves forwards in time interspersed with flashbacks to the past. These flashbacks can occur only occasionally, or frequently with a definite pattern, so that, for example, each chapter in the 'now' story is interspersed with an episode in the past. You thus end up with two linear narratives related to one another. *Holes* by Louis Sachar provides a good example of this structure.

Writing backwards

You can always try running the story backwards in time, starting at the end and ending with the beginning.

Examples include:

- ✔ Elizabeth Jane Howard's *The Long View*, which starts with the ending of a marriage and moves backwards to the moment when the two characters meet.

- ✔ Harold Pinter's play, *Betrayal*, which also became a film, starts with the lovers meeting after their relationship has ended and moves backwards in time to their first meeting at a party.

- ✔ Martin Amis let time actually run backwards in his novel *Time's Arrow*, his characters going from death to birth; so did science fiction writer Philip K. Dick in *Counter-Clock World*.

- ✔ In Helen Dunmore's *Your Blue-Eyed Boy*, the main part of the story is a conventional narrative that runs forwards, but the memories of the past, which are regularly interspersed, run backwards in time from when the two main characters separated to their first meeting.

Jumping around in time

Some complex novels jump around in time, thus creating a sense of mystery for the reader. An example is Arundhati Roy's *The God of Small Things*. Apparently, she wrote the novel as a linear narrative first, and then shuffled it up later. This technique would be very difficult to use in a play or film.

Jumping around in time is a technique for advanced writers. You really need to know what you're doing, otherwise the reader – and you – can end up completely confused.

Leaving a gap in the narrative

Omitting a part of the story or concealing it from the reader is a classic device for creating mystery in fiction. Perhaps a character has lost her memory, or the author switches to another viewpoint further ahead in the story, leaving a piece of the story the reader doesn't know about. The key to the mystery lies in this missing scene.

Joseph Conrad's *Under Western Eyes* provides a good example of this technique. At the outset, the protagonist, Razumov, is approached by a young revolutionary, Haldin, in Russia, who asks for his protection. Razumov faces the choice of helping or betraying him. The story is picked up later in time in Geneva by an English teacher, who meets Razumov and other revolutionaries from Russia. Razumov meets and falls for Haldin's sister. Only later in the novel do you discover what choice Razumov made earlier and witness the results of this action.

Reading novels haphazardly

Argentine writer Julio Cortázar's *Hopscotch* is an experimental novel written in an episodic manner. The novel has 155 chapters, the last 99 of which are, according to the author, expendable. Cortázar says the reader can read the book in direct sequence from Chapter 1 to Chapter 56 'with a clean conscience', or can hop-scotch through the whole set of 155 chapters (except Chapter 55) according to a table provided by him; the novel is an infinite loop. The novel can also be read by odd or even pages only, or by chapter in completely random order. Some of the chapters designated as 'expendable' fill in gaps in the main story, while others add information about the characters.

If on a winter's night a traveller is a novel by Italian writer Italo Calvino, published in 1979. The book concerns a reader trying to read a book called *If on a winter's night a traveller*. The first chapter and every odd-numbered chapter tell the reader what the main character is doing in preparation for reading the next chapter. For various reasons, the reading of the book is interrupted and the character starts reading other books, which are reproduced, so that the even-numbered chapters are all from whichever book the reader is trying to read.

Connecting short stories

Some books are written as a series of interrelated stories. These can be considered as story collections or novels, depending on whether an overriding narrative connects them, or the stories are related to one another simply because they're set in the same town or they have related themes. Connecting stories into a narrative or even combining them into a novel can really help your reader (see Chapter 11 on the short story).

Sherwood Anderson's *Winesburg, Ohio* is a series of stories about characters who live in the same small town and know one another. Rohinton Mistry did a similar thing in *Tales From Firozsha Baag*, stories about different characters who inhabit the same apartment block in Mumbai. In Thornton Wilder's novel *The Bridge of San Luis Rey*, the stories of six characters killed in an accident on a rope bridge in South America are linked through the conscience of a priest whose faith in God is shattered when he hears of the accident but restored through learning the stories of the six characters.

Telling a story within a story

Sometimes a novel contains a story within a story. Discovered letters or journals can serve as the vehicle for telling a story from the past and present at the same time. Often the main character of the piece is writing or telling a story about some other person or incident.

If you're using a novel within a novel, or journals or diaries, set each in a different typeface to clarify for the readers which story they're in or who's talking. Sometimes the narrator simply appears in a 'frame' around the story, being present at the beginning to introduce the story and then commenting on it at the end.

Good examples of the story-within-a-story frame are Margaret Atwood's *The Blind Assassin*, where one character is being told a science fiction story, and John Gardner's *October Light*, which contains a trashy paperback novel that one of the characters is reading. Classic novels sometimes use a 'frame' narrator, such as Marlow in Joseph Conrad's *Heart of Darkness* and Lockwood in Emily Brontë's *Wuthering Heights*.

Going around in circles stories

Circular narratives have been used by some writers, such as Toni Morrison in *Beloved*, to get away from traditional Western storytelling structures. In a circular story, the ending takes you right back to the beginning. You think the story is resolved, but then something happens that opens up the main question all over again.

Circular stories are very popular with young children, possibly because they need to keep doing the same thing over and over again in order to learn.

Chapter 10

Rewriting and Editing

*P*erhaps the main secret of creative writing is that rewriting is all. People who don't write often make the assumption that writers just put pen to paper (or fingers to keyboard); they sit down at the beginning of the book and write it straight through to the end. If only the process was this simple!

What non-writers think of as finishing a book is actually just the first stage – completing a draft. This draft is heavily revised, rewritten and restructured, often many times, before it can be considered complete. Even then, comments from an outside reader, an agent or a professional editor can send the writer back for more work.

In this chapter, I take you through the revising and editing process.

Producing the First Draft

The first draft – the unrevised, raw first words that you commit to the blank page or screen – is only the beginning; and yet without it, you can get no further. Think of it as the clay that you can later mould and work.

Write the first draft for yourself alone. Don't have anyone else read it. Use it to find out what your story is, what you really want to write about and how.

Writing the first draft should be fun. Detach your inner critic, forget about any potential readers or publishers and write whatever you feel; you can digress, put in notes and reminders, jump around in time and surprise yourself with thoughts, ideas and characters you hadn't imagined. At this stage, the important thing is just to write.

Choosing pen, computer, both or neither

Some writers like to write longhand; they say they find a closer connection between the mind and the hand exists than is possible with a computer keyboard. Writing longhand often slows you down and makes you take more time over your writing. Your pen moves more slowly over the page, and you need to pause from time to time and rest your fingers.

Other writers prefer to type straight onto the computer. They find they can write more quickly and more freely this way. Other writers do both; they write longhand, then type it up, editing and polishing slightly as they go.

Some writers still use a typewriter. They say they prefer the heaviness of it and the satisfying clunk at the end of every line when they use the carriage return.

Whichever way you prefer to write is fine. Do what feels right for you.

Don't expect your first draft to make sense. Many writers don't know what their work is about or where the story's going when they begin. You may be a writer who makes discoveries as you go along and needs to change much of the early material you write. However, don't go back and alter things immediately; just make a note and carry on.

You may have a good idea of the plot, or even a breakdown of the structure of your story or poem to start with, but find that it changes as you write. Don't worry about altering direction, either; just go with the flow.

A draft just needs to produce some material, a loose – and often baggy – skeleton for a story, poem or play. It is an A–Z: starting somewhere, ending somewhere and with a lot of material in between. Ultimately, you may not start or end in those places, but at least you have something down on paper to work with.

Many beginner writers go over and over the first three or four chapters, endlessly rewriting them and never getting any further. Try to resist doing so.

Some writers like to steam ahead and get the first draft down before they do any revising. Others like to write and then edit what they've written before they move on. No one way is right; choose what suits you.

Trying different techniques

When you're writing your first draft, take the opportunity to try out different techniques. If you're writing in the third person, but suddenly feel you want to try the first person, do it. Maybe you need to catch the character's inner voice or explore her thoughts and feelings for a reason. You can work on the reason later.

Describe places and characters in great detail, so you know what they're like; you can slim down or take out some of this information later.

Go for melodrama if it seems appropriate; don't hold yourself back. Write the things you're scared of writing; remember, no one is going to see this draft. Write what you want.

Letting it go and coming back later

When you finish your first draft and get to the end of your book or story, put it away for a while. Now is not the time to read through it. Often, when you read through a first draft, the material seems hopeless, so much less interesting and well-executed than the ideas you had in your head.

Allow yourself a few days, a week or two or even a month to bask in the fact that you've finished a whole draft. Enjoy the feeling of achievement.

The longer you leave your draft, the more objectively you can see it. And always consider Ernest Hemingway's famous dictum: 'The first draft of anything is sh**' (fill in the blanks!).

Becoming Your Own Editor

Being an editor isn't the same as being a writer. To succeed as a writer, you ultimately need to be both, but separating out the two processes as much as you can is helpful. With time, as you become more experienced, you may be able to bring your editor into play when you're drafting, but many writers never do.

When you go back to your first draft, read it all through in one go. This first read-through is to see what you've written and how it fits together. At this stage, don't bother with the small details like spelling mistakes and punctuation. Many writers find that reading from the printed page is easier than from a screen. This approach can pose a problem for the environmentally conscious person who doesn't want to waste paper! If you read better when your material's printed out, then do so, but remember to use a smaller font and print on both sides to use less paper. If you print out various drafts, use a different font so you can distinguish between them.

Read through your work from beginning to end, making notes as you go. Mark passages that need to be cut, moved around, expanded or shortened. Identify *continuity errors* – where a character has changed outfits in the middle of a scene, for instance – and points or details that need clarifying. You can correct lumpy sentences or images that don't work if you spot them, but don't get into the nitty-gritty of rewriting now; reading right through and seeing what you've got is the important thing.

In poetry, you may need to move whole lines or verses, change the rhyming scheme, write in new lines and take others out.

When you've gone through the first draft, you usually have a lot of work to do. You may need to:

- ✔ Take out whole scenes or sections
- ✔ Write completely new scenes or chapters
- ✔ Move whole sections around

When you've finished all these corrections and changes, you have a second draft. You may need to do more drastic work to make a third draft, or even fourth or fifth, if you're writing a long or complex book. When you're satisfied with the basic structure, you are ready to edit your work a bit more closely.

When you edit, you do the following:

- ✔ Cut things out
- ✔ Put new things in
- ✔ Change sentence order and structure
- ✔ Look for repeated words
- ✔ Strengthen verbs and adjectives
- ✔ Expand sections
- ✔ Trim sections

Correcting common English errors

If you really care about your work, take the time and trouble to get even the small things right. After all, if you don't take this trouble, why should you expect anyone else to invest time and effort on it?

In the following sections, I cover some of the basic ways you and I and every other writer can mangle the English language, and give you tips on how to correct those errors.

Staying on top of spelling

If you work on a computer, you can catch and take care of spelling errors fairly easily by running your spell-checker. However, you still need to read through the piece yourself as the spell-checker doesn't catch words that exist in their own right like 'tow' when you mean 'two' and 'cant' when you mean 'can't'.

Make sure your computer spell-checker is set to the right language – UK English. Far too many people leave their word-processing program set on the default US spelling. This setting gives you the wrong paper size, too!

Check the spelling of any proper names, places and brand names (the For Dummies trademark, for example, includes the capital *F* as well as the capital *D*).

Other tips to make your writing misspelling-free include:

✔ Keep a dictionary to hand and use it when in doubt about how to spell something.

   Alternatively, you can make use of the dictionary in your word-processing program; generally, you right-click on a misspelled word to bring up a list of suggested corrections.

✔ Make a list of the most common misspellings and put it near your computer.

   I did so in my first job; my words were independEnt, sepArate, bUrEAUcracy and presEnce.

✔ Add words you consistently mistype to the autocorrect list of your word-processing program. (If you use Microsoft Word, AutoCorrect is in the Tools menu.)

Grasping the basics of grammar

Grammar means the structure of a language, the order in which words can be placed so that they make sense, the types of word people use and their functions in sentences, and the forms these words can take.

Common errors to watch out for include:

✔ Using it's (it is) when you mean 'its' (belongs to it) and the other way round.

✔ Confusing homophones – words which sound the same but have different meanings. These words don't get picked up by the spell-checker because they're real words:

   • There, their and they're

   • Here and hear

   • Right and write

   • Read and red

Paying attention to sentence construction

You can write clumsy sentences that don't read well and clumsy sentences that don't make sense. Beware of these mistakes:

- ✔ A verb clause that doesn't refer to the subject of the main sentence: 'Looking out of the window as she stirred her cup of coffee, the plane came in to land.'

  The plane clearly can't look out of a window or stir a cup of coffee! This sentence should be: 'Stirring the cup of coffee, she looked out of the window as the plane came in to land' or 'She stirred the cup of coffee and looked out of the window as the plane came in to land.'

- ✔ Putting actions in the wrong order: 'Rolling over and over as he went, he fell down the hill' works so much better the other way round.

Eliminating irritating words and phrases

Repeated use of the same word within a short piece of text is annoying to read. Use a thesaurus to find another word instead.

Too many adjectives and adverbs can also be irritating as they clutter up the text and draw attention to themselves (see the 'Employing the Tools of Description' section in Chapter 7 for more on this). Avoid adverbs by using a stronger verb; for example, rather than 'she violently took hold of his hand', write 'she grabbed his hand', rather than 'she walked slowly', put 'she ambled' or 'sauntered' or 'dawdled'. Rather than several weak adjectives use one stronger one, so that rather than 'he picked up the pen with soft, pale, long fingers' say 'delicate fingers'.

When you read as much unpublished fiction as I do, you come to hate some of the little phrases people use to excess. To me, the following phrases indicate a lazy writer:

- ✔ **Suddenly:** This word is often a sign that the writer is desperately trying to liven up the writing: 'Suddenly the ceiling fell in.'

  Don't just use the thesaurus and put in 'abruptly', 'hastily', 'quickly,' 'rapidly' or whatever.

  The line 'Suddenly she remembered' is also annoying on a couple of levels: people usually remember things because something makes them recall them, and a piece of writing is so much more interesting if the trigger for a memory is the sight, sound or scent of something meaningful to the character or story.

  'Suddenly he found himself', as in 'Suddenly he found himself in a crowded street', is equally irritating. How did this happen? Did he temporarily lose his memory or get transported there by aliens?

✔ **There was:** Many writers litter their prose with the phrases 'there was' or 'here is'. These phrases are passive and don't engage the reader's attention. Look at this passage:

'He walked into the room. **There was** a small lamp standing on the desk. He went over and switched it on, before opening the top drawer and putting in his hand. **There was** a long, thin envelope in the back of the drawer. He pulled it out and was just about to look inside when **there was** a loud noise from downstairs. He rushed across to the window and looked out. **There was** a man standing by the front door.'

This passage reads much more strongly if you omit 'there was': 'He walked into the room. A small lamp stood on the desk . . .. He felt inside and pulled out a long, thin envelope . . . he heard a loud noise . . . a man stood by the front door.'

✔ **There was something:** 'There was something strange about him', 'there was something appealing about her', 'there was something awkward about the way he moved'.

To help them be involved you need to tell your readers what it is that's strange, appealing or awkward. Be specific!

Ensuring that the structure's sound

As you read through your work, look out for potential pitfalls. A piece of writing should be clear, so that the reader can follow the story. Check anything that's confusing and be aware of the fact that writers are more often over-ambiguous than too obvious. Cut out long-winded, static description, especially if it goes on for several paragraphs, or dialogues that continue over many pages. Also be vigilant for these pitfalls:

✔ **Character confusion.** Sometimes a secondary character isn't introduced properly and the reader doesn't know who she is or remember her from earlier. Make sure you introduce characters properly and find subtle ways of reminding the reader who they are when they reappear.

✔ **Too much explanation.** You don't have to explain the whole childhood history of your characters or the complete background to the Second World War in your story. Just weave in the important details your reader needs to know as they come up in your story.

✔ **Plot holes or inconsistencies, or too many coincidences.** A plot hole is a gap or inconsistency in a storyline that makes the reader or viewer doubt the characters or the storyline. A classic example is, why doesn't the main character just call the police? A writer should always find a way to plug the hole.

In Ian McEwan's novel *Enduring Love*, the main character goes to the police to say a man is stalking him, but leaves in disgust when they suggest he might be encouraging him. This scene is missed out in the film version, much to the detriment of the story.

A story that relies on too many coincidences stretches the reader's credulity. When you're editing and rewriting, try to find rational reasons for the coincidences. For example, in many spy movies the hero and enemy agent fall for one another; this scenario is much more convincing if it transpires that she's been ordered to seduce him.

Cutting and pasting to improve readability

You'll often find that changing the order of some of your paragraphs can help improve the flow of your story. Simultaneously changing other elements of the story may also be necessary to maintain continuity and prevent the reader from becoming confused. Keeping track of different versions or the changes you've made can help prevent getting in a muddle.

Cutting and pasting is incredibly simple on the computer. You highlight a paragraph or section, press Ctrl X, move the cursor to the new location and press Ctrl V to reinsert it; you can also use the Cut and Paste options on your toolbar. Rearranging things is so easy that you can go on endlessly moving bits around until, in the end, you have no idea what you moved where and why. Your text can become disconnected and lack any sense of flow as a result.

If you edit on computer, you need to read right through each new version to make sure that it makes sense. If you need to, print out a copy so that you read it with new eyes.

Saving every version as a new document can be helpful. Make sure you clearly label each version by number, though. Remember to change the name as soon as you start editing a new document, so you don't accidentally overwrite the earlier version. You may never need to go back to these versions, but keep them in case you do, in order to see what you originally intended.

When I worked as a journalist in my first job, my editor used a great phrase indicating that an article wasn't right and needed reworking: 'Run it through the typewriter again.' I'd retype the whole piece from beginning to end, without referring to the original version unless I needed to extract some factual material from it. The second version was invariably superior – clearer, sharper and better constructed. With the advent of word processing, people no longer seem to use this approach, but that's not to say that you can't try to improve a problematic passage by simply ignoring what you've written before and writing it again.

The joys of literally cutting and pasting

In the old days, before computers, writers used to cut and paste with scissors, sticky tape and glue. I loved cutting and pasting. It was enjoyably practical and reminded me of cutting out at school. Physically moving the pages around and re-ordering my work was also very satisfying.

After cutting and pasting, I had to type up the work again. As I typed, I could tweak the story to fit the revised structure. Doing so gave me the opportunity to make sure everything fitted together in the new order and still flowed.

Adding texture

For many writers, the first draft serves the same purpose as a preliminary sketch does for a painter. When you read through your work again, the first thing you need to do is flesh it out and add some texture. Description, dialogue or perhaps a memory slotted into the right place can begin to expand and deepen your narrative.

Sometimes writers rush ahead to get to the end of the story. Slowing down can be helpful, though, to let the reader really see the character, hear and see him talking or acting and know what's going on around him.

Remember to build up the narrative through concrete events; as your characters move through the world you've created, they see, smell, touch, taste, feel, think, remember the past and anticipate the future.

Paring down

Just as you need to build up your narrative, sometimes you also want to cut where you've written too much. Dialogue, in particular, often needs trimming down to make the important part stand out (see Chapter 5 for more on dialogue). Overly long description, excessive interior monologues and complex passages of exposition all need to go. You'll generally recognise when something's going on too long when you read through it after a break – trust your own instinct, but err on the side of cutting if you're in any doubt. Like good design, pleasing description or dialogue is often achieved not when you've put everything in, but when nothing remains to take out.

Eliminating backstory

When re-reading and revising your work, look out for too much information about what happened in the past, before your story began. You may have started brilliantly with your first chapter, in which John meets and falls for Siri, but in the second chapter feel you need to tell your readers all about

John's early life and everything that happened to him before he met this girl. Resist the temptation to provide all this information. Far better for John to gradually reveal his past to Siri as he gets to know her – or as much of it as has any interest for Siri or the story. Your story should always move forward; don't look back.

Finding a Trusted Reader

When you've been over your draft several times and feel your story is nearing completion, you need to find a trusted reader to help you evaluate your work. You know what you had in mind, but can't be sure that you translated it properly into words and images that communicate well enough to the reader.

In writing, a tension always exists between saying too much and saying too little, being too obvious or not obvious enough, giving the plot away completely or leaving the reader in confusion. On the inside, as the writer, seeing if you've strayed too far in one direction or the other is difficult. Your reader comes in here – almost all writers use one. Of course, some readers are more perceptive than others; everyone knows those annoying people who, when watching a film, always know what's going to happen at the end, while others are at a complete loss as to what's going on in each scene. But somewhere in the middle is your average film-goer or story reader who can follow the thread and relax and enjoy the story.

If you have more than one reader you can trust, consider using up to three. They may make the same comments, which is reassuring, but be aware of the fact that they can disagree and leave you in confusion about which one to go with.

Getting the right reader

Your ideal reader isn't a literary critic with several degrees in English literature who'll nit-pick every phrase and pull your work apart, or someone who knows nothing about writing or storytelling, who just reads your work and gives you bland and meaningless praise. You want someone who knows something about reading and writing – an intelligent, critical reader, who can point out elements that communicate well or are confusing, when something is too obvious or not obvious enough; who can pick up continuity errors, digressions, passages that are too long or laboured, or places where the reader needs more information.

Your ideal reader is:

- ✔ Another writer, or a keen and perceptive reader.
- ✔ Supportive of your work and not competitive.
- ✔ Someone who shares the same general taste in film, poetry or fiction.
- ✔ Honest but sensitive.
- ✔ Able to constructively criticise your work.

Heeding what your reader says – but not too much

If you ask people to read your work and they come back with a critique, taking it seriously is the least you can do. You won't necessarily agree with everything your readers say, but do take note.

If two or three people read your work and they all say the same thing about some aspect of it, you really do need to take notice.

Pay no attention to comments such as:

- ✔ **'I really liked/enjoyed it.'** Why? If they won't say, they probably didn't read it properly.
- ✔ **'It's not my kind of story.'** They won't be the right audience.
- ✔ **'If I were you, I'd give up writing.'** This is the most destructive thing anyone can ever say to a writer. Take no notice; they're being deliberately cruel.
- ✔ **'This is the best thing I've ever read.'** An overinflated view of your work won't really help you in the long run.

Part III
Writing Fiction

'A pop-up book proposal manuscript — how <u>very</u> original.'

In this part . . .

Perhaps you've always wanted to write fiction but aren't sure what the difference is in length between a short story, a novella, or a novel. Or you want to write for children but don't know what's appropriate for each age group. Or you want to write for stage or screen but aren't sure about the way to lay out a script. Or you're a poet, and you need some guidance on the different forms and how to structure your work . . .

This part looks at the different forms that fiction takes and helps you to choose the one that best suits the kind of writing you want to do.

Chapter 11

When Less is More: Crafting Short Stories

*T*he short story, being short, is often the first choice for beginner fiction writers. In fact, though, the short story is one of the hardest things to write well. Every word has to count, and the focus of the story has to be completely clear.

The art of story-telling goes back to the very beginnings of civilisation. Perhaps the oldest and most direct ancestor of the short story is the anecdote – a short personal account of an incident or event. Ancient parables and fables use a brief narrative to demonstrate a moral or spiritual truth; these tales anticipate the severe brevity and unity of some short stories written today. Fairy stories and mythological tales are still popular today because basic human nature hasn't changed much.

Defining the Short Story

Determining what separates a short story from longer fictional formats isn't always easy. Length is the most obvious differentiator; generally, the term *short story* refers to a work of fiction no longer than 20,000 words and no shorter than 1,000. Stories with less than 1,000 words are usually referred to as *short short fiction* or even *flash fiction*. Competitions have even been held to find the best story told in no more than 50 words. Anything more than 20,000 words, but shorter than a full-length novel is likely to be considered a novella (see the 'Growing a Story into a Novella' section later in this chapter).

A classic definition of a short story is that you can read it in one sitting, a point made in Edgar Allan Poe's essay, *The Philosophy of Composition* (1846). He also said that a short story should concern a limited number of characters and incidents, have the same style and tone throughout, and use words efficiently and sparingly – points that most writers and editors would agree with today.

Writing the Short Story

Short stories aren't just novels in miniature. The short story is to the novel what a still photograph is to a motion picture. While a novel takes time to build up to and fall away from the climax, the short story just hones in on the moment of climax – the day, hour or moment when everything changes forever. (See Chapter 9 for more on structure.)

A short story usually covers a very brief time span. You condense the action down to the shortest time possible. Write about the single event that's a major turning point in the life of a character. In the words of short-story master Raymond Carver: 'Get in, get out. Don't linger.'

Keep the focus tight. In a short story, you don't have time for any digressions. Don't provide lots of details about the past of your characters; you have to deal with them as they are here and now. Don't introduce too many characters, scenes or places.

James Joyce suggested that short stories concern an *epiphany* – a moment of profound revelation – and many short stories are built around a moment when a character realises something about himself, his relationships or his life that has a deep and lasting effect on him.

Structuring a short story

In terms of structure, a classic short story follows the same steps as a novel, film or play; an incident kicks off the story, then conflict leads up to a crisis, a resolution and an ending. However, the short story really homes in on the moment of crisis itself; if a whole novel tells the story leading up to a divorce, with details of the characters' affairs, the slow build up to the moment when all is revealed, the characters' confrontation and the decision that the marriage is over, the short story may focus just on the day or the hour when this confrontation happens. The short story cuts so closely into this climax that the story may be just that final scene; starting with the row itself, and possibly even ending before the decision to divorce happens, leaving the raw emotion open for readers to draw their own conclusions. Raymond Carver uses this structure beautifully.

Another classic short-story structure involves taking two seemingly unconnected narrative lines and crossing them over. At the point where the two stories intersect, something happens between them that changes both characters, and perhaps sends both off in different directions. The following exercise can help you to see how this technique works.

Take a simple story – a man taking his dog for a walk in the park while he thinks about the song he has to write; add another simple story – a mother who's lost her child rushes frantically to the playground; now make the characters collide.

Write about what happens. Does the man help the woman find her daughter? Does the woman later, out of gratitude, help the man with his song?

Making every word count

In a short story, every word and every sentence must be written for a reason; it must be indispensable. Many short-story writers use a spare, pared-down language that seems appropriate to the story's length. You don't have the space for long descriptive passages, for explanations about the characters' histories or any aspects of their lives that aren't directly relevant to the story.

For example, a description in a longer piece, such as:

> The little house was built with red brick and stood at the end of a long, leafy lane. The garden surrounded the house and was full of colour, with a profusion of flowers of all kinds – hollyhocks, roses, lilies and hydrangeas.

may be pared down to something like:

> The little red house stood at the end of the lane in a garden filled with brightly-coloured flowers.

Short stories are often more like poetry in the way that they condense events and explore emotion. Often the short story is dominated by an image or metaphor in the same way as much poetry. Very short stories or pieces are often known as 'prose poems'.

The history of the short story

In Europe, the oral story-telling tradition began to develop into written stories in the early fourteenth century, most notably with Geoffrey Chaucer's *The Canterbury Tales* and Giovanni Boccaccio's *The Decameron.* Both of these books are composed of individual short stories, ranging from farce or humorous anecdotes to well-crafted literary fictions set within a larger narrative story (known as a *frame story*).

Among the earliest writers of the modern short story were Sir Walter Scott, Nathaniel Hawthorne and Edgar Allan Poe. At the turn of the nineteenth century short stories were all the rage, being published in large numbers of literary magazines. Stories like those featuring Sherlock Holmes by Sir Arthur Conan Doyle were published in *The Strand Magazine* and sold hundreds of thousands of copies.

Great writers such as Anton Chekhov made the short story their own, and in the early twentieth century James Joyce, Katherine Mansfield and W. Somerset Maugham received huge critical acclaim.

American writers have remained at the fore-front of the short story, with Ernest Hemingway, Dorothy Parker, F. Scott Fitzgerald and, more recently, Raymond Carver all being acknowledged as masters of the craft.

Short stories used to be popular in both literary and commercial magazines. Today, however, very few outlets exist for literary short stories, and fewer commercial magazines publish short stories than in the past.

Joining stories together

Famously, publishers have always had a problem persuading readers to buy short stories. Publishers' sales figures show that a short-story collection sells roughly a quarter of what a novel by the same writer would sell. Reasons for this situation aren't clear, especially since a sound-bite, time-pressured culture would seem to favour short rather than long fiction. However, many readers love the fact that they can start a novel, put it down and then re-enter its world later, picking up where they left off. Starting to read a novel can be a challenge; you have to get into the story, but once in you're away. With a collection of stories, however, you have to do that hard work of connecting with the characters and setting repeatedly.

Connecting your short stories in some way can provide readers with greater continuity and enable them to become absorbed in the stories more quickly. You can connect stories in several different ways:

  ✔ **Have a theme:** You can write stories around a similar central idea: mysteries such as Edgar Allan Poe's *Tales of Mystery and Imagination* and retellings of fairy stories such as Angela Carter's *The Bloody Chamber.* The theme helps readers identify what kind of story to expect, and if they enjoy one they're likely to appreciate them all.

Twelve classic stories

If you want to master the art of the short story, read these classic examples for inspiration:

- ✔ **'The Pit and the Pendulum', Edgar Allan Poe (1842).** Classic nineteenth-century horror from the master of the genre about a man being tortured by the Inquisition.

- ✔ **'The Necklace', Guy de Maupassant (1884).** A classic story about the borrowing of a necklace, with a great twist.

- ✔ **'Ward No. Six', Anton Chekhov (1892).** In this shocking tale, a doctor finds himself in trouble when he aims to help people in an asylum.

- ✔ **'The Dead', James Joyce (1914).** In one of the most beautiful short stories ever written, a woman remembers her dead lover.

- ✔ **'The Garden Party', Katherine Mansfield (1922).** A coming-of-age story, widely considered her finest piece of short fiction.

- ✔ **'A Telephone Call', Dorothy Parker (1927).** A wonderful, bitter, funny monologue about unrequited love.

- ✔ **'The Secret Miracle', Jorge Luis Borges (1944).** A composer facing a firing squad asks God for a hidden miracle.

- ✔ **'Lamb to the Slaughter', Roald Dahl (1953).** A much-imitated classic story with a twist.

- ✔ **'The Star', Arthur C. Clarke (1955).** A brilliant science fiction story examining religious faith and humankind's place in the universe.

- ✔ **'Little Things', Raymond Carver (1980).** A separating couple fight over their baby.

- ✔ **'Far North', Sara Maitland (first published 1983 as *True North*).** Based on an Inuit myth, the story shows how the arrival of a strange man disturbs the relationship between two women.

- ✔ **'Brokeback Mountain', Annie Proulx (1997).** A modern classic about two cowboys who fall in love, made into an Oscar-winning film.

- ✔ **Set the stories in the same location:** Consider using the same town as the backdrop to your stories. Examples include Sherwood Anderson's *Winesburg, Ohio*, in which some of the main characters in one story appear as minor characters in others, and V. S. Naipaul's *Miguel Street*.

- ✔ **Involve the same characters:** Consider the detective stories featuring Sherlock Holmes, or Melissa Bank's *The Girls' Guide to Hunting and Fishing*, which started life as a collection of short stories but was then marketed as a novel.

- ✔ **Tell the same story from different viewpoints:** Use a variety of different voices and styles – such as Raymond Queneau's *Exercises in Style*.

Short-story *collections* and *anthologies* are different:

- ✔ **Short-story collection:** A number of short stories all written by the same author.

- ✔ **Short-story anthology:** A number of short stories by different authors. Some anthologies are themed; others aren't.

Exploring Short-Story Genres

Many short stories fall into clear categories. These genres are:

- ✔ **The literary story:** This is perhaps more like poetry than the novel, with its focus on the use of language, insight into character and personal revelation. Modern literary short-story writers include Lorrie Moore, Alice Munro and Raymond Carver.

- ✔ **The ghost story:** Many short stories concern the supernatural, weird or uncanny, about ghosts, hauntings or horror. Edgar Allan Poe, Henry James and Susan Hill have all written in this genre.

- ✔ **The detective story:** The classic whodunnit can easily be condensed into short episodes, as with the Sherlock Holmes stories by Sir Arthur Conan Doyle.

- ✔ **The humorous story:** This can be a kind of extended joke, often with a twist at the end – masters of this genre are Saki, O. Henry and Roald Dahl.

- ✔ **The parable of our times:** This often focuses on an issue of contemporary importance. Many such parables still resonate years later; for example, stories about the greed that led to the Wall Street Crash of 1929 are suddenly relevant to the credit crisis of recent times.

- ✔ **The science fiction story:** Many science fiction stories have proved uncannily true to developments in modern science and technology, and warned people about where the world's going. Jules Verne, Isaac Asimov, Arthur C. Clarke, Philip K. Dick and Ray Bradbury are masters of the craft.

- ✔ **The erotic story:** Short fiction has also been a favourite form for those who want to explore the erotic, perhaps because it does away with the necessity for extended character development and can focus more on the sexual act itself. Erotic fiction differs from pornography in the use of language and metaphor and in revealing human truths about people. Anaïs Nin's *Delta of Venus* is a classic example.

- ✔ **The twist-in-the-tale story:** This carefully leads the reader into expecting one outcome and then delivers a clever twist. The twist's timing is all important, as is the story's build-up, which ensures that the twist makes sense. The twist should arise naturally out of the story and characters and not appear out of nowhere. Roald Dahl and Jeffrey Archer both specialise in this technique.

- ✔ **The what-if story:** Many short stories deal with a 'what if?' scenario. What if an alien spaceship landed in your back garden? What if a man woke up one morning and couldn't see? What if a child realised she could communicate with animals? In these stories, the characters are less important than the theme and situation. What-if stories can also be written in all of the other genres. Stephen King's stories often start with this premise.

Two main types of short story exist: character driven and based on a situation or theme. Character-driven stories explore people and the human condition. Most literary short stories are of this kind. Many such stories deal with a moment of personal change or revelation; the day a character's life changed forever. Other stories explore an idea or circumstance, with perhaps a plot twist; much science fiction falls into this category.

Try writing a character-driven story. Start with a character who interests you. Put her into a situation that has possibilities for development – an unexpected visitor or telephone call, a chance meeting, some unwelcome news, a sudden accident. See how the character deals with the situation you've created. You may find out something about her that you didn't expect.

Finding Story Ideas

A short story needn't concern a grand or exciting subject – it can deal with the commonplace. A child losing her favourite toy, an old woman remembering an event from her past, a piece of domestic drama or a man losing his job, for example. In *Hey Yeah Right Get a Life* (2000), Helen Simpson wrote some brilliant short stories about modern women and motherhood based around everyday events.

Short-story ideas are all around you. Anything can be the basis for a short story – the smaller the incident, the better. You're walking down the street, you see a child with an ice cream, the ice cream falls to the ground, the child cries, the exasperated, overtired mother shouts at her. Within this little scene lies a whole story concerning the mother and her child, their hopes and expectations, and the relationship between them.

Try these exercises to generate your own short stories:

- ✔ Find a photograph or painting that interests you and includes more than three people. Look at the people. Write a story about them – what they're thinking, what's going on in the scene – based on just this one moment.

- ✔ Think about recent small events in your life – you get a phone call from an old friend, you take your cat to the vet, you miss the train, you bump into someone in the street. Use these incidents as the basis for a story.

- ✔ Read the News in Brief section in a newspaper – local papers especially are always full of odd and surprising stories. Pick one story and rewrite it in your own style.

- ✔ Focus on one emotion – jealousy, embarrassment or terror, for example – and write a story around a character who feels this emotion.

Finally, some modern short-story writers have taken old stories – fairy tales and myths – and retold them with a subversive, modern twist, often involving a new ending. Masters of this technique are Angela Carter and Sara Maitland. The issues you face today may seem superficially different, but remain at heart the same – how to grow up and leave home, face life's challenges, find the right life partner, become a good parent, grow old and face death.

Entering Short-Story Competitions

Entering short-story competitions is one of the best ways of improving your chances of success as a writer. Being selected by the judges for the main prize (*shortlisted*) means you may win a cash prize, but it can also help you attract the interest of agents or publishers.

Entering competitions helps you in other ways, too. Doing so imposes discipline because you have to finish by the deadline, gives you an incentive to polish a story and make it the best you possibly can and encourages you to keep writing and sending stories out.

Carefully read and follow each competition's rules. Most competitions state a minimum and maximum word length, and many stipulate format, theme or number of stories you're allowed to enter.

In some cases you pay an entry fee of about £10 to help with the administration costs. A small fee is fine, but beware of competitions that ask you for a lot of money upfront.

Considering some competitions

A large number of short-story competitions take place in the UK every year. Some of these are run just once, but a number are awarded annually. Here's a selection of the biggest and best-known competitions:

- **Asham Award (www.ashamaward.com):** Britain's only prize for short stories by women. The prize is offered every two years (the even-numbered years) and the prize money is over £3,000.

- **BBC National Short Story Award (www.theshortstory.org.uk):** The largest award for a single short story in the world. The writer of the winning story receives £15,000, the runner-up gets £3,000 and the three other shortlisted writers win £500 each.

- **Bridport Prize (www.bridportprize.org.uk):** This is an annual international creative writing competition for poetry and short stories. First prize in each category is £5,000; 12 runner-up prizes are also awarded.

- ✓ **Fish Publishing short-story prizes** (www.fishpublishing.com): Fish Publishing runs a number of short-story competitions. Visit the website for more details.

- ✓ **Mslexia women's short-story competition** (www.mslexia.co.uk): First prize is £2,000. All winning stories are published in *Mslexia* magazine.

- ✓ **V. S. Pritchett Memorial Prize** (www.rslit.org): This commemorates an author who's widely regarded as the finest English short-story writer of the twentieth century. The V. S. Pritchett Memorial Prize offers £1,000 for an unpublished short story and is supported by Chatto & Windus, V. S. Pritchett's publishers, and administered by the Royal Society of Literature.

A complete list of competitions is available from Story, the campaign to celebrate the short story, on their website: www.theshortstory.org.uk.

Making your story stand out from the crowd

If you enter a short-story competition, you need to find a way to make your story get noticed. Many competitions get hundreds of entries, and the judges usually employ a sifter or team of sifters who go through the entries and select a shortlist to present to the main judges, who are often well-known writers.

Engaging the reader's attention very quickly is essential. Here are some ways to do so:

- ✓ **An intriguing title:** A great title can help a story to stand out immediately, especially if you make it original and unusual.

- ✓ **A great first sentence:** The first sentence should immediately grab readers' attention and make them want to read on. Yours needs to give readers a flavour of what the story's about and draw them in. (Chapter 9 offers advice on writing attention-grabbing opening lines.)

- ✓ **An unlikely premise:** A story based on an unusual or unlikely premise is more likely to intrigue the judges than one on a hackneyed theme.

- ✓ **An unusual voice:** Writing in an unusual voice or style, as long as it isn't difficult to read, may help your story stand out from the crowd.

Don't be too clever. There's no substitute for a straightforward story, well told. In your attempt to be different, don't make the story too convoluted, mannered or incomprehensible, or so bizarre that no one can take it seriously.

Finding an Outlet for Your Short Fiction

Far more opportunities for getting short fiction in print used to exist. Unfortunately, many of the literary magazines lost their funding; others struggle on but have little space. Some magazines, however, do still publish short fiction.

Literary magazines

Magazines that still publish literary short stories include *Granta* (www. granta.com), *The London Magazine* (www.thelondonmagazine.net), *Stand* magazine (standmagazine.org) and *The Reader* (thereader.org. uk). *Prospect* magazine (www.prospect-magazine.co.uk) publishes one short story per issue.

Some specialist literary magazines also exist:

- *Mslexia* magazine (www.mslexia.co.uk) publishes themed fiction by women every quarter.
- The *International Magazine of Erotica* publishes erotic fiction (not pornography).
- *Jewish Quarterly* (www.jewishquarterly.org) publishes some fiction by Jewish writers.
- *Chroma* magazine publishes fiction by gay writers.
- *Wasafiri* (www.wasafiri.org) publishes work by black writers.
- *Time Out* magazine (www.timeout.com) has published short stories and run competitions in the past.

Anthologies

A number of publishing companies occasionally produce anthologies of writing. These anthologies can be centred on a theme or are sometimes simply collections of new writing. They may feature stories shortlisted in competitions, often combined with those by well-known writers to help the anthology sell.

Publishers of such anthologies often call for submissions, so check out short-story websites or literary magazines.

Women's magazines

Many women's magazines still publish short fiction:

- *Best* (www.bestmag.com) sometimes accepts 900–1,200-word stories. Aimed at modern women in their thirties, these often involve a twist.

- *Woman* (www.goodtoknow.co.uk), *Woman & Home* (www.womanand home.com) and *Woman's Weekly* all publish some women's fiction. Particularly geared to older women, these stories are generally easy-to-read commercial fiction. They're often romantic or historical, and are sometimes serialised.

- *Good Housekeeping* (www.goodhousekeeping.com) usually publishes work by established writers only, but sometimes runs short-story competitions.

Follow these tips when submitting short stories to women's magazines:

- Always read the magazine you're submitting to before sending off your story. Get a feel for the readership and the style of stories accepted.

- Submit by post not email.

- Type your story on one side of the paper only.

- Include a stamped addressed envelope (SAE) – although not all magazines return unused stories.

- Put your name and contact number on every page of a short story in case pages get separated.

- Send seasonal stories well in advance. Some magazines publish summer fiction supplements, stories for which are picked about six months in advance.

Payment varies from magazine to magazine. You can usually find guidelines on the magazines' websites or from the editorial department of the magazines.

Science fiction magazines

In science fiction, short stories are still very popular. A number of magazines welcome science fiction stories, including *The Future Fire*, *Interzone*, *Jupiter*, *Nemonymous*, *Postscripts* and *Black Static* (formerly known as *The Third Alternative*). Increasingly, though, Internet sites have been taking over as the forum for new science fiction stories. Dowse SF & Fantasy Hub (www.dowse.com) provides up-to-date information on science fiction and fantasy publishers and magazines.

Radio

BBC Radio 4 regularly broadcasts short stories, most by well-known writers but some by unknown authors. Sending a story in to BBC radio is a bit like entering a competition; stipulations exist regarding length, format and so on. The stories must be the right length to be read in the 15-minute time slots – roughly 2,000 words. You may need to read your story aloud to judge its timing.

According to Di Spears, Executive Producer of the Reading Unit, stories are usually grouped in fives across a week, often around a theme, such as Sleepers, Heartbreak, Passion and Addiction. BBC radio looks for terrific writing, a good story and an ear-catching voice.

Stories on radio are read by actors, and occasionally use sound effects. The way stories are read can range from a monologue in a distinct voice to the imitation of many different voices. Usually just one actor is used, though sometimes others read different parts. Music is usually used to set the mood.

Listen to a lot of stories on the radio before entering your own, to get an idea of how they're written and what works in this medium.

Stories are still usually submitted on paper, not on tape or CD or via email. Remember to include a stamped addressed envelope if you want your story returned.

Always make sure your SAE is large enough for your story to fit into. Weigh the manuscript and check that the postage is correct.

The Internet

A huge growth in Internet sites offering opportunities for short fiction writers has occurred in recent years. Many of these enable writers to post their work and hopefully get a readership. One problem with such sites is that it can be hard for writers to protect their ideas and copyright and to get paid for their work.

The Story (www.theshortstory.org) and Write Words (www.write words.org.uk) websites are trustworthy sources of information about opportunities for short-story writers. Look for sites funded by the Arts Council or supported by other reputable agencies. Fish Publishing (www.fish publishing.com) is one of the best-known sites for online short stories.

Ten classic novellas

- Herman Melville's *Billy Budd* (published in 1924) deals with a tragic incident at sea. It offers a nautical recasting of the Fall, a parable of good and evil, a meditation on justice and political governance, and a searching portrait of three men caught in a deadly triangle.

- Henry James's *The Turn of the Screw* (1897) is a ghost story which defies easy interpretation. A governess in a remote country house is in charge of two children who appear to be haunted by former employees who are now supposed to be dead. But are they? The story is drenched in complexities – including the central issue of the reliability of the person who's telling the tale.

- Joseph Conrad's *Heart of Darkness* (1902) concerns the search for a mysterious Kurtz, who's involved in the exploitation of Africans in the ivory trade.

- Thomas Mann's *Death in Venice* (1912) is a haunting story of the relationship between art and life, love and death. A famous German writer goes to Venice where he falls in love with a young boy.

- Franz Kafka's *The Metamorphosis* (1915) tells the story of Gregor Samsa, who wakes one morning to find himself transformed into a giant insect.

- George Orwell's *Animal Farm* (1945) is a famous allegory of totalitarianism.

- Ernest Hemingway's *The Old Man and the Sea* (1952) tells the story of an ageing fisherman who struggles with a giant fish.

- Françoise Sagan's *Bonjour Tristesse* (1954) concerns 17-year-old Cécile, who spends her summer in a villa on the French Riviera with her father and two other women, including Anne, with whom she vies for her father's affection.

- Anita Brookner's *Hotel du Lac* (1984) won the Booker Prize despite being novella length. It explores what happens to a middle-aged woman who runs away just before her wedding and takes refuge in a foreign hotel.

- Joyce Carol Oates's *Rape: A Love Story* (2005) reveals the after-effects of a horrific crime.

Growing a Story into a Novella

The *novella* is a strange hybrid of the short story and the novel. Generally, a novella is considered to be a work of fiction above the 20,000-word upper limit of the short story, but below the 40,000-word length that constitutes a novel.

What makes a novella is that, rather like the short story, it has a concentrated unity of purpose and design. Character, incident, theme and language are all focused on a main issue, which is usually of a serious nature and of universal significance.

Some ideas just can't be given justice in a short story and yet aren't wide enough in scope to become a full-length novel. The novella usually encompasses more time than the standard short story as well as allows room for deeper characterisation.

Like short stories, novellas aren't terribly popular with conventional publishers. Most mainstream publishing companies like novels to be at least 50,000 words in length so that they feel thick enough to give readers a sense of value for money. Some writers of novellas are asked to expand their stories, but doing so can result in padding them out and spoiling the effect. Well-known writers for whom sales are guaranteed are usually exempt from such constraints; some of Ian McEwan's novels are very short, and *On Chesil Beach*, which was short-listed for the Man Booker Prize 2007, is about 35,000 words in length.

Shorter novellas are usually published in collections along with other stories or novellas. Individual short novellas can be marketed in the same way as short stories, except that they are too long for publication in many magazines.

A longer novella can be published on its own, often simply as a novel. These are sold in the same way as novels to mainstream or small independent publishers through agents (see Chapter 22 for more information about agents).

Many of the classic novellas are concerned with one main theme, often concerning people learning important lessons or making significant journeys – see the nearby sidebar for some examples.

Chapter 12

Writing the Novel

*W*riting a novel is perhaps the most demanding form of fiction writing. A *novel* is usually simply defined as a fictional work of prose of more than about 50,000 words. So a novel is characterised mainly by its length, which presents quite a challenge to the writer.

Novels are important. The novel depicts, explores and interprets human character and behaviour. Not only are readers of novels entertained, but also they're able to reflect on human behaviour and come to a deeper understanding of life's problems. Through reading a novel, you can enter the consciousness of other people and explore the world as they see it – and understand their problems and difficulties. Through this created empathy, a novel can bring about social change: Charles Dickens exposed the reality of the poor in Victorian England and Thomas Hardy forced people to engage with the social discrimination of women.

Less serious novels can also help you pass the time, reassure and entertain you, and provide escapism from the often hard realities of day-to-day life.

Aspiring to the Literary Novel

Literary fiction is today considered by the publishing industry to be a genre of its own. By literary fiction, publishers usually mean fiction that:

✔ Has a serious theme or message.

✔ Has psychological depth of characterisation.

✔ Uses language in a fresh and original way.

History of the literary novel

While poetry and drama go back thousands of years to works such as the Babylonian *Epic of Gilgamesh* (c. 2000 bc) and the Greek play *Oresteia* (458 bc), the novel is a somewhat more recent literary creation. Fictional narratives written in prose appeared before 1700 (Giovanni Boccaccio's *Decameron* (1351–1353), the English romancer Sir Thomas Malory's *Le Morte d'Arthur* (c. 1469) and Miguel de Cervantes's *Don Quixote* (first volume 1605, second volume 1615). Many scholars date the birth of the modern novel to the eighteenth century, specifically the publication of the English printer Samuel Richardson's *Pamela, or Virtue Rewarded* (1740; a long story recounting the trials of an English girl in a battle against her seducer).

In the UK, the term *novel* didn't really come into use until the end of the eighteenth century. By the 1850s the expansion of the middle class meant that more people could read; they also had money to spend on literature. At the time autobiography, biography, journals, diaries and memoirs were popular, and people were hungry for new material.

Over the next century, English readers saw the publication of many long fictional narratives, including Richardson's own *Clarissa* (1748), Henry Fielding's *Joseph Andrews* (1742) and *Tom Jones* (1749), Tobias Smollett's *Roderick Random* (1748) and *Humphry Clinker* (1771), Laurence Sterne's *Tristram Shandy* (1760–67), and Jane Austen's *Sense and Sensibility* (1811) and *Pride and Prejudice* (1813).

The novel quickly became extremely popular. Between 1840 and 1900, many important novels were published, often in instalments, including Charlotte Brontë's *Jane Eyre* (1847), Emily Brontë's *Wuthering Heights* (1847), Charles Dickens's *David Copperfield* (1849–50), *Great Expectations* (1860–61) and *Bleak House,* George Eliot's *Middlemarch* (1871–72), William Makepeace Thackeray's *Vanity Fair* (1848), and Thomas Hardy's *Tess of the d'Urbervilles* (1891).

At the turn of the twentieth century, Henry James began to explore the idea of subjectivity and interior consciousness. In the twentieth century, Virginia Woolf, D. H. Lawrence and James Joyce were hugely influential in developing the literary novel as an art form.

The term is also used for fiction that stands the test of time and will be read by future generations. Most of the novels produced in Victorian times have disappeared without trace; only the very best are still read today. Recognising which of today's novels will still be read by the next generation is obviously very difficult.

Review coverage and being nominated for one of the many literary prizes is what makes a literary novel stand out and be successful. Being shortlisted for the Man Booker, Orange or Costa (formerly Whitbread) prizes can make an author's reputation and ensure that the nominated book and future books get reviewed and sell well.

Considering the characteristics of the literary novel

Writing a literary novel involves some degree of originality. Take a look at the most successful literary novels of the last ten years; many of these use:

- ✔ **An unusual voice:** Peter Carey's _The True History of the Kelly Gang_ is written in the voice of an illiterate Australian; Andrea Levy's _Small Island_ has a Caribbean lilt; Mark Haddon's _The Curious Incident of the Dog in the Night-time_ imitates the voice of a 15-year-old autistic boy; and Xiaolu Guo's _A Concise Chinese-English Dictionary for Lovers_ has the voice of a Chinese woman who doesn't speak good English.

- ✔ **An unusual structure:** David Mitchell's _Cloud Atlas_ is divided into six narratives, each of exactly 80 pages, split into two sections. Lionel Shriver's _The Post-Birthday World_ has the same first and last chapter, but the chapters in between alternate with two possible narratives, depending on whether she goes ahead with an infidelity or not. Margaret Atwood's _The Blind Assassin_ contains a story-within-a-story, Sarah Waters's _The Night Watch_ has a narrative that runs backwards in time (Chapter 9 covers the traditional structure of the novel).

- ✔ **An unusual or important theme:** Chimamanda Ngozi Adichie's _Half of a Yellow Sun_ describes the painful history of Biafra, Linda Grant's _When I Lived in Modern Times_ looks at post-war Israel, and Clare Morrall's _Astonishing Splashes of Colour_ concerns a woman with synaesthesia. Kazuo Ishiguro's _Never Let Me Go_ looks at the issue of cloning people for body parts, while Mohsin Hamid's _The Reluctant Fundamentalist_ concerns the relationship between the Muslim world and the West.

Literary novels use metaphor and symbolism (see Chapter 7 for more on these devices); they work at more than one level. They often refer back in structure or theme to other literary texts or even art forms, echoing classic texts such as the Bible and Dante's _Divine Comedy_, as well as other well-known literary novels. James Joyce's _Ulysses_, for example, refers back to many events in Homer's _Odyssey_, and Philip Pullman's _His Dark Materials_ trilogy refers to Milton's _Paradise Lost_ (the title is a quotation from it) and Dante's _Divine Comedy_ (the heroine, Lyra Belacqua's surname is taken from a character in Dante's work).

Writing a literary novel requires an ability to use language with originality and flair, a deep curiosity about character and the choices people make, and often a deep concern for a difficult issue that affects human beings, for example, the effects of war, discrimination, illness and disability, political freedom or the future of the planet, medical ethics or the dark recesses of the human heart.

Exploring experimental fiction

Although literary fiction is in some ways always experimental, much literary fiction that wins prizes or is commercially successful conforms to the usual rules of character and narrative. Some writers, however, push the boundaries and develop new techniques and styles of writing.

Some experimental writing involves the concept of randomness to replace the structure of conventional novels. Such authors may randomly cut up and reconstruct their work, perhaps doing so using a device such as the tossing of a coin to determine which section goes where. Some examples include:

- William S. Burroughs (*Naked Lunch*), who made much use of this technique, in his unnerving story of a drug addict's descent into hell as he travels from New York to Tangier and then into the dreamlike Interzone.

- James Joyce and Samuel Beckett, who both subverted language and structure in their works. *Finnegans Wake* is written in a unique language revolving around puns. In Beckett's novels *Molloy*, *Malone Dies* and *The Unnamable*, all sense of plot, place and time are abandoned, leaving only an interior monologue.

- David Markson, who, in *This Is Not a Novel*, ignored plot and characters, and constructed a list of quotations, anecdotes and opinions on artists, writers, composers and philosophers.

Publishers are notoriously reluctant to publish experimental fiction, mainly because so few people want to read it. However, if you really want to write such fiction, don't let anyone stop you.

Writing Commercial Fiction

In contrast to literary fiction, commercial fiction is designed less to challenge and disturb than to amuse and entertain. While literary fiction pushes the boundaries, most commercial fiction is fairly formulaic; the basic plot and structure are set, although the author has plenty of room for manoeuvre within the outlines. At its very best, commercial fiction can merge with literary fiction – sometimes referred to in the book trade as *lit lite!* Such novels usually combine a more conventional plot-line and narrative voice with greater depth of character and insight. Generally, though, little confusion exists between the two genres.

Romancing the fiction

Romantic fiction is as popular now as it ever was and follows a well-tried 'boy meets girl' formula.

Romantic fiction can range from the literary, as in Jane Austen, to the utterly formulaic, as in Mills and Boon stories. Commercial romantic fiction is usually written to specific guidelines, which publishing companies are generally happy to supply. Within these constraints, however, room still exists for creativity.

Harlequin (Mills and Boon) publish in several different categories and are adding new ones all the time. Harlequin accepts writers without an agent, and some series are produced by book packagers – that is, they come up with a concept and then hire a group of authors to write on this theme.

Conforming to the basic requirements of romantic fiction

Character, of course, is the most important element of a love story. Modern romantic heroines are far from being the fainting wallflowers of previous generations. Your heroine needs to be lively, appealing and in control of her own destiny. She must be a strong personality in her own right, capable of living without the hero and not existing simply to be rescued. Readers need to relate to your heroine and fall in love with your hero – so forget remote or dominating hunks.

Point of view is also important. Most romantic fiction is told from the perspective of the heroine, although sometimes the man's viewpoint is added too. Adding other viewpoints isn't a good idea. Romance readers want to concentrate on the relationship between the main characters, not on what other characters think.

Whether or not to include sex scenes in the romantic novel is also an issue, as is their explicitness. Read the publisher's guidelines, which usually have fairly strict parameters. Some romantic fiction novels keep sex scenes behind closed doors, while others are more explicit. However, if you find writing explicit material difficult or awkward, don't go there. Many romantic novels contain only implied sex – indeed, some of the best ever written never get beyond a kiss.

A romantic novel doesn't always have to end happily, although you should at least finish on an optimistic note with your characters full of hope for the future. Some of the really great romantic novels of the past have ended in tragedy, but this isn't usual in commercial romantic fiction.

Tips for aspiring romance writers include:

- ✔ Have fun choosing a location. Many contemporary romances have international settings, but don't give too much detail – you're not writing a travelogue. Also, avoid issues such as poverty or politics.

- ✔ Make your characters believable and think about their motivation. Have them communicate with realistic dialogue that isn't too hackneyed or stilted and think about how they'd act and behave in every situation.

✔ Make sure that the conflict always arises from the main characters and their emotions, and not from the supporting cast.

✔ Keep up the tension by alternating the drama between highs and lows, advances and retreats. Readers should be in doubt that all ends happily, even if they know in their hearts that it will.

Playing with variations on the romantic theme

Occasionally, different forms of romantic fiction become popular. *Sex and shopping* described a 1980s' type of romance involving a materialistic modern heroine and her adventures with men; they still often concluded with finding the right guy. Today, *chick lit* is the buzz category; novels involving single working women in their twenties and thirties. The novels often revolve around female friendships as well as romance.

Historical romances – those set before the Second World War – have long been popular. The first historical romances appeared in 1921, when Georgette Heyer began writing novels set during the English Regency period, largely inspired by the works of Jane Austen. Today, a vast range of books is available from all historical periods, from pre-Roman England, through the Elizabethan period, and up to and including the First World War. Much modern historical romance is well-researched and gives the heroine a more active role than in the bodice rippers of the 1970s, in which the women long to be overpowered by a man and may even be sexually violated.

Sagas often tell the story of a family over several generations. Most of these have a romantic theme, revolving mainly around the women characters and their various lives and loves. The *Aga saga* is a term coined in the early 1990s for a kind of fiction popularised by Joanna Trollope, involving middle-class women and their families. Mary Wesley and Maeve Binchy have also been put into this category.

A classic example of the family saga is John Galsworthy's *The Forsyte Saga*, which concerns three generations of one family. Daphne du Maurier's *Hungry Hill* centres on a feud between two families and spans a hundred years.

Uncovering crime and detective fiction

Crime writing has long been one of the most popular forms of fiction with readers across the English-speaking world. Crime continues to fascinate, in both reality as described in newspapers, or in imagination through books and on television and radio. A solid market exists for good crime writing, which seems here to stay.

Writing a Mills and Boon novel

Many people think writing a Mills and Boon novel is easy. It isn't. First, you have to believe in what you're doing. If you're tongue in cheek or don't take the story seriously, it'll show. If you don't read romantic fiction, it'll show. Before you begin writing, you need to read many, many books in this genre. The series that emerges as your favourite is probably the best one for you to submit your manuscript to.

According to Mills and Boon, stories should be grounded in reality and reflective of contemporary relevant trends. However, they should also be 'fast-paced', 'essentially escapist romantic fantasies which take the reader on an emotional roller-coaster ride'.

Mills and Boon stories are always written in the third person. They can be written from the male or female point of view, or seen through the eyes of both protagonists, but not from the point of view of anyone else.

Crime fiction is divided into a number of sub-categories:

- **The Cosy:** This American term describes a very traditional murder mystery, often set in a quiet backwater, such as a village, with an investigator like Agatha Christie's Miss Marple. Apart from the initial crime, not much violent action occurs and the focus is usually more on the characters than the crime.

- **The Private Eye novel:** This term refers to mainly American crime novels featuring private investigators such as those by Dashiell Hammett and Raymond Chandler. Sara Paretsky's stories are a modern equivalent. These are often told in the first person through the eyes of their hard-boiled heroes and heroines, in an idiosyncratic, original voice.

- **The Whodunnit:** This term applies to a crime novel involving a cast of characters; the reader is provided with clues from which the identity of the murderer can be deduced before the solution is revealed in the final pages of the book. The locked room mystery was a popular early form of this type of novel – a story in which a crime, usually murder, is committed under apparently impossible circumstances. Examples include many of Agatha Christie's and Dorothy L. Sayers's novels. Classic locked room mysteries are *The Four Just Men* by Edgar Wallace and *The King is Dead* by Ellery Queen.

- **Historical crime novels:** These are a more recent fashion. A classic example is Ellis Peters's Brother Cadfael novels, set in twelfth-century Shrewsbury. These novels must be historically accurate – part of the fun derives from the lack of modern forensic techniques, which places emphasis on the skill of the detective figure. Modern crime novels are set in every conceivable period, from Tudor to Victorian England, from medieval Italy to ancient Japan.

✔ **Police procedurals:** These have long been popular, with Lawrence Treat's 1945 novel *V as in Victim* the first novel of this kind. Ed McBain wrote dozens of novels in the 87th Precinct series, beginning in the mid-1950s and continuing almost until his death in 2005. John Creasey's *Inspector West Takes Charge*, written in 1940, was the first of more than 40 novels to feature Roger West of the London Metropolitan Police. In France, Georges Simenon's highly influential Maigret series is also a police procedural.

✔ **Violent or gruesome crime novels:** These have become more popular in recent years. Examples include Patricia Cornwell's Kay Scarpetta series, featuring a forensic pathologist, and those of Mo Hayder and Val McDermid, which pack a powerful punch.

✔ **Woman in jeopardy or psychological crime novels:** These usually involve a first-person narrative and revolve around a character who's put in a situation of extreme peril. The story's usually told from the perspective of the potential victim. Examples include husband-and-wife team Nicci French, Ruth Rendell (who also writes as Barbara Vine) and Lesley Grant-Adamson.

If you're interested in writing a crime novel, consider these tips:

✔ Research the market as much as you can by reading a wide range of novels in the genre.

✔ Choose a type of crime writing that you feel comfortable with and will enjoy writing.

✔ Try not to write something that is very similar to the work of a writer who's already successful – publishers look for something new.

✔ Think carefully about the setting for your crime novel as an unusual location often helps you to be original.

When writing crime fiction, you need to plan out every detail of the crime in order to cover all eventualities. You need to have some idea of how the police work and the limits that are placed on them, how dead bodies are dealt with, what tests are carried out on the corpse and the effect of various forms of death on the body. In a modern crime novel, you need to be realistic and convincing.

Much detective and crime fiction involves readers in a complex game to deduce the murderer. Remember to give the characters plausible alibis and to scatter your narrative with clues (not too obvious) to help the readers and red herrings to confuse them and lead them down a blind alley.

Increasing the excitement with thrillers

A *thriller* is a fast-paced novel with an element of suspense and conflict, and containing action and adventure. Thrillers often have complex plots, involving many twists, turns and cliff-hangers. They generally feature a resourceful, usually male, hero, who's pitted against an evil enemy, sometimes an individual, often an organisation or state.

Many of the most successful thriller writers have inside knowledge of their subject-matter, for example espionage, war, medical or legal experience. John le Carré worked in the British Embassy in Berne for the secret services and Ian Fleming for Naval Intelligence; Alistair MacLean served in the Royal Navy during the war, Robin Cook and Michael Crichton are trained doctors, and John Grisham is a former politician and legal attorney.

Thrillers can be divided into sub-categories:

- ✔ **Action:** These concentrate on fast action and adventure, and most often feature a male hero who uses his physical and mental prowess to overcome the enemy. The Jason Bourne novels by Robert Ludlum (*The Bourne Identity* is the first), about a renegade spy, are a good example.

- ✔ **Crime:** This hybrid of thriller and crime novel usually emphasises action and suspense over psychological detail. Harlan Coben's *Tell No One*, a novel about a man whose dead wife contacts him over the Internet, is an example.

- ✔ **Disaster:** These usually involve natural or human-made disasters, such as floods, volcanic explosions, earthquakes and the like. Usually a hero tries to avert the disaster and save as many people as possible from its effects. Thomas Scortia's *The Glass Inferno* about a fire in a hotel (which was a source for the film *The Towering Inferno*) and Chuck Scarborough's *Aftershock*, in which an earthquake hits New York, are good examples.

- ✔ **Eco:** Here, the main character must try to avert a biological or environmental disaster, and is often pitted against shadowy enemies from governments or multinational corporations. Kyle Mills's *Darkness Falls* explores a world that runs out of oil, and Kim Stanley Robinson's *Forty Signs of Rain* describes global warming.

- ✔ **Legal:** These feature courtroom dramas and often also involve action outside the court as the hero tries to get to the truth and make sure justice is done. John Grisham (*The Pelican Brief*, *The Runaway Jury*) is a key exponent.

- ✔ **Medical:** Here, the main character is usually a doctor or researcher who must prevent the spread of some appalling disease or avert a medical catastrophe. Robin Cook's *Coma* is a classic in this category.

- ✔ **Psychological:** Here, the conflict between the main characters is mental and emotional, rather than physical – at least until the (often violent) conclusion. Psychological thrillers often include a large element of suspense. The novels of Patricia Highsmith, such as *The Talented Mr Ripley* and *Strangers on a Train*, are good examples.

- ✔ **Spy:** In this category the hero is generally a government agent who's pitted against a rival government or terrorists. This type of novel reached its peak during the Cold War, with works by authors such as Len Deighton (*The Ipcress File*), Frederick Forsyth (*The Day of the Jackal*) and Charles McCarry (*The Tears of Autumn*). Ian Fleming's James Bond novels led to a highly influential film series.

  John le Carré (*The Spy Who Came In From the Cold* and *Tinker, Tailor, Soldier, Spy*) intentionally rejects the conventions of the thriller, and his novels are more internalised stories of mystery and intrigue.

- ✔ **Techno:** These generally feature war and military action, and provide detailed descriptions of the technology involved in the often complex plot. Tom Clancy is considered to be the originator of the genre, with works such as *The Hunt for Red October*.

- ✔ **War:** Wartime events still form a good basis for thrillers, with plenty of action and opportunities for displays of courage. Alistair MacLean (*The Guns of Navarone*, *Where Eagles Dare*) is the classic writer in this category.

Adventure stories share some of the thriller's characteristics, focusing on action and physical danger. Adventure novels can involve the exploration of exotic and dangerous places, escapades at sea or during wartime, and more usually involve male heroes. Alexandre Dumas's *The Three Musketeers*, H. Rider Haggard's *She* and *King Solomon's Mines*, and Jules Verne's *Journey to the Centre of the Earth* are classic adventures. As the world has shrunk as a result of air travel, many modern adventure novels are set in a historical period, such as James Clavell's *Shogun*.

The *Western* is often considered to be a kind of adventure story. Classic Westerns include Jack Schaefer's *Shane* and *Monte Walsh*. Zane Grey and Louis L'Amour dominated the genre for many years but their work was considered to be *pulp fiction* – cheap escapist writing for the general entertainment of mass audiences.

Today, the Western has become more mainstream, and the image of the American Old West is likely to be more realistic. Examples are Larry McMurtry's Pulitzer Prize-winning *Lonesome Dove*, which describes a 2,500-mile cattle drive, and Cormac McCarthy's *Blood Meridian*; both are recognised as works of serious literary merit.

Imagining science fiction and fantasy

Science fiction is hard to define as it covers such a wide range of subjects and treatments. Some people dismiss science fiction as non-literary, but consider George Orwell's *1984*, H. G. Wells's *The Time Machine* or Cormac McCarthy's post-apocalyptic novel *The Road*, which won the Pulitzer Prize. Fantasy novels such as J. R. R. Tolkien's *The Lord of the Rings* have also achieved classic status.

Science fiction broadly includes writing set in the future or in an alternative reality, which may also portray the moral problems inherent in the development of technology. Some science fiction involves space or time travel.

Much science fiction has been extraordinarily prophetic; Arthur C. Clarke 'invented' the fax machine and the geostationary communications satellite before the actual technology for them was developed.

Categorising science fiction

Science fiction (SF) is a broad genre containing a large number of sub-categories. Some authors involve speculative or existential perspectives on contemporary reality in their novels, and so are considered to be on the borderline between science fiction and mainstream literature. Examples include:

- Philip K. Dick's *Do Androids Dream of Electric Sheep?*
- Stanislaw Lem's *Solaris*
- Kurt Vonnegut's *Slaughterhouse-Five*

Sub-categories within science fiction include:

- **Hard SF:** This usually involves cutting-edge physics, astronomy, mathematics and chemistry to postulate new worlds that advances will make possible. Classic writers in hard SF are Arthur C. Clarke and Isaac Asimov.

- **Soft SF:** This makes less use of science and technology and is more concerned with human issues. Authors in this genre include Ray Bradbury, Ursula K. Le Guin and Philip K. Dick.

- **Post-apocalyptic:** This considers what would happen to humanity after a major nuclear war or other catastrophe. This category includes many literary works, such as Doris Lessing's *The Memoirs of a Survivor*, Paul Auster's *In the Country of Last Things* and Nevil Shute's *On the Beach*. A classic SF text is Walter M. Miller's *A Canticle for Leibowitz*, first published in 1959 and never out of print.

✔ **Military SF and the Space Western:** These stories involve warfare between man and aliens from other planets, or between different galactic empires or the conquest of space. The popular TV series Star Trek is an example of space replacing the Wild West as the 'final frontier', as is Frank Herbert's best-selling novel *Dune*.

✔ **Alien encounters:** Many SF stories and films involve meetings with alien intelligences. Sometimes these encounters are benign and sometimes they threaten human life and civilisation. Examples include Walter Tevis's *The Man Who Fell to Earth* (filmed in 1976 by Nicolas Roeg), Robert A. Heinlein's influential *Stranger in a Strange Land* and Douglas Adams's brilliant and comic *The Hitchhiker's Guide to the Galaxy*.

✔ **Cyberpunk:** These novels are usually set in near-future dystopian societies. Common themes in cyberpunk include advances in information technology, especially the Internet and cyberspace, and the development of artificial intelligence. William Gibson's *Neuromancer* is one of the first and best examples.

✔ **Alternative history:** This subcategory explores what would have happened had the course of history taken another route. Examples include Philip K. Dick's *The Man in the High Castle*, in which Nazi Germany and Imperial Japan won the Second World War. Robert Harris had a similar idea in *Fatherland*.

✔ **New wave:** This term is used for SF writing characterised by a high degree of experimentation, both in form and content, and a highbrow and self-consciously 'literary' or artistic sensibility. Michael Moorcock (*Breakfast in the Ruins*) was one of its main exponents.

Focusing on fantasy

While science fiction often deals with the realm of what may one day happen, *fantasy* concerns alternative worlds that will never exist. Some of these alternative worlds are more technological, and the books may be considered as science fiction; others are based on alternative, possibly historical, realities.

Fantasy novels usually involve magic and mythical beasts, and are often inspired by mythology and folklore. Prominent fantasy writers include Anne McCaffrey, whose Dragonriders of Pern series is set on a colony of Earth which has reverted to medieval times, and Marion Zimmer Bradley, whose *The Mists of Avalon* is a feminist take on the Arthurian legend.

Many fantasy novels have been written for children, such as C. S. Lewis's seven stories about Narnia and J. K. Rowling's Harry Potter novels. However, much fantasy fiction is too complex or violent for children, may involve romantic or sexual themes, and is very much designed for adults.

Sub-categories within fantasy include:

- ✔ **Sword and sorcery:** This is generally characterised by heroes engaged in exciting and violent conflicts, usually with swords and primitive or magical weapons. An element of romance is often present, together with magic and supernatural forces. Robert E. Howard's tales of Conan the Barbarian fit in this category, as do Michael Moorcock's Elric series.

- ✔ **Superhero fiction:** These novels usually feature beings with extraordinary capabilities and prowess. They generally help the citizens of their countries or world by using their powers to overcome natural disasters or threats by other superbeings. Superman, Spider-Man and Batman are examples. Jonathan Lethem's *The Fortress of Solitude* involves two teenage friends who discover a magic ring that turns them into superheroes.

For your fantasy novel to convince the reader, you need to develop your world's rules, geography, language and history in great detail.

Embracing horror

Horror fiction usually involves an element of the supernatural – ghosts, spirits, vampires, demonic possession and so on. However, some more modern horror fiction simply involves gruesome, morbid or extremely violent events, told using a high degree of suspense.

Horror fiction plays on fear of death and repressed superstitions and beliefs. It also exploits the feeling that life may involve more than rational beliefs allow for. Horror often features doubles, shadow figures or the return of the dead – things ancient peoples believed in and that still exist in repressed form in modern psyches. When something happens that seems to confirm these old beliefs, a feeling of the uncanny is unleashed.

Classic horror novels include Mary Shelley's *Frankenstein* and Bram Stoker's *Dracula*. Stephen King is a modern master of the genre, many of whose novels have been made into successful films (*Carrie*, *The Shining*).

In modern horror fiction, the sense of the uncanny needs to be balanced by a realistic narrative. The more authentic the setting and characters, the more easily you can convince the reader that a supernatural threat may be real.

Trying erotic fiction

Today, a big market exists for commercial erotic writing. At one time writing about sex at all without a novel being censored or banned from publication was almost impossible. This situation changed with the trial of

D. H. Lawrence's novel *Lady Chatterley's Lover* in 1960. Lawrence had courageously described the sex act in great detail and using four-letter words, but within a serious literary work. After the paperback publication was allowed, the floodgates opened until sex scenes became a normal, if not obligatory, part of modern fiction.

Of course, pornography has always existed, and always will exist, but its definition changes with time. Pornography is writing which is specifically and solely designed to produce sexual feelings in the reader. Erotic fiction fills a rather different niche – while it may also be arousing, it can also have a serious literary intention.

Very few pornographic books refer to themselves as such, more often preferring the term 'erotic fiction', and it can sometimes be hard to draw a dividing line. While most pornography is aimed at men, series such as Black Lace are written by women for women. Erotic lists are now published for all tastes, including gay men and women, and people who like sadomasochism (S&M).

Anaïs Nin (*Delta of Venus*) and Marguerite Duras (*The Lover*) have written literary erotic fiction, and many contemporary novels focus mainly on sex, such as Nicholson Baker's *Vox*, which transcribes a long telephone conversation between two people who meet over a phone-sex line, and Helen Zahavi's *Dirty Weekend*, in which a woman avenges herself on various men who make obscene phone calls, accost her or force her into having sex.

Writing about sex

Writing about sex can be challenging, but within the context of a serious story or novel it offers a unique opportunity to see your characters at their most open and vulnerable. A person's true character may be revealed during sex, or no better or other way to reveal the truth about the relationship between two people may present itself.

Try to avoid hackneyed phrases or sentimentality – forget manly chests and heaving breasts. Finding a suitable vocabulary for writing about sex and in particular the sexual organs is difficult, though. Anglo-Saxon words can seem crude, Latin medical terms can sound clinical and the various euphemisms can sound coy. Making the vocabulary you use fit the characters is the best approach – use the words that they would use.

How much sex you describe depends very much on the genre in which you're writing. Most pornography contains little else, erotic novels feature explicit sex scenes fairly frequently, and most other fiction may include just one or two sex scenes that are vital for understanding the characters or moving the plot forward. Don't be tempted to go overboard on the sex scenes – in this area of writing, less is often more!

Chapter 13

Once Upon a Time: Writing for Children

In This Chapter

▶ Recognising that writing for children is tougher than it seems

▶ Understanding the needs of different age groups

▶ Going arty with comic books

▶ Delving into non-fiction

*B*efore you pick up your pen to start writing for children, you need to do some careful thinking and some research. Books for children need to be very tightly focused on the specific age group you're writing for – huge differences exist between writing for toddlers, early readers and teenagers. You also need to consider the relationship between illustrations and the text and ensure the vocabulary fits the age range you're aiming at.

When writing for children, many people think of the classic books they enjoyed when small, many of which are still in print today. However, just because these books are still read doesn't mean that publishers want more of the same. Today, editors are looking for something new, original and related to the fast-paced modern world. Contemporary children are easily bored and so much competition exists for their attention that a book needs to entice them straight away.

Dispelling the 'It's Easy to Write for Kids' Myth

You may think that writing for children must be easy. After all, a story for young children is short, doesn't use complicated vocabulary and should be fun. Actually, writing for children is extremely difficult. Before you begin, consider these factors:

✔ The vocabulary, content and length have to be exactly right for the age group you're writing for.

✔ Even if you set it in the past, a story for children must relate to the modern world. You need to avoid anything that may seem old-fashioned.

✔ Writing for school-age children almost demands that you become familiar with the national curriculum and the kinds of books used in reading schemes.

Research your market to see what currently sells and excites young readers without simply copying what's there – the publishing world really doesn't need any more Harry Potter imitations.

Before Schooling Begins: Writing for the Under 5s

Children's books give a child experience of different types of language, rhythms and sounds. Books put children in contact with topics that don't always come up in conversation or are outside their everyday world – foreign lands, exotic animals and even everyday places such as hospitals and factories.

Books for very young children may not involve the written word at all. They may simply be a series of images or a collection of words with pictures – an A–Z perhaps or numbers one to ten. These books are designed rather than written. Babies ultimately graduate to very simple rhymes and stories, and at this point the writer comes in.

Following the three 'Rs'

Almost all stories for very young children involve three elements:

✔ Rhythm

✔ Rhyme

✔ Repetition

I talk about each element in the next sections.

Realising the benefits of early exposure to books

Children should be introduced to books long before they can read. Books can be familiar objects, with exciting, colourful images. Books made of cloth or stiff card, which make sounds or have moving parts, can all introduce young children to the idea that books are fun long before they can distinguish a book from any other kind of toy. Babies benefit hugely from being exposed to books. The effort of focusing on pictures helps them to develop their eye muscles. Handling the book and learning to turn the pages helps develop hand–eye co-ordination.

Each time a child hears a particular word, it is imprinted more strongly in his or her brain. Children love to imitate sounds, which helps to develop their speech, and looking at books is one of the easiest ways to expand a young child's vocabulary.

Research shows that preschool children who are exposed to plenty of language through both books and conversation tend to do better at school. In addition to its educational value, reading to young children is a wonderful way to bond with them and is also very calming, an ideal activity for bedtime.

Feeling the rhythm

Children love rhythm. They love to be bounced, sung to and able to expect something that then happens. This sense of anticipation followed by fulfilment helps babies and young toddlers to feel that the world's stable and predictable, and it makes them feel secure.

When you write for a very young child, think of a rhythm like that of a train, a horse trotting or galloping, or a simple song. Make sure that you keep the beat going.

Poetry with a traditional *metre* (the basic rhythmic structure of a verse) usually follows a very simple pattern. When writing for young children, stick to a strong and simple rhythm, such as *tum-ti-ti*, *tum-ti-ti*, or *ti-tum-ti-tum ti-tum*. Read some children's verse and clap out the rhythm as you do so.

Think of a rhythm and write something that fits it exactly. Enjoy the way you have to find words that fit the beat.

Taking time to rhyme

Children love rhyme because, like rhythm, they can anticipate what comes next. Many books for young children involve rhyme, which, in combination with the importance of rhythm, makes writing for young children so much like writing poetry.

Take a simple sound – such as 'ine' or 'ock' – and write a story based on that rhyme. Keep the rhyme going as long as you can.

Submitting picture books

Print your story on single-sides of A4 paper, just the text which will appear on each page or with page breaks marked. Remember to number the pages. Most picture books are 32 pages long (a convenient format for the printer), which gives you 12 or 14 double-page spreads, allowing for the title page and other front matter. Don't give much detail about illustrations, only marking where the illustration needs to show something that isn't obvious from the text.

Repeating yourself

Young children love repetition – of a refrain, for example, or the same sentence with slight variations. Many popular books for young children use this technique – examples are the opening of *Funny Bones* by Janet and Allan Ahlberg, *The Elephant and the Bad Baby* by Elfrida Vipont and *We're Going on a Bear Hunt* by Michael Rosen. Many nursery rhymes also use this technique, such as 'Winding the Bobbin Up':

Winding the bobbin up,
Winding the bobbin up,
Pull, pull, clap, clap, clap.
Point to the ceiling
Point to the floor
Point to the window
Point to the door
Put your hands upon your knee
Now you clap out 1, 2, 3.
Winding the bobbin up,
Winding the bobbin up,
Pull, pull, clap, clap, clap.

Write a story in which you use the same phrase over and over, just changing one or two words each time.

Sounding out words

When writing for children, thinking about the sounds words make is important. Fiction for young children often uses *alliteration*, repetition of the same initial sound in a series of words, and *onomatopoeia*, words that sound like the thing they're describing – animal noises like 'oink', 'moo', 'woof' and 'meow', and sounds like 'tick', 'boom', 'clunk', 'clang', 'buzz' and 'bang'.

Reading schemes

Schools rely less on reading schemes nowadays, preferring to use books produced for the mainstream market. However, some publishers still produce books aimed at use in schools, with a very limited vocabulary and consistent format.

Reading-scheme books are graded in several levels, with a gradual but clear progression in terms of subject, style, narrative length, sentence structure and vocabulary, giving children the satisfaction of making measurable progress.

Making things come to life

Young children want things to be animated. When they play with toys they pretend that the wooden or plastic objects come to life, and they love the same to happen in stories. Classic tales such as *Mary Poppins* and *The Nutcracker and the Mouse King* and the film *Toy Story* all involve toys coming to life.

As a children's writer, you can animate anything – a teapot, a car, a computer. And, of course, talking animals fill the pages of much young children's fiction.

Take an everyday object in your house – a spoon, book, jug, piece of fruit, lamp or rug. Draw a simple picture of the object, with eyes, nose, mouth and arms. Now write a little story about this character.

Showing coping skills

Much fiction for young children rests on the world seeming a dangerous and unpredictable place, in which the small child has little power. Stories often involve overcoming a threat of danger to reassure children that they can cope with their fears and be safe.

Think of the dangers that might face an animated object you're writing about; a teapot may get broken, a book discarded, fruit eaten, a rug trodden on. Consider how the object can try to escape this fate or cope with the problem successfully.

Learning to Read Alone: Writing for 5- to 9-Year-Olds

By the time children are four and start school, they should be familiar with books and ready to start reading. You need to target writing for children aged five to seven at both them and the adults who'll be reading it aloud. Stories need to appeal to adults in some way as well because they mainly choose books for this age range. Be careful not to aim just at adults, though.

Your story has to grab the child at the outset with a surprising or striking opening. Children this age don't have the same attention span as older children or adults. An adult might give a book or poem a chance, but a child will toss it away or fidget until the story's over.

Fiction for children in this age group is always illustrated. For the 5- and 6-year-olds, the illustrations are usually in full colour and take up the larger part of the page. Books for children who've started to read alone are in large print and often a black and white illustration is provided on every second or third page.

Many children learn to read largely from the illustrations. However, the text comes first and has to tell a lively and interesting story.

Approaching a children's story with a child's world view may sound like common sense, but many authors do so using adult-sized words and ideas. Remember not to try to do too much; keep the idea simple and the concept clear.

Ten classic stories for the under 5s

As well as the all-time classics such as Beatrix Potter's stories, notably about Peter Rabbit and his siblings, Jean de Brunhoff's Babar books, and more recent series featuring Eric Hill's Spot the dog and Lucy Cousins's Maisy mouse, try some of these:

✔ Janet and Allan Ahlberg's *Peepo!*

✔ Angela Banner's *Ant and Bee*

✔ Quentin Blake's *Mister Magnolia*

✔ Eric Carle's *The Very Hungry Caterpillar*

✔ Julia Donaldson's *The Gruffalo*

✔ Judith Kerr's *The Tiger Who Came to Tea*

✔ David McKee's *Not Now, Bernard*

✔ Maurice Sendak's *Where the Wild Things Are*

✔ Dr Seuss's *The Cat in The Hat*

✔ Elfrida Vipont's *The Elephant and the Bad Baby*

Make sentences fairly simple and don't use long or unusual words, unless you have a very particular reason to do so. Children don't appreciate long or more complex sentences until they're also reading longer books (at around 6 to 8 years of age.) Even then, condensing one long sentence or dividing it into two shorter ones is usually better.

Always bear in mind that children:

- ✔ **Are smarter than you think:** Don't talk down to your readers. Children know when they're being patronised. Aim your story at both children and adults and so you don't make this mistake.

- ✔ **Enjoy a challenge:** They like to learn something new when they read. Stories can take them outside situations they're familiar with and somewhere new. Children enjoy learning the odd new word or made-up words, especially when they sound exciting (think of Margaret Mahy's *The Great Piratical Rumbustification* or Mary Poppins's *supercalifragilisticexpialidocious*).

- ✔ **Want to read about children, not adults:** Some of the most popular stories are those in which children display the independence and freedom of adults. Children like stories in which their peers are heroes and heroines, saving the day and outshining their parents and teachers.

- ✔ **Love anthropomorphic characters:** Young children love stories featuring talking animals and living objects. They enjoy a sense of magic, excitement and wish-fulfilment.

- ✔ **Prefer happy endings:** Most of the best-loved children's stories involve an element of threat, darkness or danger, but also provide an upbeat and encouraging message. Young children aren't usually mature enough to appreciate a sad or horrifying ending – despite old tales such as Chicken Licken, which ends with all the animals being eaten by a fox!

Ten classic stories for 5- to 9-year-olds

Children enjoy many of these stories first when they're read aloud by an adult. Later, beginning readers can tackle these titles themselves:

- ✔ Lynne Reid Banks's *The Indian in the Cupboard*
- ✔ Lewis Carroll's *Alice's Adventures in Wonderland*
- ✔ Roald Dahl's *Charlie and the Chocolate Factory*
- ✔ Clive King's *Stig of the Dump*

- ✔ A. A. Milne's *Winnie the Pooh*
- ✔ Dodie Smith's *The 101 Dalmations*
- ✔ Jill Tomlinson's *The Owl Who Was Afraid of the Dark*
- ✔ Jill Murphy's *The Worst Witch*
- ✔ E. B. White's *Charlotte's Web*
- ✔ Jacqueline Wilson's *The Story of Tracy Beaker*

Ten classic novels for 9- to 13-year-olds

Children of this age often read alone and can handle much more adult themes and vocabulary. They still enjoy an element of escapism, though.

- Richard Adams's *Watership Down*
- Louisa May Alcott's *Little Women*
- David Almond's *Skellig*
- Nina Bawden's *Carrie's War*
- Anne Fine's *Flour Babies*

- C. S. Lewis's *The Lion, the Witch and the Wardrobe* (from the Chronicles of Narnia series)
- Philippa Pearce's *Tom's Midnight Garden*
- Michael Morpurgo's *Private Peaceful*
- J. K. Rowling's *Harry Potter and the Philosopher's Stone*
- T. H. White's *The Sword in the Stone* (from The Once and Future King quartet)

Captivating the Confident Reader: Age 9 to 13

Children aged nine and over should be fluent readers. Stories for this age group start to resemble adult fiction in terms of characterisation, plot and structure. Stories for this age group are distinguished by:

- **The age of the protagonist:** Ideally, your main character is the same age or a little older than your target readership.

- **The use of imagination:** Many stories for children involve imaginary worlds or approach the world from a new or fantastic angle. Others involve children experiencing adventure and create a sense of mystery.

Moving Towards Adulthood: Teenagers

Fiction for teenagers is a tricky area, because by the mid-teens most good readers are tackling adult novels. They still read books on the school curriculum such as Charles Dickens's *Oliver Twist* or *David Copperfield*, Jane Austen's *Pride and Prejudice*, Charlotte Brontë's *Jane Eyre*, William Golding's *Lord of the Flies*, John Steinbeck's *Of Mice and Men* and Harper Lee's *To Kill a Mockingbird* – all perennial favourites on secondary school English courses. Most of these stories involve young people and are considered accessible for teenage readers.

Ten classic novels for teenagers

Teenagers venture into adult fiction but may also sometimes like to read books for slightly younger children too. They may want to read about serious themes or escape into books that involve fantasy and the imagination.

- John Boyne's *The Boy in the Striped Pyjamas*
- Melvin Burgess's *Junk*
- Susan Cooper's *Over Sea, Under Stone* (The Dark is Rising trilogy)
- William Golding's *Lord of the Flies*
- Mark Haddon's *The Curious Incident of the Dog in the Night-time*
- S. E. Hinton's *The Outsiders*
- Michelle Magorian's *Goodnight, Mister Tom*
- Louis Sachar's *Holes*
- Mildred D. Taylor's *Roll of Thunder, Hear my Cry*
- J. R. R. Tolkien's *The Hobbit* and *The Lord of the Rings*

However, teenage children still enjoy escapism and magic, which accounts for the huge popularity of writers such as J. K. Rowling, J. R. R. Tolkien, Philip Pullman and Susan Cooper. Teenagers also enjoy science fiction – Douglas Adams's *A Hitchhiker's Guide to the Galaxy* is a favourite – and adventure stories, such as Anthony Horowitz's popular Alex Rider books.

Writing for teenagers involves a number of challenges. Many aspiring writers make the mistake of assuming that today's children are exactly the same as teenagers were when they grew up. In many ways they are, but the pressures of modern life, the accessibility of 24-hour television, the Internet and new media mean that teenagers are much more aware of what's going on in the world than previous generations. In particular, they're more aware of war and crime, and sexual and environmental issues. Contemporary teen writers have tackled issues such as teenage pregnancy, drug abuse, the perils of Internet chatrooms and environmental disasters.

If you pick a serious theme for a teenage novel, take care not to preach or be negative. Teenagers don't like a story that's too depressing.

So-called *crossover fiction* – books that appeal to adults and teenagers alike – is a recent development. Examples include Mark Haddon's *The Curious Incident of the Dog in the Night-time* and Danny Rhodes's *Asboville*. Some publishers have produced adult and children's versions of the same books, with different covers, as in the Harry Potter series by J. K. Rowling. Other books loved by both adults and older children are Sue Townsend's *The Secret Diary of Adrian Mole Aged 13³/₄* and its sequels and Philip Pullman's *Northern Lights* (His Dark Materials trilogy).

Reading decreases as children get older

A recent study has shown that children's reading habits slump dramatically after they start at secondary school. The typical 8-year-old reads nearly 16 books a year but, by the time a child reaches 15 or 16, this has dwindled to just over three books per year. The big drop-off starts after the first year of secondary school, when the number of books read falls from nearly 12 a year to just six.

The study, based on interviews with nearly 30,000 pupils aged 7 to 16, also shows a growing trend towards reading comics, magazines, newspapers and online articles, and playing computer games.

Retelling Old Tales

Many children's writers retell old stories for a modern audience. Popular subjects include:

- ✔ Biblical stories
- ✔ Fables – Aesop's and others
- ✔ Fairy stories
- ✔ King Arthur and his Knights of the Round Table
- ✔ Myths from different countries and cultures
- ✔ The adventures of Robin Hood

Sometimes the retellings are quite traditional – just shorter versions of the stories using simpler vocabulary. Some new versions are much more imaginative, using the characters and main events as a springboard for a story, sometimes set in modern times. Sometimes the new versions subvert the old stories, often giving girls and women stronger roles, for example Marion Zimmer Bradley's *The Mists of Avalon* relates the Arthurian legends from the perspective of the female characters.

Your story needs to present the material in a new and original way to succeed in convincing a publisher that a new edition is worth releasing.

Crafting Comic Books

Comic books are extremely popular, especially with boys and children who don't like reading conventional novels. Classic comic books include Hergé's Tintin series and Goscinny and Uderzo's Asterix stories. Dav Pilkey's Captain Underpants series has also been hugely popular.

Many teachers are realising that such books hold great appeal for many students and can be of educational benefit in encouraging boys, especially, to read. Instead of being treated as junk-reading and dismissed as not being proper books, comics are proving to be invaluable reading tools in a world dominated by video games and films.

Manga-style comic books (comics and print cartoons developed in Japan in the twentieth century) have been extremely popular and include serious works such as the manga *Macbeth*.

According to Open Education, a website that tracks changes in education, the best comic books for primary school children are:

- ✔ J. Bone and J. Torres's Alison Dare series
- ✔ Jay Hosler's *Clan Apis*
- ✔ Jeff Smith's Bone series
- ✔ Jimmy Gownley's *Amelia Rules!*
- ✔ Chris Wilson's *Beowulf*

Considering Non-Fiction for Children

Recently, non-fiction for children and teenagers has been revolutionised by highly illustrated series of books in presentations and formats attractive to young readers. Publishers like Usborne and Dorling Kindersley (DK) have produced a wide range of books about the arts, the sciences and the natural world. DK produce the Eyewitness guides, the Made Easy series, the Young Scientist series and a variety of encyclopaedias and reference books. Usborne publish the Things to Make and Do and The Little Book Of series, as well as many puzzle books, treasuries and anthologies.

Series such as Scholastic's Horrible Histories, Horrible Science and Horrible Geography have been hugely popular with children. They aim to provide accurate factual information in an entertaining way, in an inexpensive paperback format with black and white illustrations.

If you want to write non-fiction for children, your research must be comprehensive and accurate. You must be able to impart facts clearly and simply, in an engaging and informal manner. Familiarising yourself with the National Curriculum is useful so that you know what children are studying and when. Because the research involves so much time and effort, gaining a commission before you write a non-fiction title is almost always best.

If you think you've found a gap in the market, send the series editor a two-page outline, together with information about why you're the ideal person to write such a book and any ideas about promoting it.

Chapter 14

Penning Plays

*D*rama is fiction that results in a performance. Writing drama is a collaborative process. Unlike other forms of writing, many plays are finalised only when the director and actors become involved; many an actor has refused to speak certain lines and many a director has deleted a particular scene that didn't work. Many of Shakespeare's plays exist in different versions for this reason.

Drama is unique because live actors and a live audience create a state of tension and excitement not found in other forms of fiction. Writing for the stage requires some knowledge of how the theatre works – you need to see a lot of plays to appreciate what works on stage and what doesn't. Many great writers of novels have failed miserably when attempting plays – the spectacular failure of novelist Henry James's *Guy Domville* on the West End stage is one example.

Writing a play can be a long and hard road; plays tend to be developed through readings and workshops before they're fully produced. No substitute exists for visiting the theatre as often as possible, reading reviews and play-scripts, and attending writing workshops, often run by theatre companies – and, of course, reading this chapter.

Setting Up the Dramatic Structure

A play is usually more highly structured than prose fiction; a play can last only a limited time and must hold the attention of the audience throughout.

The history of the play

Greek dramas – comedy, tragedy and satire – were the earliest known plays. Works by the great Greek dramatists – Aeschylus, Sophocles and Euripides, and the comic writer Aristophanes – are still performed today.

The Romans were influenced by the Greeks, though their plays are less well-known today. In medieval times, mystery and morality plays on religious themes were performed, but drama really took off in the Elizabethan period with the genius of William Shakespeare, Christopher Marlowe and Ben Jonson.

Modern drama is usually considered to have begun with the Scandinavian playwrights, Henrik Ibsen (*A Doll's House, Hedda Gabler*) from Norway and August Strindberg (*Miss Julie, A Dream Play*) from Sweden. The Russian writer Anton Chekhov (*The Cherry Orchard, The Seagull, Uncle Vanya*) was also hugely influential. Ireland's George Bernard Shaw (*Pygmalion, Major Barbara*) was the first major British playwright of the twentieth century. He authored 47 full-length plays and many one-act plays, becoming the most prolific playwright in British history.

Bertolt Brecht (*The Caucasian Chalk Circle*), the German playwright, pioneered a new kind of drama – *epic theatre* – intended to create a heightened social and political awareness among the audience, rather than involve them emotionally in a realistic or naturalistic situation.

Samuel Beckett (*Waiting for Godot*) was one of a number of playwrights in the 1940s and 1950s who worked within the framework of the *theatre of the absurd*, which presents the human condition as fundamentally ridiculous and meaningless.

Romanian playwright Eugène Ionesco (*Rhinoceros*) also rejected logical plots and character development, creating his own anarchic form of comedy to convey the meaninglessness of modern humankind's existence in a universe ruled by chance. Contemporary playwrights such as Harold Pinter (*Betrayal, The Caretaker*) have been highly influenced by these writers.

Contemporary British playwrights of note include Edward Bond, Caryl Churchill, Michael Frayn, David Hare and Tom Stoppard.

Aristotle, in his *Poetics*, stressed the three *unities* of drama:

- ✔ **Unity of action:** A play must have one plot and no subplots.
- ✔ **Unity of place:** The action should take place in one physical location.
- ✔ **Unity of time:** A play should take place over 24 hours only.

Even today, plays that conform to these rules can be very powerful, and are simple and easy to stage.

Shakespeare helped to overcome these rules; his plays feature many different locations, subplots and even jumps in time. Attempting something very ambitious is fine, but also be aware of the costs and logistical problems involved in staging such a work.

Before writing for the stage, reading up on the history of the theatre and familiarising yourself with some of the great works, including the classical Greek dramas that are still influential today, is a good idea.

Sticking with the classic three-act structure

The classic three-act structure is still useful today; it consists of:

- **The set-up:** Introducing the characters and the dramatic conflict.
- **Complications:** The plot thickens!
- **The resolution:** The conflict is resolved.

Usually the three acts are of fairly equal length. In fact, even if you have a one-act play, the same structure can apply.

Getting started

Begin with an idea. Be inspired by an unusual person, a meaningful event, an interesting place or an important point that you think needs to be expressed. Plays are a great medium for voicing a concern or highlighting an issue.

Plays are all about conflict. Take an inner struggle – a woman wondering whether to leave her husband – and consider how you could dramatise it; she can talk about her dilemma; pack and unpack her suitcase; make plans to leave, which are foiled by events such as someone arriving just as she's about to walk out of the door; and so on.

Recognising that plays are about language

Unlike the cinema, which relies heavily on images, plays are about words. Everything has to be conveyed through dialogue and action. When writing a play, you can't rely too much on stage directions – you have to let the language speak for itself.

Remember, too, that a play open to a number of interpretations is often richer. Don't make the dialogue too obvious. Create the sense of a *subtext* – something lying beneath the surface of a character's spoken words – and let the character's actions imply what remains unsaid. Consider also that characters may be lying to one another (see Chapter 5 on dialogue).

Most dialogue needs to be realistic. However, in a play, sometimes using heightened, poetic forms of language in a way that wouldn't be appropriate in a film or a more realist medium is acceptable.

When writing dialogue, you need to focus on exactly what your characters want and are trying to say with each line – the structure of a play doesn't allow for rambling.

Try these exercises for maintaining focused dialogue:

- ✔ Write a dialogue between two characters, in which each can speak a maximum of three words per line.
- ✔ Write a monologue. Make the character speak for ten minutes.

Contradictions, disagreements and misunderstandings are what make dialogue interesting. A good monologue resembles a character having a conversation with a different aspect of himself, so that even within this one-sided conversation an argument or dispute occurs. Dialogue also becomes more engaging when you know what characters want and can predict, based on what's said, if they're likely to get it.

Putting a Play Together

The written script is only the first stage in a larger artistic process. The main steps are:

- ✔ The written script.
- ✔ The interpretation of the script by the director.
- ✔ The actors' performances.
- ✔ The reception of the play by the audience.

As the play takes shape, the director or actors may want to make changes to the script, and often authors sit in on rehearsals so that they can adapt it as required.

If you want to become a playwright, collaborating with an amateur dramatics society in your area is the best approach. The members can produce your plays, and you can gauge what works and what falls flat in front of a live audience. This relationship can mutually benefit many amateur dramatic groups and budding playwrights.

Consider getting together a group of actors in your area to put on your play and contacting your local radio station to publicise it. Local radio may also be a good resource for finding actors and listening to them taking part in other productions.

The role of the dramaturge

You're likely to work with the theatre's dramaturge when you have a play produced. The responsibilities of a *dramaturge* vary between theatre companies but can include the hiring of actors, developing a season of plays, sometimes with a particular theme, assisting in the writing and editing of new plays by resident or guest playwrights, and organising educational services in collaboration with schools. They often conduct research into the historical and social conditions, specific locations, time periods and/or theatrical styles of plays chosen by the company to assist the playwright, director and design team in their production. The dramaturge also locates and translates worthy scripts from other languages, writes articles and makes media appearances promoting shows and community programmes, and helps develop original scripts.

Never submit a play to theatres or publishers until you've at least held a reading with professional or semi-professional actors to try it out. You can't tell if a play works until you hear it read out or see it being performed.

Don't send a play script to a publisher before it's been performed. Most publishers won't accept plays that haven't first been produced. Send your play to theatres and competitions first. Most plays are only published when they've achieved a certain measure of success on stage.

Sorting Out Types of Play

A play can vary in length from a short monologue to a five-act, four-hour drama. Here are the most common formats:

- ✔ **Ten-minute play:** A good ten-minute play isn't a sketch or an extended gag, but rather a complete, compact piece, with a beginning, middle and end. It typically takes place in one scene and runs to no more than ten pages. Many competitions for short plays insist on a ten-page, ten-minute format.

- ✔ **One-act play:** One-act plays can run anywhere from 15 minutes to an hour or more. A one-act play usually isn't long enough to last for a full evening. The most popular length for one-act plays is around half an hour, so they can run with other plays of a similar length. Thirty minutes is also a good length for a competition play.

Pick just one main action or problem; if possible keep your play to one set and as few scenes as possible.

✔ **Full-length play:** These usually run from 70 or 80 minutes and upwards, though not usually much more than two hours. A play of this length usually has at least one interval, which you need to factor in when writing to ensure that it comes in an appropriate place.

Formatting Your Script

Make sure that your script is in the recognised format and thus looks professional. Follow these guidelines:

✔ Use A4 paper (with holes so the play can be kept in a ring binder).

✔ Print on only one side of the page.

✔ Use 12-point type and a regular font such as Times New Roman.

✔ Set top, bottom and right margins at 3 centimetres (an inch). The left margin, where the binding is, should be 4 centimetres (1.5 inches).

✔ Start page numbering on the page where the actual play and dialogue begins. Place page numbers in the upper right-hand corner (in the header).

✔ Put the title of the play and the author's name on the first page and the cast of characters on the next – don't number these pages.

✔ Begin each act or scene at the top of a new page.

✔ Lay out dialogue with the character's name in capitals at the left-hand margin and a colon introducing the text. Set the text on a hanging indent (in Word, highlight the relevant text, then select Paragraph from the toolbar, followed by Special, and then Hanging).

✔ Set your stage directions on new lines, in square brackets.

Women writing for the theatre

Women have always been underrepresented in the theatre. Aphra Behn (1640–1689) was a prolific Restoration dramatist and one of the first English professional female writers, but she is one of only a few known today. The number of plays by women writers staged now still lags far behind men. Sarah Kane made a huge impression with her first play *Blasted*, but she died tragically young. Astonishingly, the first original play by a woman to be performed on the Olivier stage at the National Theatre was *Her Naked Skin* by Rebecca Lenkiewicz, first performed in 2008.

Agatha Christie's *The Mousetrap* has the honour of being the longest-running play on the London stage.

Today, many projects exist to encourage more women to write for the stage and greater opportunities are certainly available. So, if you're a woman, don't be put off – get writing!

Figure 14-1 demonstrates how to lay out a script.

Act One

A living room in a modern apartment. ANNA is holding a mobile phone; she is scrolling through the messages, reading as she goes. MICK enters.

MICK: Is that my phone?

ANNA: Don't try to deny it this time – I've read the text.

MICK: What text?

ANNA: [Holding out the phone] This text.

MICK: [Looking at the phone] Oh, that. It's not what you think.

ANNA: What do you mean, it's not what I think? How could it possibly mean anything else? It says –

MICK: I know what it says.

ANNA: It's from Anji.

MICK: I know it's from Anji. It's some dialogue from the play we're working on.

ANNA: What?

MICK: I forgot a line of dialogue, and I asked her to text it to me.

> *Silence. ANNA stares at him. MICK glances around the room, as though looking for something. Then he bursts out laughing.*

MICK: You really have got the wrong end of the stick, haven't you? You thought – you actually thought – [He doubles up]

ANNA: I don't believe you.

MICK: [Still laughing] Well, it's true. Ring her and ask her.

ANNA: I can't just ring her.

MICK: Why not?

Figure 14-1:
An example
script.

ANNA: You know why!

MICK: Anna, I'm tired of this. Just give me the phone.

Seeing Theatre Spaces

Always consider where your play may be staged. Obviously some spaces work better than others. Large modern theatres such as the Olivier can allow for dramatic scene changes and special effects; other plays have to be performed in far more limited spaces.

Types of theatre include:

- **Proscenium:** This is the most common type, with a stage in front of the audience. The stage is raised above the level of the audience or the seats are in tiers so everyone can see. The actors must generally face forwards so they can be seen and heard clearly.

- **In the round:** In this layout the actors are in a central playing area, and the audience surrounds them on all sides. Actors may have to enter and exit through the aisles and need to take care to face different parts of the audience at various times so everyone feels included.

- **Black box:** This performance space looks exactly as it sounds: a black-painted square or rectangle. Here, the audience can be seated to match the staging needs of your play, instead of organising your play around the audience.

- **Touring:** A touring play may have to be adapted for a variety of different stages. If you intend to tour, bear in mind the following:

  - Keep sets simple so that they can be installed and taken down in minutes and easily transported.

  - Use props and costumes that can be packed into a large box.

  - Avoid lighting cues beyond 'lights up' and use only sound cues that can be done from a CD player.

  - Use a small cast (anything much larger than four is asking for trouble).

Writing for Radio

Radio is an extraordinarily flexible medium, in which many of the limits that apply to stage plays don't count. A radio play can take place anywhere and move rapidly through time and space – it can be set on a desert island, in a plane or on a ship; on other planets (like Douglas Adams's *The Hitchhiker's Guide to the Galaxy*); or in a character's memory.

Radio is very good at dramatising what people are thinking, and can convey a character's thoughts directly in a way that is harder to achieve on stage, where monologues can seem contrived. In radio, the listener can be instantly transported inside the head of a character and hear every secret, private thought – things that are often better left unsaid! You can also show the contrast between what people say and what they think in a very effective way. For these reasons, radio drama has been described as the 'theatre of the mind'.

In radio, you write in sequences rather than scenes. A sequence is very similar to a scene in a play but, because you don't need to change sets or move scenery around to indicate a change of location, can be very short. A sequence in a radio play can thus vary from several pages to simply one line.

Radio gives you much more freedom than a stage play. You can:

- ✔ Cast as many characters as you like, because the actors can play more than one part.
- ✔ Take the listener anywhere in the world with appropriate sound effects.
- ✔ Set your play against any kind of background, in any kind of weather, in daylight or darkness.

The radio is fatally easy to switch off! When writing for radio, the beginning is all-important. You must grip and hold your audience from the outset.

Listen to as much radio drama as you can – Radio 4 airs a play at 2.15 p.m. every day. Tape programmes you like and analyse them, noting how many changes of scene occur, how long each scenes is, how many characters are involved and what sound effects are used.

Note the names of producers whose work appeals to you and send your script to them.

Using sound

A variety of sounds can be used to vary the background and help create interest. Remember to alternate scenes in noisy places – a pub or factory – with scenes in a quiet place, so the listeners' ears don't tire. Use the contrast between indoor and outdoor settings: an echoing library, traffic in a busy street, a bird singing in a garden or running water.

Use sound effects that try to tell the story, such as car doors slamming or feet crunching on gravel, sparingly or they can sound silly. 'Hello Jamel (crunch, crunch, crunch), I like your new car (door slams), do come in (door creaks open), would you like a gin and tonic?' (sound of ice in glass and liquid being poured). Let the listeners imagine some things for themselves!

Utilising music

Like film, music is also important in creating atmosphere and mood in radio drama. Use music to enhance your play – the sound of music on a radio before it is switched off, a character humming to herself, a choir rehearsing in a church hall, spooky or mysterious refrains to create a sense of danger or of the supernatural.

If you use actual songs or previously performed works – even just short clips – you need permission to use them, which may be expensive.

Tapping into Resources for Playwrights

If you're trying to write plays, you need all the help you can get.

Writernet (`www.writernet.co.uk`) is a useful resource for aspiring playwrights. This website can help you find your nearest writing group and provides details of courses, agents and competitions. It also offers a script-reading service, which provides feedback on drafts.

Writernet also curates the Playwrights Network, which links regional organisations developing playwrights' work across the UK.

Some theatres also offer a professional script-reading service for a small fee, which is one of the best ways of getting useful feedback on your work.

Playwriting competitions

Many competitions and opportunities exist for young playwrights. The Bruntwood Playwriting Competition for the Royal Exchange Theatre in Manchester is probably the best known. You can download the information from `www.writeaplay.co.uk`.

Writernet also provides a regularly updated list of competitions and awards.

Sources for new playwrights

Some initiatives helping new playwrights to develop their work are:

- **Tinderbox Theatre Company, Belfast:** Tinderbox commissions plays from both emerging and established writers and supports the development of scripts from initial idea to full production. The talents and skills of new playwrights are developed through a range of specially designed initiatives. Recently, Tinderbox has engaged with venues staging new material to develop a strategy aimed at building new and wider audiences.

- **Soho Theatre, London:** Anyone who wants to write plays should know about Soho Theatre. Founded in 1969, this company presented new works by playwrights such as Sue Townsend, Hanif Kureishi, Timberlake Wertenbaker, Tony Marchant and Pam Gems.

    Now situated in a state-of-the-art building in the heart of London's West End, Soho Theatre presents challenging and entertaining theatre, late night comedy and cabaret, and a programme of talks.

- **SCRIPT, Birmingham:** This agency (also a registered charity) aims to discover and develop writers in the West Midlands to the point where they can work professionally. SCRIPT offers services to writers at all levels, from earliest aspirant stages through to first commission and beyond. These services include script-reading, workshops, writer development programmes and a monthly newsletter. SCRIPT works with writers for all dramatic media – stage, screen and radio.

- **The Playwrights' Studio, Scotland:** This initiative is designed to celebrate, promote and develop Scotland's culture of writing for live performance. It aims to secure a future for playwrights and their work by improving and sustaining artistic quality, raising awareness and increasing opportunities and access.

Chapter 15

Writing Screenplays

*W*riting for film and television is very different from doing so for stage and radio – and for the printed page. Much of what's told in film is told visually, through the actor's expressions and body language, action and even scenery. In writing for the screen, language takes second place – a glance between two characters can tell more than pages of dialogue.

A screenplay is basically a story told with pictures. Many film-makers use the technique of *storyboarding* – making a cartoon-like strip of the visuals. Storyboarding helps keep you focused on the fact that, even though a script has dialogue, you need to tell the story through setting and action too.

Breaking Down the Stages of a Screenplay

Before you begin, you need to have a clear concept for your film. You can use a *logline* – a one-sentence summary of your script. A logline resembles the short blurb in TV guides telling you what a film's about, which helps you decide whether you're interested in seeing it or not. You need to be able to express your idea in a short, succinct way. You use your logline as your *pitch* – what you tell people in the industry when they ask you that dreaded question, what's your screenplay about? You want to grab them with the concept and then you can enlarge upon it if and when they ask you for more details.

You may find yourself saying, 'but my idea is so complex I can't possibly summarise it in a sentence or two'. Fair enough – but if you want to sell your screenplay successfully, you'll almost certainly have to!

When you're starting out, going for something that isn't too expensive to film or make is best – a domestic drama is far cheaper to film than a sci-fi extravaganza. On the other hand, you need to use your imagination to create something new and original, within the strict conventions of the form.

Starting with the synopsis

A *synopsis* is a short summary of a screenplay, which introduces the characters and describes in outline the plot of the story, with the beginning, middle and end. Importantly, your synopsis needs to show how the story is told, not just what the story is about.

When writing a synopsis, include answers to the following questions:

- ✔ Who's the main character?
- ✔ What's the main character's goal?
- ✔ What place or time is the setting?
- ✔ Where does the story begin?
- ✔ What is the source of conflict?
- ✔ What is the resolution of the story?

Write the story of your film in 50 words. Refine that paragraph until you've covered as much as possible in that word limit.

Moving on to a treatment

A *treatment* is a longer synopsis, going into a little more detail. It can be two or three pages, or a more detailed scene-by-scene breakdown of the story. A treatment describes each scene in your script, but without including dialogue, unless one or two lines are of crucial importance.

Sometimes treatments are produced to help sell an idea or get funding to develop a project further, without having to commission an entire screenplay. You may also produce a treatment as a first stage to writing a script.

Sketching out a storyboard

A *storyboard* is a series of sketches demonstrating the camera shots the director uses to create the film from a script. The result resembles a comic book version of the film – minus the speech bubbles. Storyboarding was originally developed for cartoons, but is now widely used in the film industry.

As a writer, you don't need to storyboard your screenplay, but sometimes having a good visual image can help. A storyboard can help you think visually about how your film is going to look.

However, most storyboards are produced by the director, not the writer. The director uses it on set as a reference to show the camera crew where to move their camera and lights, to tell the art department which parts of the location are going to be in shot and to give the actors a feel of what they're going to be doing.

Storyboarding is especially useful for complex visual sequences, especially elaborate shots or special effects. Sometimes a film only uses storyboards for difficult sequences; in others the entire film is storyboarded. Some directors storyboard extensively, as doing so means they shoot only the sequences they need, reducing the need for complex editing and saving both time and money.

Speculating on a Screenplay

Most scripts are produced *on spec* – that is, they're speculative works that haven't been commissioned by a studio, production company or television network. Scriptwriters generally write on spec and send their work in. If you don't sell your script you don't get paid for writing it, so you really need to have faith in your idea.

Screenwriting is always a collaborative process, and most scripts are radically altered by the time they reach the screen – if they ever get made at all! If you want to maintain artistic control of the project, writing your idea as a novel or story first and getting it published is the best approach – then whatever's done to the film, at least the original story remains yours.

Proven screenwriters are often used to rewrite scripts – the amount of rewriting can vary from a bit of polishing to crafting a completely new draft. *Script doctors* are often called in late in the process to iron out problems, sometimes even after shooting has begun.

Keep your screenplay as tight and focused as you can, so that your concept is clear and needs altering as little as possible.

Episodes for television series are often written by several writers who're involved at different stages before the project is finalised. Comedy scripts are very often written by two people; a partnership is the best way to create the tension and quick repartee necessary for successful comedy.

Making your own film

Some screenwriters skip out the selling their script stage, and get together with others to make their own films, often on a very low budget. Your friends can play the various roles, or you may be able to recruit some drama school students. Often people get involved on a profit-sharing basis should the film ever make any money.

Video cameras and digital editing software have made film-making much cheaper and more accessible for would-be film-makers. Such films can be burned onto DVD and sold directly, or entered for competitions.

Adapting an Existing Story

Many films, perhaps even a majority, are adaptations of novels, stories, plays or memoirs that already exist. Some of these are famous, classics in their own right – consider the number of adaptations of Jane Austen's *Pride and Prejudice* and many of William Shakespeare's plays – others are obscure, little-known stories – Asif Kapadia's film *Far North* was based on a short story by Sara Maitland that had no dialogue and was just nine pages long.

You can adapt a story to a range of different degrees:

- **Based on** means that the script stays fairly close to the original source.
- **Adapted from** means that quite a lot of changes are made.
- **Inspired by** means only the characters and style are taken from the original work.

When adapted for film, the story usually needs to be considerably simplified. Several pages of description in a novel can be a single image in a film. Dialogue is pared back to the essentials, and often minor characters and sub-plots are left out.

In several film and TV versions of Leo Tolstoy's *Anna Karenina*, for example, only the main story of the relationship between Count Vronsky and Anna is featured; the novel's other main story, of Levin and his wife Kitty, is completely omitted.

Merging several characters into one, leaving out some minor characters altogether, is a common feature of adaptation. Often a major character can do something a minor character does in the book, reducing the cast and number of actors and characters that the film audience needs to keep track of. Whole strands of a story can be reduced or taken out altogether.

Securing Options

Before you start work on adapting an existing novel, play or story, you need to secure the rights. If you don't do so, you may find that someone else holds an option on it and that all your work is wasted. An *option* gives the owner – usually a writer or producer – the right to develop the idea and try to sell it to a film or TV company or raise the finances to produce it independently. During the period a work is optioned, no one else can develop it. Options usually last for only six months to two years, though some can be extended.

You need to involve a lawyer or agent in drawing up an option agreement as they can be quite complicated.

Works published more than 70 years ago are out of copyright, so you don't need to worry about their ownership. However, do find out if anyone else is developing the idea before you get to work.

Formatting a Screenplay

A screenplay is *the* most structured form of writing – your script has to meet very strict criteria. You need to follow the standard format or your script won't be read.

Formatting your script properly helps you to get noticed. It suggests a professional approach to your writing, and the script is easier to read, assess and ultimately use. Perhaps more importantly, writing to a particular format is helpful because it makes you think and write in visual terms. The screenplay must contain all the information needed by the producer, director, actors, production manager, director of photography, production designer, sound recordist, costume designer and all the other people involved with the making of a film. The standard format makes the screenplay easy to read, understand and use on set.

Don't litter your screenplay with technical details such as complex camera angles and minute descriptions of people's appearance or clothing.

Today, you have no excuse for not presenting a screenplay properly because numerous computer software programs do the job for you. Try Final Draft and Movie Magic Screenwriter.

Each page of script counts as a minute. Most feature films run to about 90 to 120 minutes; if you write for television, one-hour dramas or serials of 30 to 60 minutes are the norm. Your script can't be too long or too short.

When printing your screenplay, follow these guidelines:

- ✔ **Typeface:** Use 10-point Courier, which resembles an old-fashioned typewriter (10 point means ten characters to an inch.)
- ✔ **Margins:** Leave a good margin all around the screenplay – one-and-a-half inches for the left margin, and one inch for right margin, top and bottom of page. These margins leave room for the producer, director, actors and others to make notes as filming progresses.
- ✔ **Page numbering**: Never forget to number your pages! Top right corner in the header is best. Don't number the title page, though.

The cover page, providing the title of the screenplay and your name in capitals, is called the *title page*. Put your contact details in the bottom right corner of this page.

THE HAUNTED LIBRARY

by

MAGGIE HAMAND

Maggie Hamand

Address

Phone number/email

The elements inside the script require specific formatting too:

- ✔ **Scene headings** show where and when the action takes place. These are always in capital letters. You need a new heading for each scene. The headings begin at the left margin. Use the abbreviations *INT* for interior and *EXT* for exterior, one or the other of which should start every scene heading.

```
INT. LIBRARY. NIGHT.
```

✔ **Action** shows what the camera sees and what the actors are doing.

```
The librarian takes off her glasses and rubs her eyes
sleepily.
```

✔ **Characters' names** are always in capital letters (also known as upper case) when first introduced. If the character is speaking, the name is in capitals and placed four inches from the left side of the page or two-and-a-half inches from the left margin, followed by a colon.

✔ **Dialogue** is the words the actors speak. Dialogue begins two-and-a-half inches from the left side of the page or one inch from the left margin, and ends at five inches from the left margin:

```
                    SANDRA:

          I'm so, so scared of the dark.
```

✔ **Parentheticals** are adverbs that tell the actors how to say the lines and are used only when the dialogue doesn't make clear how the words are spoken.

```
                    SANDRA:

               (ironically)

          I'm so, so scared of the dark.
```

✔ **Reaction shots** explain how other characters react to what's said or done. They begin at the left margin. Remember that all characters' names are in capitals on first mention in the script or when they're speaking.

```
FRED rolls his eyes
```

✔ **Transitions** tell the director when and how to cut from one scene to the next. These directions are in capitals, placed at the left margin and followed by a colon.

Types of transitions include:

- CUT TO:
- FADE TO:
- FADE OUT:
- DISSOLVE TO:
- INTERCUT: To cut between two different scenes.

```
INTERCUT:

Sandra closing down the library, Fred putting on his
vampire outfit
```

- **Montage** means dissolving two or more shots into one another to create a series of images. Put the word MONTAGE (in capitals), followed by a colon. List each shot on a separate line and letter them in order:

```
MONTAGE:

        A) Books piled up on the table

        B) The door slowly opens

        C) Glasses being dropped onto the floor

        D) A vampire's face at the window
```

Table 15-1 lists terms used for technical directions, their abbreviations and some examples.

Table 15-1	Technical Terms		
Term	*Definition*	*Abbreviation*	*Example*
Close up	A camera shot close to the subject.	CU	CU: SANDRA'S EYES
Point of view	The camera angle is from a character's point of view.	POV	'SANDRA'S POV – FRED' means the camera points from where Sandra is standing, at Fred.
Voice-over	The audience hears a character's thoughts.	VO	FRED VO: I've always wanted to attract Sandra's attention
Off-screen	The audience hears something but doesn't see where the sound is coming from.	OS	A voice SCREAMS OS SCREAMS is in capitals to draw attention to the sound effect.

Figure 15-1 demonstrates how a screenplay page should look.

```
                              THE TEXT

FADE IN:

INT. BEDROOM. EVENING

A modern warehouse apartment in East London with river view. ANNA, a striking
woman in her early 30s, is standing by the window holding a mobile phone, her
back to us. MICK, a good-looking man of about the same age, comes in, looking
around for something, agitated. Then he sees Anna.

                              MICK
                    You got my phone?

                              ANNA
                         (turning to face Mick)
                    I've read the text.

                              MICK
                         (puzzled)
                    What text?

                              ANNA
                         (holding out the phone)
                    This text.

MICK walks over, looks at the phone, steps back, shaking his head.

                              MICK
                    It's not what you think.

                              ANNA
                         (with controlled anger)
                    What do you mean?

                              MICK
                    It's from the screenplay that
                    we're working on.

                              ANNA
                    What?

                              MICK
                    I forgot some lines of dialogue, so I asked her to
                    text them to me.

                              ANNA
                    I don't believe you.

CUT TO:

INT. OFFICE. DAY

ANJI is sitting at her desk, watching a DVD on the computer screen. The DVD
shows a couple having sex.

The phone rings and she picks it up.

                              ANJI
                    Mick?
```

Figure 15-1:
One
complete
page of
formatted
script.

Writing for TV

Writing for television is similar to writing for film, but more varied in terms of length and structure. Also, many television programmes are series – soaps like *Eastenders* or *Coronation Street*, dramatised serials of works by classic authors like Charles Dickens and Jane Austen, detective series or, more rarely these days, original dramas.

Each type of drama necessitates a different type of writing. A script for a continuing prime-time soap in 30-minute episodes is very different in scope and style to that for a one-off crime series in 60-minute episodes or a 60-minute single drama with an adult theme designed for late-night viewing. In some series, each episode tells a self-contained, character-driven guest story, while others normally interweave multiple storylines.

Knowing your market is crucial. Watch as much TV as you can – see what genres and formats are currently popular, and what does and doesn't work for you. Read programme reviews and consider whether or not you agree with them. If you propose writing for a specific show, rent or borrow past episodes and familiarise yourself with the characters, their histories and personalities, and everything that's happened so far.

Remember that writing for established formats (series that have been running for some time) isn't the same as writing to a formula – it still allows for a certain amount of creativity and individual expression. Many writers cut their teeth on established formats; this approach can be very helpful for teaching you what does and doesn't work on screen.

Make your story opening as dynamic as possible – switching channels is all too easy. You need to hook the viewers' attention immediately so that they want to stay tuned and also to come back for the next episode.

TV is a visual medium, so revealing your characters and their stories through the action as well as the dialogue is important.

If you're writing for a commercial television channel, you need to structure your story around advert breaks. If you're writing a two-part drama, for example, structure the plot around the breaks and include a minor cliffhanger before each one. End the first episode with a major cliffhanger to lead viewers into the second part.

TV scripts are written in exactly the same way as film scripts, using the same formatting and language. The BBC website provides helpful details on its preferred script style. Usually the left margin is wider than a conventional film script, and the BBC may favour a different typeface, such as Arial or Times New Roman.

You can download a whole range of scripts from the BBC archive at `www.bbc.co.uk/writersroom/insight/script_archive.shtml`.

Chapter 16

Rhymes and Reasons: Writing Poetry

*P*oetry may be the hardest of all the creative arts to define. A good poem can in fact be the closest people can get to saying the unsayable. A poem is a way of expressing a profound emotion or something true about the world and how it appears to you. Ideas that are too deep to express in the usual way you use words can be articulated through poetry.

Traditional poetry relies on structures such as rhyme and rhythm, and devices such as starting many words with the same letter or sound, and using unusual words and images. Modern poetry ignores many of these elements, especially the need for rhyme and a set structure, and yet often works through tension with the old forms.

Poetry was originally a spoken form of literature, and even today it often works best when read out loud. Rhythm, rhyme and other structures were used in the past as devices for helping people to memorise poems. Today, poetry as a live performance, often with venues staging open mike nights for aspiring poets, is increasingly popular.

Getting Started

Literally anything may inspire a poem. A poem can communicate something very simple – a passing mood, a yearning, the sight of something seemingly trivial or an unusual image. It can also express the profound – the fear of death, joy of love or meaning of life. These large themes are often enclosed in or revealed by something small; William Blake's 'whole world in a grain of sand'.

You can write a poem anywhere. All you need is a pen and something to write on. You can draft one while waiting to see the doctor or dentist, lunching in a café or sitting in the park.

Always write a poem in longhand. Putting pen to paper seems to connect the fingers and brain better than typing on a keyboard. Those slips of paper form a history of your various drafts and help you know what changes you made in case you decide to use an earlier phrasing after all.

While the first draft of a poem may come quickly, most published poetry has been worked over many times. You may be lucky and draft a whole poem in a morning, but some take days, weeks or even years to complete.

If you're stuck, try some simple exercises to write a first draft of a poem:

- ✔ Choose a colour – something subtle such as burgundy, azure or ochre.

  Look around you, leaf through art books or magazines or go for a walk, and then compile a list of items you found in that colour. Now write a poem linking these images.

- ✔ Arrange small pieces of scrap paper into two piles. On those in the first pile write a selection of emotions; on the second a range of random objects. If you're lost for inspiration, ask someone to supply lists of emotions and objects.

  Shuffle the individual piles of paper and then select one piece from each – linking an emotion with an object. You may pick the kettle of rage, the rose of jealousy or the sausage of happiness. Use these word pairs as the bases for some short poems.

A poem is so tightly structured that every word must count and serve a purpose. Don't use any words that the poem can function without; a good poem is complete when nothing else can be taken away without losing what you want to express. Be concrete, not abstract. Play around with your poem until it feels right.

Considering the Elements of Poetry

Three main elements comprise poetic form: using rhyme, in simple or complex patterns; manipulating rhythm to emphasise certain words and ideas; and arranging text into regular or irregular verses. This section looks at these three elements of poetry in more detail.

Why write poetry?

Poetry may seem an odd art form to write today. Having your poems recognised or published is very difficult, and many people admit that they never read poetry. Simultaneously, though, schemes such as Poems on the Underground, which displays short pieces with the ads on the Tube, bring poetry to the attention of ordinary people who clearly appreciate what it has to say.

To many modern readers, poetry seems as out of date and constricting as a crinoline, an artificial form that takes them back to school essays and English Literature exams. A poem usually demands concentration, and can benefit from both knowledge of the circumstances in which it was written and an understanding of the history of poetry.

A good poem can, however, also reach out and speak straight to the heart, moving people in a way no other art form can.

Writing in rhyme

One of the first things a child learns about poetry is that it rhymes. A *rhyme* is a repetition of identical or similar sounds in two or more different words.

Rhyme helps to structure a poem and gives readers or listeners a sense of satisfaction and security – they know what to expect. Often rhyme is enjoyed simply because the repeating pattern is pleasant to hear. The regular use of a rhyme helps to mark off the ends of lines, thus clarifying the structure for the listener.

Types of rhyme include:

- **Perfect rhyme:** The stressed vowel and all following sounds are identical.

- **End rhyme:** The final words in one or more lines rhyme. Usually, people think of rhymes as coming at the end of a line, so an end rhyme scheme offers the audience security and comfort.

- **Internal rhyme:** A rhyme that appears within a line as well as or rather than at the end of a line.

- **Partial rhyme:** Using words that sound very much like one another but don't rhyme exactly. Examples are alone and home, size and five, fun and mum.

- **Eye rhyme:** Makes use of words that look as if they should rhyme but are pronounced a little differently. Examples are earth and hearth, wind and kind, laughter and slaughter.

- **Wrenched rhyme:** The stress of a word has to change to make a rhyme. Examples are bent/acc*ent*; free/poe*try*.

Keeping rhythm or metre

Metre is a systematic regularity of rhythm used in poetry. It creates and organises the content of the poem, emphasising some of its words or elements. The more regular the metre, the more expressive small departures from the norm can be.

Metre makes a poem memorable and conveys tempo and mood. In a skilled poet's hands, the metre can provide a convincing approximation of the rhythms of everyday speech.

You don't need to know all the technical terms to use various rhythms in your poetry, but trying them out to internalise them, recognise them in poetry you're reading and understand how they work can be helpful.

Repeating patterns

Metre can be completely regular, with the same repeated rhythm, or irregular, where the rhythm varies.

Below is an example of a regular metre:

> Ti-**tum**, ti-**tum**, ti-**tum**, ti-**tum**, ti-**tum**.

The *tum* is stressed and the *ti* isn't. So, in a poem, a line following this metre would read:

> The **man** looked **up** and **saw** the **bird** fly **down**.

This ti-**tum** rhythm is known as an *iamb*.

Here are some other common rhythms:

- **Trochee:** A **tum**-ti pattern in which the stress starts on the first sound and alternates from there. For example: '**Thus** was **born** my **Hia**watha.'
- **Spondee:** A **tum-tum** pattern in which both syllables are stressed throughout. A spondee is usually used as a change in rhythm within a poem. For example: 'When the **blood creeps** and the **nerves prick**.'
- **Pyrrhic foot:** A ti-ti pattern in which neither syllable is stressed;the when the and the and the are pyrrhic feet in 'When the blood creeps and the nerves prick.'

If you use three syllables within each foot (I discuss feet in the next section), you get patterns such as:

- **Anapest:** The stress is on the last syllable – ti-ti-**tum**, ti-ti-**tum**.
- **Dactyl:** The stress is on the first of each triplet of syllables – **tum**-ti-ti, **tum**-ti-ti.

In practice, much poetry gains its power from changes to the regular metre, for example:

- A *caesura* creates a break in the middle of one line with a full stop or comma.

- An *enjambment* runs a sentence over the end of one line into the next, straddling two lines.

- *Mixed feet* change the mood of a poem or create an effect.

Moving forward in feet

Each 'ti-tum' two-syllable rhythm pattern is called a *foot*. The ti-**tum** rhythm is called an *iambic* foot or an *iamb*. Lines with different numbers of feet have different names:

- **Dimeter:** Two feet to a line.

- **Trimester:** Three feet to a line.

- **Tetrameter:** Four feet to a line.

- **Pentameter:** Five feet to a line.

- **Hexameter:** Six feet to a line.

Shakespeare's sonnets are structured using the regular rhythm of the iambic pentameter, for example:

> Shall **I** com**pare** thee **to** a **sum**mer's **day**?

Separating poems into stanzas

Poems are often divided into *stanzas* (also called verses), which usually share common features such as the same number of lines or pattern of rhymes.

Again, some technical terms apply. A *couplet* is two lines, a *tercet* three, a *quatrain* four, a *quintrain* five, a *sestet* six, a *septet* seven and an *octet* or *octave* eight.

Stanzas in *free verse* may follow no pattern, although they may sometimes separate changes in rhythm, mood, point of view or emphasis in the poem, acting in miniature rather like chapters in a book.

Try the following exercise to make you think about writing in stanzas.

With eyes shut, pick a book from your shelf, open it at random and copy a line or phrase you like. Play with and alter this phrase until it becomes your own. Write a further four lines of verse, of similar length to this first line, creating a five-line stanza. Now write a second five-line stanza, following the pattern of the first.

Listening to the Language of Poetry

Poetry uses many figures of speech that are rarely found in other forms of writing. For example, similes and metaphors are used in prose writing but can be left out; in poetry they're almost essential.

Looking into imagery

Poetry works best when the readers feel that they actually see, hear, smell, taste or touch the images portrayed by the poet.

Simile and metaphor are the two main tools for creating vivid imagery. A *simile* is a comparison using the word 'like' – the sea is *like* glass. Similes are useful for making comparisons between things, and can also be useful for bringing in memories of the past. They can also be used ironically - as in 'as subtle as a sledgehammer' - to create humour.

A *metaphor* is more complicated than a simile: simile describes one thing in terms that are suggestive of another; a metaphor says that one thing actually *is* another – the sea *is* glass.

The English language is littered with metaphors. People use them constantly, often without realising; consider an old flame, boiling mad, things going smoothly, glowing praise, a shady character, a sour note, the sweet smell of success and music to my ears. You use metaphor when you say that time is money, you're running out of time, that cost me a lot of time or worth your while.

Spatial metaphors often communicate mood: they were feeling up or down, high or low; were climbing the wall or falling into a trap. Metaphors of war are often engaged in an argument: she shot down his argument, won the debate, attacked his point of view; her position was indefensible. Some metaphors are so frequently used that they've degenerated into *dead metaphors* or *clichés* (hackneyed phrases). They no longer have the effect, that a good metaphor has, of looking at something afresh and seeing it in a new way. Clichés such as 'explore every avenue' or 'leave no stone unturned' no longer create a visual image in your mind.

Writing a good metaphor involves the ability to see the similarity between two very different things and is surprisingly hard to do well. Metaphors fail completely when the audience can see no similarity at all.

Allegory is a form of extended metaphor in which a particular story or poem is used to illustrate the truth about something else.

Other language devices used in poetry include:

- **Metonymy:** Calling a thing or concept not by its own name, but by that of something intimately associated with it. For example: saying 'sweat' rather than 'hard work'.

- **Synecdoche:** Often understood as a type of metonymy, a synecdoche uses a specific part of something to refer to the whole. For example, in a love poem, you refer to an attribute of the beloved, such as eyes or lips, or use 'mouths' to indicate hungry people.

- **Pun:** A play on words, using a word with the same sound but two different meanings. For example, *a mouse* for a small rodent or a computer device; *lie* meaning to tell an untruth or to recline.

- **Oxymoron:** A word or phrase that contradicts itself. For example: deafening silence, dazzling darkness and sweet pain.

- **Personification:** Describes inanimate things as if they were alive or human. For example, talking to an object: 'O Rose; thou art sick' (Rose is not a girl's name but a flower); making a thing behave like a person: 'Death lays his icy hand on kings.'

- **Symbolism:** Uses an object to stand for something else and point to more than its literal meaning. Symbols are hard to pinpoint as they often have individual, cultural or universal meanings; however, an example is the ocean, which is often used to symbolise infinity, humankind's power-lessness against natural forces or depth. It can also represent the divine, with the human soul as the individual drop that merges into the ocean. A ring is a symbol of fidelity in love, of the eternal (it has no beginning or end), of completeness (a whole circle), but can also stand for bondage and ownership (slaves bore rings, which can represent shackles).

Hearing sounds

Use of language and sound is fundamental to poetry. An awareness of the standard terms and techniques is helpful:

- **Assonance:** The repetition of vowel sounds to create internal rhyming within phrases or sentences. For example: the hound howled loudly outside the house.

✔ **Dissonance:** When sounds clash or sound awkward together. Surprisingly, dissonance can be very effective – consider the effect of saying black glass, man's smudge.

✔ **Sibilance:** The repeated use of hissing sounds. For example: the sea snake hissed when she swam into the snow and ice.

✔ **Alliteration:** The repeated use of consonants, often but not always at the beginning of a word. For example: Bob bashed the bucket with his big black boots.

✔ **Repetition:** Use of the same word for poetic effect. For example: on a dark, dark, night; break, break, break.

Finding a Form

Some poetic forms are well established and imitating them may be a helpful approach when you're starting out. You may not want to write 'old-fashioned' poetry, but you can learn a lot about how poetry works by writing in these forms. Among the most common are:

✔ **Ballad:** Often set to music, a ballad is usually a quatrain (four feet) in which the lines alternate between four and three stresses. An example is William Wordsworth's 'A Slumber Did My Spirit Seal'.

✔ **Ghazal:** Consisting of rhyming couplets and a refrain, each line in a ghazal must share the same metre. The Persian poet Rumi wrote love poetry in ghazal form, where the beloved is a metaphor for God.

✔ **Haiku:** This Japanese form of poetry has become very popular, partly because of its brevity. In English, a haiku consists of three lines, of five, seven and five syllables, and often centres on one image. Below is an example by seventeenth-century Japanese poet Etsujin:

Covered with flowers,
Instantly I'd like to die
In this dream of ours!

✔ **Limerick:** A five-line verse that follows a strict form. For example: 'There was an old man from Dundee / Who decided to climb up a tree. / When he got to the top / He fell down with a flop / That silly old man from Dundee.' Edward Lear is famous for writing limericks.

✔ **Ode:** Odes originated in ancient Greece and are a form of stately verse. They can be written with different metres. 'Ode to a Nightingale' and 'Ode on a Grecian Urn' by John Keats are examples.

✔ **Rondeau:** This form of French poetry comprises 13 lines of eight syllables plus two refrains; it uses only three rhymes. John McCrae's First World War poem 'In Flanders Fields' is a well-known example.

✔ **Sestina:** An elaborate form of French poetry dating to the Middle Ages. A sestina consists of 39 lines: six stanzas of six lines and a final stanza of three, called a *tercet* or *envoi*. The final words of the lines of the first stanza are repeated as the final words of the following five, but in a different order, creating an elaborate pattern. A modern example is Seamus Heaney's 'Two Lorries'.

✔ **Sonnet:** This form originated in Italy. Sonnets have 14 lines, usually written in iambic pentameter (see the earlier section on 'Keeping rhythm or metre'). An English sonnet has three quatrains followed by a couplet, and follows an ABAB CDCD EFEF GG rhyming scheme (for example, the first and third lines rhyme, and so on), as in the works of William Shakespeare.

✔ **Villanelle:** Another complex medieval French form, it has five three-line stanzas rhyming ABA, followed by a four-line stanza rhyming ABAA. Entire lines are repeated as a refrain. Dylan Thomas's 'Do Not Go Gentle into that Good Night' is a modern version of a villanelle.

Offering prose poems

People still argue about whether a *prose poem* – a short piece of poetic prose – falls into the category of poetry or short fiction. Essentially, a prose poem is laid out like prose, but reads like poetry. Ranging in length from a few lines to several pages, a prose poem may explore a wide range of styles and subjects.

Novels can be extremely poetic – consider the prose of Virginia Woolf, or a work like Elizabeth Smart's *By Grand Central Station I Sat Down and Wept.* Prose poems have been written by authors as diverse as Oscar Wilde, Charles Baudelaire, Allen Ginsberg, Gertrude Stein and Aleksandr Solzhenitsyn.

Choosing blank verse or free verse

Blank verse and free verse are forms of poetry differentiated as follows:

✔ **Blank verse:** Poetry that has no rhyme but a very definite rhythm (commonly iambic pentameter – see the 'Moving forward in feet' section earlier in this chapter). The Elizabethan playwrights Christopher Marlowe and William Shakespeare made great use of blank verse in their plays. The romantic English poets William Wordsworth, Percy Bysshe Shelley and John Keats revived blank verse as a major form, and a little later, Alfred Lord Tennyson used blank verse in many of his longer poems. Among American poets, Wallace Stevens used blank verse in extended compositions at a time when many other poets were rejecting it in favour of free verse.

✔ **Free verse:** Poetry with no regular rhyme or metre; it is made recognisable as poetry by being laid out in lines, having strong rhythms and using imagery and other poetic devices.

Writing free verse may seem easier than writing to a formula, but demands a great deal of thought and effort in working out where line breaks should appear and how the poem should be structured. Free verse is certainly no easy way out.

Look for internal rhythms in your poem; this feature may help you recognise how it should be arranged. Consider how the different parts of your poem connect. A poem can have an argument just like a piece of prose, asking questions and giving answers.

Performing Poetry

Performance poetry is a form of accessible contemporary verse including music and drama, storytelling and even stand-up comedy. Performance poetry can resemble rap or reggae, with quick word-play, rhythm, rhyme and repetition – although almost anything goes. Benjamin Zephaniah is a great contemporary performance poet.

If you want to perform your poetry in public, bear these tips in mind, starting with ones to prepare you for the big night:

✔ Learn some elements of the actor's trade: relaxation, breath control, articulation, voice projection and modulation.

✔ Memorise your poems at least partially, so that you only need to glance at the script occasionally.

✔ Prepare how you make your entrance, place your script and face the audience.

✔ Rehearse the performance so thoroughly that the actual reading seems easy and natural.

✔ Work out where you appear in the line-up, so you're prepared.

✔ Wear something that makes you look good but also feels comfortable.

✔ Check the stage space, lectern, microphone, lighting and other equipment.

And finally:

✔ Entertain your audience; secure their attention, address them directly and play to their responses.

✔ Enjoy yourself; if you have a good time, the audience will have one too.

Getting Your Poetry Published

Before even thinking of getting poetry published, you need to work on your writing. Make use of some of the large numbers of poetry workshops, courses and writing groups all over the UK, many of which are taught by skilled and published poets. Universities also offer creative writing programmes that include poetry.

Submitting your poetry to magazines is the best way to get published. A number of excellent poetry magazines can help you to build a reputation for yourself. Always read several issues of the magazines first to see what kind of poetry they publish.

The Poetry Library in London is a valuable resource and offers a comprehensive listing of all presses and magazines on its website (www.poetry library.org.uk). You can read back issues of leading poetry journals at (www.poetrymagazines.org.uk).

You can also enter poetry competitions (type **poetry competition** into an Internet search engine to find suitable choices). Getting shortlisted for a good competition can really advance your reputation.

Some small presses are prepared to publish a pamphlet or *chap-book* of about 15 to 20 poems. However, bear in mind that developing a body of work sufficient to justify publication of a book-length manuscript can take years.

Self-publishing your poems is also an option; many great writers have done so. However, with no editorial feedback or control, and without the reputation of a publisher behind you, being taken seriously is very difficult. Beware of vanity presses, which can charge a great deal of money to publish your book.

Nobody ever wrote poetry to make money. Even if you are published, poetry sells in very small quantities, and you're unlikely ever to make much of a living as a poet. Most poetry books sell fewer than 1,000 copies and the royalties are less than £500. Poetry sales account for less than one per cent of the book market and only ten imprints publish most of the significant poets: these publishers include Anvil Press, Bloodaxe Books and Carcanet Press.

Part IV
Exploring Non-Fiction

"'My goodness, Snow White", said her friendly, kind generous, loving & <u>extremely</u> beautiful stepmother "I wouldn't eat that apple if I were you.'"

In this part . . .

Writing non-fiction can be very creative – from journalism and travel writing to biography and blogging, you can tell stories, discuss issues and visit places in your imagination. Many of the writing skills you need are the same as those for fiction if you want to convey a sense of place, portray a historical period, or sum up a life. You need to get your readers hooked and keep them reading to the end.

This part gives you all you need to know to enter the world of journalism and non-fiction writing.

Chapter 17

Breaking into Journalism

* *

* *

*J*ournalism may not sound much like creative writing, but many novelists, poets and playwrights also pen articles to help support their writing. Many journalists' columns have been turned into books and many a novel sprang from or was inspired by a piece of journalism. Journalism can be highly creative and can also act as the cutting edge where new ideas, concerns and styles of writing are born.

Journalism is a highly competitive, insatiable industry, always demanding material for new stories. To be a journalist, you need to work hard and have the ability to think of fresh ideas. And, if you keep plugging away, you can make an impact. You need to master the tools of the trade, be prepared for many rejections along the way and be tough.

Journalism demands a high standard of English, fluency and brevity of expression, and the ability to get to the kernel of a subject. It also demands a lively and inquiring mind, intuition about people, the ability to sniff out when something's not quite right, and the toughness to enable you to write about difficult or emotional subjects.

The mass media is a huge industry, and opportunities always exist for new people. That said, resting on your laurels is never an option because someone new is always looking to supplant you. If you want to get into journalism, no substitutes prevail for reading newspapers and magazines, watching television news and documentaries, listening to the radio and taking an interest in current affairs.

Writing the Facts: News and Features

News articles are the bread and butter of journalism. To write a news story, you need to:

- ✔ Gather the information.
- ✔ Check the facts.
- ✔ Talk to the experts.

Usually, you gather far too much information. You need to sift through it and decide on what is and isn't important before you begin writing your article.

Working through the five Ws

According to an old piece of wisdom in the journalistic trade, every news story should involve the five *W*s:

- ✔ **Who:** Who's the subject of the story? Who's been killed or murdered? Who won an election or an award?
- ✔ **What:** What exactly took place? What action did the subject of the story take or what happened to him?
- ✔ **Where:** Where did the event take place?
- ✔ **When:** When did the event happen – at what hour precisely, on what day?
- ✔ **Why:** What reasons and forces behind this event led to its happening?

Often, too, a sixth element is needed – how – to add detail on how the event happened and what was involved.

Giving the story structure

A news article follows a different structure from much other writing in that you first need to summarise the story and then give more information as you go down to fill it out. As the reader may only read the first paragraph, this summary has to make sense in itself.

For example:

> Three gunmen *(who)* shot a man dead *(what)* when they attacked a news-agents shop in Wapping *(where)* at 9 p.m. last night *(when)*.

> The gunmen used a sawn-off shotgun *(how)* and stole a total of £486 from the till *(why)*.

Then you add any additional information:

> The police say the gunmen used a blue van to make their getaway.
>
> Police in Wapping have been concerned by a recent spate of similar attacks on small newsagents . . .

The rest of the story may consist of background information, which can be cut if necessary.

In the old days of hot metal setting, a story was always cut from the bottom up, regardless of whether doing so made sense. Journalists thus made sure the story would be understood even if the last paragraph was deleted, and always put the least important information last. Even today, news stories have to be put together at great speed, and people don't have time to read them through and think about how to cut them; they just lop off the bottom. Never put a vital piece of information at the end of a news story.

Following some rules of news writing

Many journalistic rules apply to all forms of writing – accuracy, correct grammar, clarity and ease of communication are all virtues. However, in news journalism, facts are more important than style. The writing must be simple, direct and completely straightforward – no frills allowed!

- ✔ **Always write in the active tense:** Doing so is more direct and engaging. For example: 'Three gunmen shot man dead' is better than 'A man was shot dead by gunmen'.

  Use this approach even if your story's negative. For example, 'The government has abandoned plans to expand the M25' is punchier than 'The government decided not to implement plans to expand the M25'.

- ✔ **Use short quotes:** A direct quote from a politician, crime victim or sports personality enlivens a story. Always try to capture the individual voice of the person concerned; quote what he actually said, not what you wanted him to say.

- ✔ **Avoid using 'official' language:** Police spokespersons and politicians often use jargon to camouflage what they're actually saying; make your story easily understood. Also avoid pompous words such as 'whilst' rather than 'while', 'proceed' rather than 'walk', 'apprehend' rather than 'arrest'.

- ✔ **Beware of hackneyed phrases:** Avoid over-used terms such as:
  - At the end of the day
  - At this moment in time
  - With all due respect

- A raft of measures

- 24/7

- It's not rocket science

Others to avoid include 'literally' when someone's using a metaphor (for example, 'I was literally dead on my feet'), and 'I personally' before an opinion is expressed – unless you're quoting directly.

✔ **Use few adjectives:** If it doesn't add something to the story, don't add too much description. Avoid vague adjectives; be specific. For example, say 'red' or 'yellow' rather than 'brightly coloured', or 'six foot' rather than 'tall', or 'Greek' rather than 'foreign'.

✔ **Beware of acronyms:** *Acronyms* are abbreviations formed using the initial components in a phrase or name. Do you really know what OECD or IPPF stand for? If you don't, will anyone else? (Organisation for Economic Co-operation and Development and the International Planned Parenthood Federation, if you care.) Write the organisation's name in full at first usage, unless the context makes it absolutely clear.

✔ **Don't use complicated words:** Avoid showing off your extensive vocabulary, but don't talk down to your readers either.

Brevity and clarity are crucial in journalism. Consider the following newspaper headline:

JOHN LENNON SHOT DEAD

Many people remember scanning this headline several times, frantically hoping they'd misread it and that the words must convey some other meaning.

Be very specific. Write about actual events, as they happened, in a way that makes them vivid for the reader.

If, for example, you want to write about the rise in the number of suicides during a recession, don't start your story:

> In a recession or financial crisis, like the one we are going through, large numbers of executives who lose their jobs decide that life is no longer worth living, and resolve to end their lives.

Instead, begin:

> On Sunday 16 January 2009, Henry Pound, a 45-year-old head banker at the Money Exchange Corporation, drove his car to a lonely field in Wallingford, Oxfordshire, took out a Smith & Wesson 9mm semi-automatic revolver, and shot himself in the head.

Generally, people aren't interested in hypothetical or vague information; they identify with real human stories. Any old person hasn't died; *this* man, with *this* family, in *these* particular circumstances has.

Putting out Press Releases

News journalists rely heavily on press releases circulated by publicists or press officers in organisations and government departments. A *press release* announces or reacts to news, puts across the organisation's point of view or clarifies information, gains news coverage of an event or product or announces current developments.

A good press release saves journalists a lot of work and puts them onto a story. Journalists sometimes use press releases verbatim if they come from reputable sources and the information doesn't need checking. If a release comes from a known organisation, experience with that source can help you determine whether it's usually honest (like a charity or pressure group), bragging about a product (a commercial company), conveying a particular party line (a political party or government agency) or trying to suppress the truth.

Press releases follow a distinct format: the top line or letterhead displays the organisation's name and logo – make it as eye-catching as possible; on the following line is the date or the words 'Embargoed until' and a future date.

Embargoed information is news the media is requested not to print or broadcast until a later time or date – often the time an announcement is made. The media don't always respect an embargo, but usually do. Never embargo information if when it appears doesn't matter. You can't embargo an event that has already taken place.

Here's a sample press release incorporating the five Ws of a good story.

> Superbooks
>
> Random Street
>
> London NW4 3AB
>
> **Embargoed until: 14 June 2009**
>
> PRESS RELEASE
>
> Maggie Hamand *(who)* is launching her new publishing company Superbooks *(what)* at 12.00 noon on Thursday 14 June (when) at the Groucho Club *(where)*.
>
> Superbooks is a fresh concept in publishing, aiming to give unknown writers a voice through a unique scheme making new fiction available in special promotions through 300 independent bookshops in England and Wales *(why)*.

Superbooks is backed by a consortium of independent bookshops and publishers with funding from the National Lottery *(how)*.

For further details or to talk to Maggie Hamand, contact: *(details)*.

A press release may not seem creative, but in terms of conciseness and clarity is unbeatable.

Penning Features

Writing features is a little different from news reporting. A *feature* is a longer news story that isn't always directly tied to a timeframe (though having a news peg to hang a feature on always helps).

Features often provide background information to news stories. For example, a feature may fill out the life of a significant person who's been in the news; give a history of air travel or government policy; or detail case studies illustrating an issue. Features can also be independent of the news, detailing social trends, fashion, arts and entertainment; covering talking points of the day; or digging up forgotten scandals (especially common at the anniversary of such events).

Although most newspapers and mass media use staff for news, features are very often written by freelancers.

Journalists don't call their articles stories for nothing. A really good article, though it covers something factual, reads like a good story and has a beginning, middle and end.

Features are usually longer than news stories – sometimes several thousand words – and follow a more traditional story structure, often keeping back important information until the end. If features are cut, they're usually edited more carefully and deletions can be made throughout the story.

Features need to be highly planned and structured. They should, be full of facts and information, be highly readable with a strong narrative drive and should never digress. They must hold the reader's attention despite the distractions of all the other articles and stories in the newspaper or magazine.

When you're *commissioned* – asked to write – a feature, you'll always be given a word length. Stick to it; the editor will have a particular slot in mind and won't have room for more. If you send a feature in *on spec*, without a commission, always follow the length of that newspaper or magazine's usual features.

Evaluating Reviews

Most reviews are commissioned by in-house staff or regular freelancers who know their subject well and have a particular insight into the subject. For example, most reviewers of fiction are published novelists, and non-fiction book reviewers are academics or experts in that particular field.

When writing a review, you need to:

✔ Give the reader some idea of what the book, film or play is about.

✔ Comment on how well the idea is put into practice.

✔ Give some detail that helps bring the work of art to life.

✔ Never give away the ending!

Most reviews are fairly short, so don't waffle on. Don't try to impress potential readers with your knowledge of film or literature; your role is to give your opinion, but also to help readers decide if they want to see a film or play or read a book.

Sometimes new reviewers make the mistake of panning excellent novels or films because they think it demonstrates how clever they are. This review can come back to haunt them, when the novel wins the Man Booker Prize or the film a series of Oscars. Years later, when the reviewer's own novel is published, that other writer may also take revenge – authors never forget a bad review!

Lining up Columns

Writing a column is one of the most sought-after jobs in journalism. A *column* offers regular exposure and gives the journalist the opportunity to sound off about whatever the big talking point of the week is. Many columnists have more or less complete control over what they write – a freedom not often found in journalism.

Often, the way something's said in a column is more important than the topic itself. People read a particular column because they like the writer's style: the sardonic wit, particular slant on the news of the day, obsessions, prejudices and opinions. Sometimes people even read columns because they enjoy disagreeing with and getting angry about what the writer has said.

A columnist needs to have a clear identity and writing style to attract regular readers, and must never be boring.

People think that writing a column must be easy, but nothing's further from the truth. Finding a good topic to write about week after week can be extremely demanding, especially because the columnist must never repeat themselves.

Transcribing Interviews

Interviews with celebrities, politicians or people who've been in the news are a staple of journalism. Most interviews with personalities or celebrities are set up by their publicists; if you want a big story, be polite, not pushy, and keep plugging away until you get the opportunity you're after.

Always record your interviews as legal back-up should you be accused of making something up or sued for libel. You can also refer to your recording to ensure your quotes are word perfect (allowing for editing out ums, ers and repetitions).

Always take a small recorder with you, something unobtrusive that you can put on the table and forget about. Don't make a huge song and dance about getting your recorder out and making sure it works; ideally, you want your interviewee to forget it exists. Make notes as well in case you encounter a technical problem and the recording isn't audible.

Tips for recording an interview include:

- Buy a reliable compact digital or mini-disc recorder.
- Check it before you begin – preferably outside the room.
- Make sure you have several spare batteries, tapes or discs.
- Set the volume level before you begin.

Before you go to the interview, make sure you've done as much research as possible about your subject. Search on the Internet and talk to people who know the person. The more you know, the less time you waste on asking your interviewee things you could easily have found out beforehand. Your research can also often lead to interesting questions.

Always write down the questions you want to ask ahead of time – even if you don't stick to them, they're to hand if you go blank.

Remember that your interviewee's meant to be doing the talking, not you – make your questions as short and specific as possible so that you get more out of your subject. Staying quiet and nodding encouragingly can be very effective for drawing people out.

Always be punctual and polite, even if you don't like the person you're interviewing or find his or her opinions offensive.

You're likely to get one hour at most – don't waste a minute of it.

Pitching Stories

Selling your stories isn't easy when you're a beginner or new to a particular publication. The more straightforward and professional you are about selling your work, the more likely you are to succeed.

Getting the market right

Knowing your market is one of the key skills in journalism – identifying exactly who you're writing for. Are you writing for men, women or young adults; how old and how educated are they? How knowledgeable are they on the subject you're writing about? What tone do they expect – dead serious, or light and entertaining?

Before you attempt to write for any publication, reading it first is essential. Check out what particular editors like. In particular, you need to find out what stories have appeared recently so that you can offer them something new.

Style and vocabulary are also very important. You need to adapt your style to suit every publication. Decide whether you need to make your writing very simple or are expected to use longer words and insider jargon for a professional publication. You may need to use longer sentences and paragraphs in some publications than in others.

Getting to know a publication is the best way into journalism. Read a few issues, or go to the library and look up back-issues. Identify the kind of topics the publication favours and work out what's missing. Write a brief summary (just two or three sentences) of some ideas you think the editor would like.

Making contact

Try starting with small and local papers and magazines. You can contact more mainstream publications after you've had one or two pieces in print. If you have experience in a particular area, try writing for a publication that covers this topic.

From the inside cover of a magazine or its website, identify the news or features editor and then email her two or three of your ideas, together with a simple introduction. If you've been published before, say so – 'I haven't written for you before, but my features have been published in x and y magazines.'

If you haven't heard from this editor after a week or ten days, follow up your email with a phone call. Just ask if she got your message, and briefly recap the two or three ideas, asking whether she's interested. If she's not, thank her for her time and ask if she'd like to see some more ideas in the future. Editors usually say yes, so after a bit of thinking, submit a few more proposals.

If you get a bite:

✔ Ask for the word length and stick to it exactly.

✔ Follow any brief to the letter.

✔ Check the deadline and meet it.

✔ Don't be afraid to ask what their rate is; you need to know how much to invoice for.

Considering Radio and Television Journalism

Radio and television journalism has exploded over the last decade with the expansion of cable television channels, rolling 24-hour news, the growth of more local radio stations and Internet radio. Many opportunities are out there, but breaking into this field isn't easy.

Regular, immediate radio

Radio is the fastest and most up-to-date medium for conveying news; despite the existence of rolling 24-hour television news coverage, reporters often revert to radio mode as live events happen, talking about what's going on over a static image. Radio also offers reviews, interviews and magazine-type programmes that feature a number of stories or interviews.

Local radio stations, both BBC and independent, offer the best way in to radio journalism. Many of these are always looking for good local stories and material. Hospital and student radio stations can also offer opportunities.

Asking if you can do work experience, usually unpaid, is one way in, but there's no substitute for attending a proper radio journalism course if you're serious (choose one approved by the Broadcast Journalism Training Council).

Many freelance journalists make a *package* – a recording of a story plus clips from interviews. Putting together a package requires some knowledge of radio editing.

If you put together a package for radio, consider these tips for reading aloud:

✔ Keep things short and clear – often two sentences work better than one. If your sentences are too long, the listener will have forgotten the beginning by the time you get to the end.

✔ If you're reading the news, make sure your voice goes up and down – doing so helps the listener take in the beginning and end of sentences.

✔ Emphasise more words than you would in ordinary speech. For example:

> ARMED MEN have ROBBED a JEWELLERY store in MARYLEBONE, making off with a FORTUNE in GOLD and DIAMONDS.

✔ Read more quickly than is generally natural, and make your voice sound lively and interesting.

✔ Never pause for more than an instant; silence makes people assume their radio is playing up.

Internet radio

Internet radio is growing; you can now make your own podcasts at home and let people download them from your website. Making a podcast is fairly straightforward; you just need simple digital recording equipment. You upload your recording onto your website via easily available software and people can download it to listen to on their computer, iPod or MP3 player.

Reasons for making a podcast include wanting to:

✔ Host your own talk show.

✔ Publicise an issue and get your message across to a wider public.

✔ Make your own radio plays available directly to the public.

✔ Interest people in reading your work or buying your book by offering a few spoken pages or regular instalments of it.

You need to find ways of attracting an audience to your website – for ideas, see Chapter 21 on blogging.

Television journalism

Television is the most difficult area of journalism to break into. You almost certainly need to start at the bottom and work your way up. Check out job opportunities for assistants, freelancers or part-time work. Friends of friends are often hired to do run-around jobs or help out in the studio with particular projects so make as many contacts in the industry as you can.

Many training courses are aimed at people who want to become television journalists, presenters, interviewers and so on. Check out courses offered by reputable organisations such as the National Union of Journalists or the National Film and Television School (NFTS). The Broadcast Journalism Training Council (www.bjtc.org.uk) accredits all courses and is a partnership of all the main employers in the UK broadcast industry. Check out Skillset, the Sector Skills Council for the audio-visual industries, at www.skillset.org.

Of course, many television journalists started in print or radio journalism and moved over to TV after they'd made their reputations – so do consider that route in too. Chapter 15 covers writing television drama.

Chapter 18

Writing from Life

. . . .

In This Chapter

▶ Making yourself the subject of your work

▶ Linking fiction, autobiography and biography

▶ Finding a subject for biography

▶ Imposing a structure

. . . .

*I*n a sense, all writing is autobiographical, in that, as the writer, you're always present, observing and interpreting the world and creating from your own consciousness. However, autobiography and fiction are very different – although many autobiographies are fictionalised and many novels draw heavily from life.

Writing biography may seem a very different task but all biography includes an element of autobiography too, especially if you know the person you're writing about. Your own interests and opinions always influence your writing about another person.

Writing biography and autobiography isn't easy. Without a fictional frame-work or many of the tools of fiction writing, your prose can ultimately be deadly dull and of interest only to yourself (and maybe some people who know you). But life writing can be significant: many books that would have been considered devoid of interest when they were written have become important historical documents in subsequent years. Autobiography and biography can reveal the past and also give a voice to those who were previously marginalised in historical accounts.

Writing about Yourself

Most people are curious about and fascinated by the lives of others. They have a great desire to know what other people felt in different circumstances and feel a sense of recognition when they realise that others have experienced life as they do. Reading autobiography offers the possibility of entering another person's life and world and discovering what being someone else is like.

Autobiography means writing about your own life. Using this form enables you to reach out and communicate with others so that your own experiences and insights may touch a chord with them and emphasise a common humanity.

Even though you know your subject matter intimately – none better! – you may occasionally get stuck. Use these tips to prompt your memories and your writing:

- ✔ **Record your dreams.** Keep a journal by your bed and write down everything you can remember as soon as you wake up. At first you may only recall snippets, but with practice you'll remember more and more.

- ✔ **Use your emotions as a prompt to get you writing.** What made you sad, angry, happy or frustrated today? What are you hoping for, or dreading?

- ✔ **Describe an old photograph and everything you can remember about the place or time it was taken.** Perhaps you have a picture of yourself aged four, sitting on a beach. Describe what you're wearing and how you're sitting. Who's in the photo with you? Describe the view, the feeling of the sun on your back, your eyes scrunched up against the light, the rough sand in your fingers and stuck to your skin.

   Try to create a little narrative from this story. What did you learn from this day? Perhaps that a sandcastle only lasts until the sea comes in and destroys it, but is still pleasurable to build. Maybe you saw your mother in a new light, or tasted ice cream for the first time. Go with your memories and see what comes up.

- ✔ **Read through your old school reports.** Almost everyone can remember their first day at school; write about it. Maybe you remember certain teachers, their names and faces. Describe a lesson or an interaction between you and another child or a teacher. What did you learn from the experience? Why does this memory stick out?

   Apparently, you remember best those events that have an emotional connection. Almost all your early memories are thus related to an emotion. Don't be afraid to tap into these emotional memories.

- ✔ **Make a folder or scrapbook of photographs of yourself, your family and friends;** add memorabilia such as travel tickets, theatre programmes, school reports, letters, newspaper cuttings – everything you've hoarded over the years can be useful to your writing.

A history of autobiography

The term *autobiography* comes from the Greek *autos* (meaning 'self'), *bios* ('life') and *graphein* ('to write'). The poet Robert Southey first used the term in 1809 in the English periodical *Quarterly Review*, although the writing of memoirs and journals dates back to antiquity.

Saint Augustine's *Confessions*, written around 400 AD, is one of the oldest autobiographies in existence; it tells the story of his life and conversion to Christianity, as well as a great deal of philosophical reflection. Completed in 1002, *The Pillow Book* of Sei Shonagon is a collection of a Japanese court lady's thoughts and memories, written while she was serving Empress Sadako during the 990s and early 1000s in Japan.

The diaries of the English seventeenth-century Member of Parliament and civil servant Samuel Pepys were successfully published (after his death) in 1825 and drew attention to the possibilities of the diary as a form of autobiographical writing. Pepys's diary is a combination of personal revelation and eyewitness accounts of highly significant events, including the Great Plague of 1665, the Second Dutch War and the Great Fire of London.

In the twentieth century autobiographies came to be written in protest against totalitarian regimes, such as Nadezhda Mandelstam's *Hope Against Hope* (1970), which describes the moral and cultural degradation of the Soviet Union of the 1920s and later, and Jung Chang's *Wild Swans: Three Daughters of China*, which tells the story of twentieth-century China through the lives of grandmother, mother and daughter.

In the 1980s and 1990s the celebrity memoir became a staple of publishing houses; many of these were *ghostwritten* (written by someone else) and not very insightful, revealing only what the celebrity wanted people to know.

Politicians are almost expected to write their political memoirs, though many of these are quite unreadable. Memoirs written by important and inspirational figures have sold extremely well, however, such as South African political prisoner then President Nelson Mandela's *Long Walk to Freedom* and US President Barack Obama's *Dreams From My Father*.

Finding the Form

Writing autobiographically can vary from scribbled notes in a journal to a highly polished autobiographical novel (see the 'Inventing the autobiographical novel' section later in this chapter). Some writing is destined never to be seen – some people actually lock their diaries with a key or even burn them later – while others are designed from the beginning to be read by a wide audience. Whatever you intend, autobiography comes from you and must be a place where you can feel free to explore your own inner world and possibly as a result reach out to others.

When you start writing, don't worry about the form your work takes. Getting your thoughts and experiences down on paper is what matters.

Shocking misery memoirs

Some inspirational memoirs set the bar for a popular genre:

✔ Dave Pelzer's *A Child Called It* was the first of its kind when published in 1995, and became an instant bestseller. The book recounts his childhood, growing up with an alcoholic mother who beat, starved, stabbed and burnt him, and even force-fed him ammonia.

✔ Stuart Howarth's *Please, Daddy, No* (2007), reported even worse abuse, recalling how his father repeatedly raped him and forced him to eat pigswill. Howarth was then abused by paedophiles and became a homeless, cocaine-addicted arsonist before finally killing his father and ending up in prison.

Misery memoirs sell mainly on the basis that they're true. Some authors, however, have been exposed as inventing at least some of the details, and in some cases fabricating the whole story.

Some critics have also seen the genre less as inspirational stories of overcoming appalling suffering and more as a form of emotional pornography. Some accounts can become quite literally pornographic, too. Dwelling on these stories of untold misery also tends to normalise what in fact are very rare instances of extreme abuse.

Revealing misery memoirs

Inspirational memoirs is the term usually used by publishers for books focusing on how the author survived appalling experiences. In recent years this misery memoir genre has accounted for nearly 10 per cent of the British book market, although interest is now waning. If you have a story to tell, don't be put off however; just be aware that you need to offer a new angle to make yours stand out.

Sharing letters, journals and diaries

Writing letters or keeping a journal or diary are easy ways to start an autobiography. You get into the habit of writing regularly and produce lots of material to work with.

Penning letters

Letters are becoming a dying art in the modern world of telephone and email communication. However, no reason exists why you shouldn't still put pen to paper and write to people.

Early novels were often written in the form of letters – Pierre Choderlos de Laclos's *Les Liaisons Dangereuses* is one example – and letters from both well-known and ordinary people in the past can be as fascinating as any other story. The 20-year correspondence between Helene Hanff and Frank Doel, chief buyer of an antiquarian bookseller, became a bestselling book, and later a stage play and film, named after the bookshop's location at 84 Charing Cross Road.

If you want to write, letters can be a good way to begin. Letter-writing also has one potential advantage over keeping a journal – you're always addressing another person, which can make you focus on being clear, amusing and interesting. Further, the person you write to will hopefully reply, which gives you something to respond to; letters always open up into a dialogue of sorts and can thus be more interesting than simply relying on one voice and perspective only.

If you have a friend who also wants to write, come to a reciprocal arrangement. Or consider composing letters to an imaginary person or someone you knew who's now dead.

Exposing diaries and journals

Does a difference exist between a diary and a journal? Often the words are used interchangeably. A *diary* is more often used for a simple log of what you do or what happens to you, while a *journal* implies a personal and reflective chronicle. However, a personal diary and a journal are in essence the same thing: a notebook, book or, nowadays, computer file in which you write down your thoughts and feelings and describe events that happen to you.

If you decide to keep a journal, buying a special notebook helps. Choose one with an attractive cover and paper that is smooth and pleasurable to write on. Some people like to use the same kind of journal for each year, while others experiment with different types. The choice is yours.

You may prefer to write your diary on the computer. Always copy and back it up.

Some people keep a journal and write in it every day; others write just when they feel they have something to say. Writing regularly is important, though, even if you don't write every day.

Writing as therapy

Writing is a recognised and valued form of therapy for people who've suffered abuse or have mental health problems. Writing therapy is also used in prisons to help people address the reasons why they've committed crimes and give them insight into their difficulties.

Over the past 20 years, a growing body of literature has demonstrated the beneficial effects that writing about traumatic or stressful events has on physical and emotional health. In the first study on expressive writing, carried out by James Pennebaker and his colleague Sandra Beall in 1986, college students wrote for 15 minutes on four consecutive days about 'the most traumatic or upsetting experiences' of their entire lives, while the control group wrote about superficial topics. Those who wrote about their traumas reported significant benefits in both objectively assessed and self-reported physical health four months later, with less frequent visits to the health centre and a trend towards fewer days' absence through illness.

The theory developed to account for these findings was that suppressing trauma involved inhibition and a degree of psychological work, expending energy that could otherwise be used to improve these students' health.

Writing the story of your experiences can create more coherent and meaningful accounts of major events in your life and put them in perspective. The process of writing things down may help you develop a greater understanding of what happened and why.

Some people, instead of repressing traumatic events, may repeatedly go over them in their minds. After these memories are written down, they've recorded them and can therefore let them go. This experience can be very liberating.

To begin with, don't worry about what you're writing; just get into the habit of writing something. Try to write at the same time every day – first thing in the morning when you get up, last thing at night before going to bed, or in your lunch hour. The world is full of discarded diaries. You start in the New Year and peter out somewhere in the middle of February. Make a real commitment to yourself to write every day, even if only for five minutes.

Really only two kinds of journal exist; those written privately purely for the author, and those written consciously with the thought that others will read them, or even that they may eventually be published. You may think that you're writing your journal for yourself, but then become aware that you're addressing others, or are censoring yourself because you fear someone else is going to read it.

Unless you die suddenly, or your diaries are published posthumously, you can edit them and choose what you do and don't want to reveal. So try not to censor yourself; doing so rather undermines the point of keeping a diary in the first place.

Your diary can become the recipient of your secrets, your mirror or tool for self-evaluation. If you leave your journal for a while and then go back to it, you'll be amazed at what you can learn about yourself.

Inventing the autobiographical novel

Almost as old as autobiography is the *autobiographical novel* – based on your own life story, using yourself as the main character.

At what point the autobiography becomes a novel is almost impossible to say, as the one merges imperceptibly into the other. In general, a point arrives when enough names have been changed, locations altered and events compressed and edited that calling a work an autobiography doesn't seem right.

Novels portraying settings and situations with which the author is familiar aren't necessarily autobiographical – all fiction writers describe places they know. Nor are novels including only some aspects of the author's life. Most people consider that a true autobiographical novel must have a protagonist who's modelled closely on the author and a central plot that mirrors the major events in the author's life.

As a writer, you may prefer to call a piece of work a novel because it protects you from attack by other people involved, and can save you from hurting people's feelings.

Also significant is how a book is marketed. Generally, autobiographies by people who aren't well known don't sell well, unless the story is exceptional, so publishers may hope to generate more sales if a book is sold as a novel. A work of fiction can be entered for major literary prizes and is more likely to be reviewed. Ultimately, though, whether you choose to acknowledge your story as autobiography or novel depends on what you feel most comfortable with.

Protection from the ever-present threat of libel is another reason why some writers prefer to fictionalise their stories. If you write something damaging about someone, and that person can identify herself, she can sue you (refer to Chapter 1). But if you change enough details that the person can't be identified – for example, her age, gender, physical appearance – and some biographical details, often you can still convey the emotional truth of what you experienced without risking a lawsuit.

Recently, the author Julie Myerson sparked controversy when she wrote a book about her son's drug problems and the breakdown in their relationship. The 20-year-old boy spoke out against her publishing intimate family secrets and the author was accused of exploiting her child for commercial gain. Writing a novel on the theme and concealing the identity of the people involved might have been kinder.

Novels involving more characters or where the narrator is in some ways different from the author or where what happens is more distanced from true events are sometimes called *semi-autobiographical novels*.

Classic autobiographies

Many autobiographies describe exceptional experiences or lives that are outstanding in some way. A good autobiography provides insight into human nature and offers the reader a window into a very different kind of life. Classic examples include:

- Brian Keenan's *An Evil Cradling* (1991) is an insightful account of his incarceration as a hostage in Beirut for four and a half years. It describes the experience vividly in beautiful prose and sheds light on man's inhumanity to man.

- Primo Levi's *If This is a Man* (1947) is a harrowing memoir of his experience of imprisonment in Auschwitz from March 1944 to January 1945. Of the 650 Jews who entered the camp with him, 525 died in the gas chamber. Levi survived, and writes elegantly and precisely about his experience with no trace of self-pity.

- Eva Hoffman's *Lost in Translation* (1989) is a beautifully written memoir capturing the experience of being an exile, recounting the author's move from Poland to Canada in 1959 and her resulting sense of dislocation.

- Mary McCarthy's *Memories of a Catholic Girlhood* (1957) is a collection of eight autobiographical pieces following the death of her parents during the influenza epidemic of 1918, when she shuttled between two sets of grandparents and three religions; Catholic, Protestant and Jewish. The book includes memories of her education in a Catholic convent, where she lost her faith, and an unforgettable portrait of her grandmother, Augusta.

- Thomas Merton's *The Seven Storey Mountain* (1948), the autobiography of a Trappist monk, was an unlikely bestseller. Finished five years after he entered Gethsemani Abbey in Kentucky, Merton offers a moving account of his spiritual journey, which struck a surprising chord with readers looking for personal meaning and direction in their lives.

- Edmund Gosse's *Father and Son* (1907) is a classic memoir describing the author's early years in a devout Plymouth Brethren home. The book focuses on the father's response to new evolutionary theories, especially those of his scientific colleague Charles Darwin, and Edmund's gradual rejection of both his father and his fundamentalist religion.

- Maxim Gorky's *Childhood, Boyhood, Youth* (1913) examines the author's experiences through individual portraits and descriptions of events, including his upbringing by a brutal grandfather and his uneducated but loving grandmother. Gorky was considered a founder of social realism and was closely associated with the tumultuous revolutionary period in Russia.

- Paul Auster's *Hand to Mouth* (1997) is a record of his inauspicious early years struggling to make money while writing, describing his work at a summer camp, attending Columbia in 1968 at the height of the student uprisings, his work on an oil tanker, and for a French Mafia-style film producer in Paris and for a rare-book organisation in New York.

- Simone de Beauvoir's *Memoirs of a Dutiful Daughter* (1958) is a superb autobiography by one of the great literary figures of the twentieth century. It offers an intimate portrayal of a girl growing up in a bourgeois French family, rebelling as an adolescent against the conventional expectations of her class.

- Barack Obama's *Dreams From My Father* (1995) is a well-written and insightful memoir of his childhood in Indonesia and Hawaii and his relationship with his father whom he hardly knew. The book provides a fascinating insight into the man who went on to become the first black President of the United States.

Examples of autobiographical novels include J. D. Salinger's *The Catcher in the Rye*, Christopher Isherwood's *Goodbye to Berlin*, J. G. Ballard's *Empire of the Sun*, Roddy Doyle's *Paddy Clark Ha Ha Ha*, Sylvia Plath's *The Bell Jar*, Robert M. Pirsig's *Zen and the Art of Motorcycle Maintenance* and Jack Kerouac's *On the Road* and *The Dharma Bums*.

Classic novels that are heavily based on the authors' own lives include Charlotte Brontë's *Jane Eyre*, Charles Dickens's *David Copperfield* and Arthur Koestler's *Darkness At Noon*.

Writing about Others

Biographies used to be considered dry, uninteresting works; lists of facts and events of interest only to academics and researchers. Modern trends in the writing of biographies have changed this image, however. Nowadays, they read like narrative non-fiction, with gripping stories, vivid details of where the characters lived, what they wore, what they'd have said and how they'd have said it, and consideration of their relationships with other people. In particular, a modern biography may ask a question about the character that makes you want to read on and find the answer.

Some tips on writing biography:

- ✔ Write down all your sources and references in a safe place. Nothing's worse than having to go back and research something all over again because you can't remember where you found something.

- ✔ Do your own picture research as you go along. Photographs of your subject and the world he or she lived in are invaluable material for your biography.

- ✔ Visit the places where your subject lived, worked and travelled. You can then describe what your subject would've seen – even if everything has been modernised since.

- ✔ Access archives, local libraries and museums, county and parish records, and the National Archives (formerly the Public Record Office; www.nationalarchives.gov.uk). You may find out-of-print books in the British Library at St Pancras (www.bl.uk), and the National Newspaper Archive is at Colindale (which is part of the British Library and will move to the St Pancras site by 2012).

- ✔ Track down the descendents of your subject. They may own items that belonged to your character, perhaps letters and diaries, portraits and photographs and other memorabilia. Old friends may also have memories and tales to share.

A history of biography

The ancient Greeks are often credited with developing the biographical tradition. *Parallel Lives* by Plutarch, a Greek writing during the days of the Roman Empire, is a series of short biographies of eminent men, compared and contrasted in pairs, one Greek and one Roman.

In the Middle Ages, monks and hermits wrote biographies of church fathers, martyrs, popes and saints. Their works were meant to be inspirational to people and serve as vehicles for conversion to Christianity. These accounts were not intended to be historically accurate and stressed the virtues of their subjects and omitted their faults – a technique which became known as *hagiography*. This term is still used to describe a biography that is overly flattering to its subject.

By the late Middle Ages, biographies became less church-orientated as those of kings, knights and tyrants began to appear. During the Renaissance, artists and poets became the focus of biographies, such as Giorgio Vasari's *Lives of the Artists* (1550). Vasari turned his subjects into celebrities and the *Lives* became an early 'bestseller'.

The so-called Golden Age of English biography began in the late eighteenth century. A classic work of the period is Boswell's *Life of Johnson*. In the twentieth century, accounts of the lives of historical figures became immensely popular, with authors such as Lytton Strachey pioneering a new form of biography that combined psychological insight and realism with wit and style. Strachey's aim was to free the biography from its heavy Victorian shackles in which everything that was known about the person had to be mentioned. Instead, he thought that the biographer needed 'a brevity which excludes everything that is redundant and nothing that is significant'. Among his most popular works are *Eminent Victorians* (1918) and his 1921 biography of Queen Victoria.

Modern biography is interested in the psychology of the people concerned and tends to have a stronger narrative element. Examples of modern biographies include Antonia Fraser's *Mary, Queen of Scots* and *Marie Antoinette: The Journey*, Claire Tomalin's *Samuel Pepys: The Unequalled Self* and *Katherine Mansfield: A Secret Life*, Edna O'Brien's *Byron in Love* and William Hague's *William Pitt the Younger* and *William Wilberforce: The Life of the Great Anti-Slave Trade Campaigner*.

Having the last word on any subject is impossible. New material is always coming to light, and attitudes towards people and issues change. All you can do is the best you can in the time you have available.

Entwining biography with autobiography

Autobiography is, of course, a form of biography – a biography in which the subject is yourself. Biography also involves writing from life – but this time the subject is someone other than yourself.

Sometimes a biography can be very close to autobiography. If you're writing about someone you know well – a sibling, parent or child, friend or colleague, inevitably you come into the book as a major character or as the person who views, interprets and comments on the events you describe. If the book focuses on the relationship between yourself and the other person, deciding whether the final book is a straight biography or is more autobiographical can be difficult.

In some cases, of course, a biography is about a person you've never met, possibly someone who died long before you started to write the book. Here, you may think that in no way do you, as the author, come into it. Actually, for the writer of a biography to come into the text as the researcher, explorer or literary detective who discovers the facts and uncovers the truth about a character is increasingly common. How you research and find out about the subject of the biography can become a gripping part of the narrative.

Choosing your subject

Key to a successful biography is the writer's curiosity and desire to get as close as possible to the truth about the subject of the book. You must, in some way, fall in love with your subject. You must be driven to know as much as possible about him, to uncover his hidden motivations, secret desires and passions. Biographers sometimes choose to write about people they hate – figures such as Stalin and Hitler – but usually experience the same degree of obsessional interest.

Possibly you won't have to find your subject – he may choose you. Maybe you've always been fascinated by and wanted to write about someone – so just start writing!

Many people start writing a biography because some important document fell into their hands – a grandfather's diary after his death, an unpublished autobiographical novel written by an aunt or uncle, a long correspondence with a person no one knew about.

Biographies can also be prompted by the discovery after a parent's death that you were adopted or aren't your mother or father's child. A parent's long-lost love or a family secret may be revealed on someone's deathbed.

Often an autobiography and a biography of someone you know and don't know can merge. For instance, in *Bad Faith: A Story of Family and Fatherland* (2006), the publisher and author Carmen Callil tells the story of two lives: those of Louis Darquier, Nazi collaborator and Commissioner for Jewish Affairs in the Vichy government of Occupied France, and his daughter Anne Darquier, the offspring of his marriage to an Australian alcoholic. The starting point of this fascinating book was Callil's arrival in England from Australia in 1963. Suffering from depression, she was referred to the psychiatrist Dr Anne Darquier. Anne had hardly known her parents, who'd left her in foster care, and, in Callil's words, 'she told me secrets she could have kept to herself' – secrets which, after her suicide in 1970, led Callil into a long journey of research into the extraordinary story of both Anne's life and that of her anti-Semitic father, producing a gripping blend of autobiography, biography and history.

Rather than just one person, you may be interested in a group of people, period or particular issue. If so, you may need to do some thinking about which character provides the most interesting route into the subject matter. Sometimes focusing on the most well-known person is best, on the grounds that more people have heard of and want to read about them. Recently, though, biographies have tended to focus on little-known members of a famous circle, in order to do something a little new and different.

Another recent trend is covering familiar subjects from new angles. Charles Nicholl's *The Lodger: Shakespeare on Silver Street* and Frances Wilson's *The Ballad of Dorothy Wordsworth* aren't like old-style literary biography, telling the story of their subjects from cradle to grave. Instead, they focus on just one episode in a life, in the process revealing more about the whole.

Look at what other books have been written about this person, and what you have to offer that's new if there have been books on the subject before. If there's enough interest in a figure, there's always room for a new book.

Researching your biography

Research is the key to a good biography. First, you need to find out as much information as you can about the person's life, work and family circumstances. Second, you need to research more widely into the historical background; what was going on in society during the time, and the key events that may have shaped the subject's life.

When writing a biography, recreating the background for your subject is important; without appreciating the context, understanding your subject is impossible.

People are inevitably a product of the times in which they live and the views that were generally held then. A historical biography can be brought to life by vivid descriptions of places, of insight into the clothes people wore and what wearing them felt like, how children were reared, educated and treated within the home, how medical science worked and illnesses were treated, how people related to servants and what issues excited and shocked them.

Questions to consider in your biography include:

- Did an event in your subject's childhood shape his personality?
- Did a personality trait drive him to succeed or result in tragedy?
- What were the major turning points in his life?
- What was his impact on history, and why?

Contacting family, friends and people you know

If you're writing about a family member or someone you know, the research may be comparatively easy. You can look in the attic and find papers, diaries or letters. You can talk to people who knew her, discover the family myths and stories, and form your own view of what happened.

No substitute exists for talking to the people concerned, tracking down figures from the past and hearing everyone's side of the story. Remember, however, that people don't always want to talk about the past. You may stir up old and painful memories, or be revealing information that they don't want to hear or think is best forgotten.

If you intend interviewing people, bear the following tips in mind:

- ✔ Agree an interview time, confirm the appointment and stick to it.

- ✔ Make a list of questions to ask, even if you don't follow it – otherwise you may forget something vital and not get another opportunity to meet.

- ✔ Send questions in advance, so that the interviewee can do some research herself and find the answers.

- ✔ Ask open-ended questions to avoid 'yes' or 'no' responses.

- ✔ Always be courteous, respect people's privacy and conduct the interview in a professional manner. Watch out for fatigue, too – being interviewed can be tiring, especially for older people or if the subject-matter is highly emotional.

- ✔ Ask for permission, in writing, to use the information you're given. Doing so can help avoid misunderstandings later on. A letter from you at the outset, stating what you're doing, can help; having on record that you're writing a book means she can't then turn round and say she didn't know it was for publication.

- ✔ Think about the best place to meet. Visiting her at home may offer greater insight, but she may feel more comfortable in a hotel lounge, bar or café.

- ✔ Record the interview if possible so that you can be more relaxed about taking notes and recording every detail of the conversation.

- ✔ Always thank the interviewee for her time and trouble.

Discovering strangers and historical figures

If you don't know the subject of your biography, the research can seem daunting. For a contemporary figure, you can still talk to people who knew him, his family and friends. If you're writing about a historical figure, an immense amount of research may be necessary. You can't escape detailed research – you have to know what happened and, especially in the case of a distant historical figure, have to go back to printed sources.

Two types of sources are available to you – *primary* and *secondary:*

✔ **Primary sources:** These are documents written at the time to which they refer – diaries, letters, birth, death and marriage certificates, tax-forms, census returns and so on.

✔ **Secondary sources:** These are interpretations of history – newspaper articles, history books or other biographies. A secondary source may be contemporary with the event it describes or may have been written much later. Some secondary sources are clearly more reliable than others; don't assume they're always accurate.

Remember that even primary sources aren't infallible. An account may have been written with partial knowledge, to interpret the author's actions in the best possible light or even to deliberately deceive people.

Finding your sources

Find as many primary sources as possible; these form the bedrock of your biography and help you build your story firmly on fact and record. Start with the obvious traditional sources. These include:

✔ *The Oxford Dictionary of National Biography* (www.oxforddnb.com) contains details of 55,000 people who shaped the history of Britain and beyond. You need to subscribe for the full version, but some material is available free.

✔ *Who's Who* (www.ukwhoswho.com; www.internationalwhoswho. com) details information about people alive today, but you can also look up back-issues.

✔ Newspapers and journals provide a huge amount of information. *The Times* index goes back the furthest, but you can look up all old newspapers, including local ones, at the National Newspaper archive, part of the British Library. Most documents are still offered on microfiche (a compact analogue storage system – ask the librarians how to use it), but increasingly material is being scanned onto computer. Local newspapers also keep back-copies or they may be archived locally.

✔ Libraries often have archives containing a wealth of local information. The staff are often highly knowledgeable and can help you find what you're looking for and also suggest profitable lines of research.

The National Register of Archives contains guides to archive collections throughout the country and may help you to find material stored in a place that isn't obvious.

✔ School, local authority, church, estate and business records, electoral rolls and local Post Office directories can all enable you to check facts such as which schools people attended and when, the periods at which they lived at certain addresses, and information about their business dealings. You can locate these documents through schools and local education authorities, the local council who hold estate and business records, the parish church, and local or national libraries.

✔ If your subject is a lawyer, doctor or engineer, try bodies such as the Law Society, Royal College of Medicine and Institute of Civil Engineers. If your subject is titled, try *Debrett's* or *Burke's Peerage and Baronetage*. For clergy, try *Crockford's Clerical Directory*.

✔ National collections and libraries such as the British Library (`www.bl.uk`) and the National Archives (`www.nationalarchives.gov.uk`) are invaluable. The latter provides easy access to indexes and certificates of births, marriages and deaths, indexes of adoptions, Census returns and other important sources.

✔ Wills provide fascinating information and those from 1858 onwards can be easily accessed through the Probate Search Room at the High Court (First Avenue House, 42–49 High Holborn, London WC1V 6NP). Its website (`www.hmcourts-service.gov.uk`) provides opening hour details. The National Archives can tell you where to look for wills before 1858.

✔ Museums store a wealth of material not on public view. The Imperial War Museum keeps letters from soldiers and other memorabilia and the National Maritime Museum holds Admiralty and dockyard records, together with shipping companies' business papers.

✔ Immigration information is also recorded and a number of websites list people who emigrated from the UK to Australia, Canada and New Zealand. You can glean a lot of information from GENUKI (UK and Ireland Genealogy) at `www.genuki.org.uk/big/Emigration.html`. Immigration records from Ellis Island, New York have also recently been made available online at `www.ellisisland.org`.

According to Dr Johnson: 'A man will turn over half a library to make a book.'

When writing a biography, having the almost legendary advantage of what are known as 'hitherto unpublished documents' is extremely helpful. Every researcher's dream is to discover such papers mouldering away in an attic or hidden in the depths of a drawer in an obscure library. Being lucky enough to find such documents or new evidence will certainly help you generate interest in your book.

Nothing's as exciting as viewing the piece of paper on which your subject actually wrote. As Antonia Fraser said: 'The delicate white gloves now demanded by Conservation made it particularly exciting when I inspected the single surviving Wardrobe Book of Marie Antoinette in the *Archives Nationales* in Paris – to say nothing of the presence of armed gendarmes behind me, quite ready to defend this treasure of France to the death (mine).'

If you're writing a historical account, don't make anachronistic judgements. Always consider the famous opening line of L. P. Hartley's novel, *The Go-Between*: 'The past is a foreign country; they do things differently there.' In the past, perfectly decent people supported views that we now consider to be abhorrent or evil. For example, slavery was a perfectly normal part of life and commerce, and the British Empire was built on it. In the Middle Ages, women were considered 'misbegotten men'; the male foetus was thought to be 'ensouled' at three months and a girl not until five months. Blaming a historical figure for holding a view that we now hold to be wrong is pointless. Possibly people in the future may consider children not being allowed to vote and chimpanzees not having human rights scandalous!

Considering different types of biography

People have written and read biographies for a very long time (see the 'A history of biography' sidebar earlier in this chapter). Below are the most common types:

- **Historical biography:** Probably the most common form, a historical biography reveals not only the life of the main character, but also what living in that period was like. Historical biographies describe history while also being entertaining, perhaps the main reason for their enduring popularity.

- **Literary and arts biography:** Many people have written about the lives of great writers, to discover how their work was influenced by their experiences, and why they wrote the way they did. The same applies to artists, musicians and composers. Not all artists are tortured geniuses but many had unconventional lives, which make for good reading.

- **Celebrity biography:** People want to read about celebrities and discover the truth behind the glamorous exteriors. Most celebrity biographies are comparatively easy to research because of the wealth of material available about the person concerned. Writing about a dead subject, like Marilyn Monroe, is much easier than a live one, as you don't face legal threats if you reveal things that the person doesn't wish to be public knowledge.

- **Scientific biography:** The story of twentieth-century science is inseparable from the lives of the scientists who made the important discoveries that have shaped the world and people's understanding of the universe. Biographies of scientists are popular because they show the human face of science. Biography is also an important tool in explaining modern science to the non-scientific public.

  To write this form of biography you need some understanding of science and scientific methods; historical research is also necessary.

Structuring Your Book

Although autobiography and biography are in many ways different, exactly the same issues arise when you organise and structure the material. The birth of the subject isn't always the best place to start and neither is death the obvious conclusion (especially if you're writing an autobiography!).

Being selective is the most important consideration when writing any work from life. You can't put in everything that happened in the course of a person's life; not only would space be an issue, but also most of it would be deadly dull. Instead of piling up fact after fact, you need to select the most interesting parts of a life and describe only what's significant and revealing.

Always consider the timeline. What are the most important events in a person's life, and where does his story become interesting? Maybe a character had an unusual and fascinating childhood that shaped the person he became – so include it. Many people who go on to achieve something unusual had a very ordinary childhood, however, which doesn't make good reading – so pass over it in a paragraph or two or refer to it in short flashbacks and memories.

If you decide to write about a whole life from beginning to end, skipping over periods when nothing much happens is fine. If you're describing your own life, you can cover them in a few sentences.

If you're writing a historical biography, stating 'we know very little about what happened to Joe Bloggs in the years after he left school and before he started working in the theatre' is better than speculating wildly about what might have happened or not mentioning the lack of sources for this period. If it later transpires that something very significant happened you avoid looking foolish.

Sticking to a strict chronological sequence isn't necessary either. You can start with the most interesting bit of your or your subject's life, and fill in the gaps later. You can supplement the book with a timeline or chronology in an appendix for anyone who wants to check.

Working out the main episodes in a life and writing a chapter for each is a useful approach. Choosing an appropriate title for each section can help you to focus on the main events and not digress to other areas. You can also easily check if any major events or periods in a character's life have been missed out.

Writing and researching an autobiography or biography may not seem like the most creative form of writing. Yet you still need imagination, flair, an understanding of narrative structure and the ability to describe character, places and events in a way that brings them to life and makes the most of your story. You need to fill in gaps and speculate on what you can't know, in the same way that a novelist brings life to their characters and reveals their inner thoughts and motivations.

Chapter 19

Crafting Narrative Non-Fiction

· ·

In This Chapter

▶ Defining narrative non-fiction

▶ Finding the story and doing the writing

▶ Considering the range of stories

· ·

*N*arrative non-fiction is a relatively new term for writing that's essentially based on fact, which uses real characters, places and events but also employs many of the techniques of fiction writing, such as characterisation, dialogue, description and narrative structure. This genre is known by several different names: creative non-fiction, literary non-fiction, literary journalism and the non-fiction novel. *Faction* is another, although this term tends to be used disparagingly.

Narrative non-fiction needs to be essentially true to the facts – some books sold as memoirs or real-life stories transpired to be faked, sparking huge controversy. However, while journalism strives on the whole to be objective, readers of narrative non-fiction are usually happy to accept the account as biased, reflecting the point of view of the narrator.

Exploring the World of Narrative Non-Fiction

Narrative non-fiction is essentially a hybrid – a marriage of storytelling and factual journalism. It aims to make the world of real people, places and events as dramatic and involving as a novel. It usually has a central narrative, is told through a series of scenes that involve action and dialogue, depicts complex characters and tells the story in a compelling voice.

Narrative non-fiction is a wide genre, which can embrace autobiography, biography, investigative journalism, travel writing, history and medicine. What distinguishes it from other works in these genres is the strong element of storytelling, which often leads to the selection of the more dramatic material, and the omission of aspects of the background that don't fit into the narrative structure.

History of narrative non-fiction

The contemporary genre of narrative non-fiction is generally accepted as emerging from the New Journalism movement of the 1960s and 1970s, led by such notable writers as Truman Capote, Norman Mailer and Tom Wolfe. *In Cold Blood*, Truman Capote's probing account of a shocking crime, is usually recognised as the first book written in this genre.

Increasingly in the modern publishing industry, the boundary between fact and fiction has blurred. Prize-winning novels, such as Pat Barker's Regeneration trilogy, use real characters – the war poets Wilfred Owen and Siegfried Sassoon, and psychiatrist W. H. R. Rivers are featured in prominent roles – as well as fictional ones.

Television has seen the rise of the *drama documentary* or *docudrama*, where actors play the roles of real people and where historical events are reconstructed:

- *Documentary drama* refers to programmes that are largely dramas, but include documentary-style research and delivery.

- *Dramatised documentary* refers to programmes that are largely documentaries, with documented journalistic research, but also contain large elements of dramatisation.

In relation to fiction, narrative non-fiction and the drama documentary, critics and writers continue to debate whether these techniques blur the boundary between fact and fiction, mislead viewers and sacrifice factual accuracy in the creation of dramatic storytelling.

In fiction, some novels contain a large element of fact, while works of narrative non-fiction involve elements of narrative and description that are surmised rather than documented. With both film and prose, creating a watertight divide between these forms is impossible.

The need to convey factual material in a highly readable and accessible way in an era when information is increasingly available through the news media and online explains the increasing popularity of narrative non-fiction. Further, as the twentieth century progressed, the idea that an 'absolute truth' existed, which could be recorded and written about, was gradually replaced by the notion that truth is subjective, and that all accounts of historical events are coloured by the individuals who participated in and witnessed them, and by those who write about them. And if all accounts are subjective, why shouldn't an author provide her own view on or construction of what happened.

Because narrative non-fiction is easy to read and follows a strong narrative, it usually appeals to a far wider audience than straightforward history, science, biography or memoir. In addition, the book can be easier to publicise because it describes 'true' events; the launch can be tied to a historical peg, such as the anniversary of a particular event, or the author can appear on television chat shows talking about her experience.

Top works of narrative non-fiction

Many narrative non-fiction books have become bestsellers. All these books shed light on an aspect of reality in such a way as to both inform and entertain readers.

- Truman Capote's *In Cold Blood* (1966) is the classic inside story of a murder investigation into the cold-blooded killing of two members of a Kansas family in the 1950s.

- Tom Wolfe's *The Right Stuff* (1979) tells the story of the US pilots who became the first astronauts in the early years of the Space Race.

- Sylvia Plath's *The Bell Jar* (1963) is a selective autobiography of the poet exploring her relationships and episodes of mental illness.

- John Berendt's *Midnight in the Garden of Good and Evil* (1994) explores a murder that took place in Savannah, Georgia.

- Jon Krakauer's *Into Thin Air* (1997) blends true mountaineering tales with the suspense of a good thriller.

- Frank McCourt's *Angela's Ashes* (1996) is the author's depiction of his childhood in Ireland.

- Joan Didion's *Salvador* (1983) captures the futility of this tiny nation's war with itself.

- Michael Herr's *Dispatches* (1977) offers a devastating account from the frontline of the Vietnam War.

- John Hersey's *Hiroshima* (second revised edition 1989) is a classic 1946 account of the nuclear bombing that brought the Second World War to an end and exposed the horrors of radiation.

- Linda Grant's *Remind Me Who I Am, Again* (1998) offers insight into her mother's deterioration from dementia.

- Ed Husain's *The Islamist* (2007) is a well-informed insider's guide to the netherworld of British Islamism.

- Blake Morrison's *And When Did You Last See Your Father?* (1993) is a son's memoir of his father and of coming to terms with his death.

Writing Narrative Non-Fiction

Writing narrative non-fiction requires both the skills and tools of a novelist and the fact-finding zeal of a good journalist. Most narrative non-fiction is issue-based – a story you want to tell, some facts you want to explain. But the more grippingly and imaginatively you tell this story, the wider the audience is likely to be.

Research your subject

First, do the research and get your facts straight. This can be a time-consuming task, involving reading a huge number of newspaper cuttings and interviewing experts in the subject or people who took part in or witnessed the events you cover. Many non-fiction novels are written by journalists, precisely because they have the necessary research and reporting skills.

Although a lot of information is available on the Internet, it often isn't enough for narrative non-fiction writing. You need to actually talk to experts and get their opinions and check the accuracy of newspaper reports.

If you're writing a purely factual account of an event, some details might not matter. But eyewitnesses can provide the kind of information a non-fiction novel demands – the smell, taste and sensations, the thoughts that went through someone's mind. Most people are willing to talk to someone writing a book connected with their experiences, and even those who aren't keen may want to have their say to 'get the record straight'.

Even better than recording someone else's experience, though, is actually undertaking it yourself. Someone may tell you what climbing a mountain feels like – but unless you do so yourself, you won't be able to describe it half so vividly. Obviously you may want to write about extreme experiences – being in a plane crash just to find out what it was like is possibly one step too far!

Research, then, often involves actually going to a place – to see what it really looks like, soak up the atmosphere and sometimes observe how time's changed it. Many historical books can be made more interesting by revealing how you, the writer, uncovered facts – turning what could be a dull account into something of a detective story.

Many of the great non-fiction novelists have completely immersed themselves in the subject they're writing about. Tom Wolfe, for example, was able to write *The Electric Kool-Aid Acid Test* by hanging out with Ken Kesey and the Merry Pranksters on their tour of the United States for over a year. Anne Rule, whose *The Stranger Beside Me* is a 1980 true crime novel about serial killer Ted Bundy, knew Bundy personally before and after his arrest for a series of murders.

Focus on people

Fiction is always first and foremost about people: their hopes and fears, motivations and relationships with others. The same applies to narrative non-fiction. The story must always revolve around the individuals involved, who need to become as well-developed and present to the reader as characters in a novel.

Of course, you need to find out as much as you can about the real individuals who are to be the central figures in your story. In order to speculate with some accuracy on how they thought and felt and what lay behind their actions, you must know them very well. Read as much as you can about them; find people who knew them; locate their letters, journals or writings; find photographs; discover what happened in their childhoods and how events may have shaped them.

Don't write:

> The great stock market crash of 1929 was the result of a speculative boom that had led hundreds of thousands of Americans to invest heavily in the stock market and even borrow heavily to buy more stock.

Do write:

> Joe Trader stood on Wall Street, his hands in his pockets, staring up into the bright blue sky. Just a few weeks ago his stocks had been worth $200,000, now they were worth only 10 cents.

Reflect on what you know

Often you need to spend some time thinking over the information you've gathered and sifting through it to see which details are really important.

Be ruthless in stripping away unnecessary information and irrelevant details. You may be tempted to put in something just because you have that piece of information, but unless that detail is necessary to the telling of the story, leaving it out is best.

Actually putting aside all the information you've gathered and simply writing the story, using your research to fill in the details as and when you need them, may be a helpful approach.

Involve the senses

As when you are describing things in fiction, try to use all the senses: sound, smell, touch and taste, as well as sight. Be specific about colours, scents and textures; try to make the readers feel that they're in the story.

Unlike a straightforward factual account, narrative non-fiction enables you to use imagery, similes and metaphors to enliven your writing. Chapter 7 covers involving the senses in your descriptive writing.

Add dialogue

Adding dialogue that you may never have heard, or not know was actually spoken, may seem odd. You can, of course, use people's memories of what your subjects said, but writers usually feel free to invent dialogue in narrative non-fiction.

Researching the way people actually spoke and using the words they might have used can invest your story with the sound and feel of real accuracy and truth, however. You may be able to find letters, diaries or recordings of the people who appear in your story, which can help you to imagine what they may have thought and how they would've spoken.

When reporting court cases and the like, you have a great deal of recorded dialogue to draw on; here, the problem is selecting what to use and what to leave out.

As with all dialogue, create an authentic voice for each character and make the dialogue work to take your story forward.

Create a structure

Perhaps the most challenging aspect of writing narrative non-fiction is creating a structure and timeline that work to both reflect the facts you're dealing with and also tell a good story.

As in fiction, many narrative non-fiction books start in the midst of the story, filling in background information through flashbacks. The non-fiction novel often starts later and ends sooner than a more traditional account of an event, which may spend more time describing its background and build-up, and then its aftermath and effects.

Many non-fiction novels use one of the great universal story themes to shape their narrative: rags to riches, redemption, the rise and fall of individuals and empires, the quest – I explore traditional plots and plot-related issues in Chapter 8.

Every story must pose a narrative question – something that readers wants to find out and which propels them forward. Many of the best works of narrative non-fiction have a secret or question buried within them – why did historical characters make the choices they did, who carried out the true crime, what happened to someone who set out on an adventure? Keeping this narrative question in the forefront of your mind helps you to sort your material, to see what you should put in and what you should leave out.

Examining Genres within Narrative Non-Fiction

If you want to write narrative non-fiction, reading similar books to see how the authors have treated their subjects is useful. Narrative non-fiction crosses over a number of other genres, and can be hard to categorise, but the following sections provide some examples of the main variants.

Adventure

True-life adventure stories can be highly readable. Jon Krakauer's books on exploration and mountaineering, *Into the Wild* and *Into Thin Air*, became best-sellers, as did Joe Simpson's *Touching the Void*, the story of his miraculous survival after an accident caused his climbing partner to leave him for dead. Piers Paul Read's *Alive: The Story of the Andes Survivors* is a classic tale of survival after a plane crash, and Steve Callahan's *Adrift: Seventy-Six Days Lost at Sea* tells how he survived at sea alone in an inflatable raft after his sloop capsized.

Autobiography and memoir

Autobiography at its best can read like a novel – and the line between the two genres can be very slim. In autobiographical narrative non-fiction, though, readers expect the events to be true, even though they know the account won't contain everything that happened, but only the most significant events.

Examples of highly readable autobiographies include Primo Levi's work, *If This is a Man*, *The Truce* and *The Periodic Table*. Frank McCourt's *Angela's Ashes* became an international bestseller. It tells the story of his childhood in Brooklyn and Ireland, and won the Pulitzer Prize for Autobiography in 1996. US President Barack Obama's *Dreams From My Father: A Story of Race and Inheritance* tells the story of his childhood in Hawaii and Indonesia and his troubled teenage years, community work and visit to his father's homeland in Kenya before his entry to law school.

Joan Didion's *The Year of Magical Thinking* is a beautifully written account of her husband's death and the year she spent mourning him.

Biography

Biographies can range from seriously scholarly works with footnotes to highly readable narratives such as the following:

- ✔ Jung Chang's *Wild Swans* tells the true story of three generations of her family in China, using the techniques of a novel.

- ✔ William Wharton's *Wrongful Deaths* describes the deaths of his daughter, her husband and their two daughters when a stubble fire burning out of control engulfed their car on the interstate highway. Wharton describes the book as a 'documentary novel'.

- ✔ Joyce Carol Oates's *Blonde* is referred to as a novel, but is actually a fic-tionalised biography of Marilyn Monroe.

Faking it

Some works of narrative non-fiction, especially memoir, have been exposed as more or less complete fabrications, cynically written to make money or grant fame to their authors.

James Frey's *A Million Little Pieces* tells the story of his years as an alcoholic, drug addict and criminal. The book was Oprah Winfrey's selection for the world's most powerful book club until police reports, court records, interviews with law enforcement personnel and other sources gave the lie to key sections of Frey's book.

Author Margaret B. Jones admitted that her bestselling memoir *Love and Consequences* (2008) was largely fabricated. She was not a half-white, half-Native American who grew up in a foster home and once sold drugs for the Bloods street gang; instead, she was a white woman who was raised with her biological family in Sherman Oaks and graduated from Campbell Hall, an exclusive private school in the San Fernando Valley.

Worst of all, perhaps, are the numerous 'memoirs' exploiting public interest in the Holocaust. Jerzy Kosinski's *The Painted Bird* (1965) was originally published as his

memoirs; however, he later admitted much of it was fabricated and the book's now sold as a novel. Misha Defonseca's memoir, *Surviving with Wolves* (2005), describes her childhood trauma when her Jewish parents were seized by the Nazis, forcing her to wander Europe alone until she was adopted by a pack of wolves. Later, a journalist exposed the reality that she didn't wander Europe, was raised by her grandparents and wasn't even Jewish. In 1993, Helen Demidenko won the Vogel Literary Award for her book *The Hand That Signed the Paper*, which describes her family's experiences in the Ukraine during the Holocaust. Later she admitted that her family had never lived in the Ukraine, but were from Britain and named Darville. In 1997, Binjamin Wilkomirski received the Jewish Quarterly-Wingate award for *Fragments: Memories of a Wartime Childhood*. The book purported to follow the author's childhood experiences in Auschwitz and Majdanek, but it later emerged that the author had never been in a concentration camp and had spent the Second World War in Switzerland.

Essay

Most people tend to think of essays as boring works written in dry academic prose, but this isn't always the case. Tom Wolfe's *From Bauhaus to Our House* tells the story of modern architecture with piercing insight and poetic language.

History

Dava Sobel's *Longitude*, telling the story of John Harrison's breakthrough in navigation at sea, was an international bestseller that spawned a whole series of similar books focusing on historical and scientific events. Sobel followed this book up with *Galileo's Daughter: A Historical Memoir of Science, Faith, and Love*, which brings the famous scientist vividly to life and offers a unique perspective on his trial for heresy and subsequent years under house arrest.

Serena Vitale's *Pushkin's Button* relates the story of the fatal duel that killed Russia's greatest poet and was hailed as 'a new literary form'. Charles Nicholls's *The Reckoning* describes the murder of the great playwright Christopher Marlowe, making it as gripping to read as a detective novel.

Medical and scientific

Frank Huyler's *The Blood of Strangers* is a series of true short stories from the emergency room of a US hospital, told by a physician in New Mexico. Oliver Sacks's books, such as *An Anthropologist on Mars* and *The Man Who Mistook his Wife for a Hat*, tell the stories of some bizarre medical case histories.

Reportage

Reportage is also known as *literary journalism*, and several fine books have been written by journalists. James Fenton's account, *The Fall of Saigon*, recalls how, as a 26-year-old freelance reporter, he witnessed the chaotic and terrifying final act of the Vietnam War. Ryszard Kapuscinski's *The Soccer War* tells the story of the 1969 conflict between El Salvador and Honduras. Both are highly acclaimed, as is *Salvador*, Joan Didion's account of the later civil war.

Travel

Travel writing has recently enjoyed a huge boom, with classic works such as Bruce Chatwin's *In Patagonia* and *The Songlines* and John McPhee's hypnotic tour of Atlantic City, *In Search of Marvin Gardens*, becoming bestsellers.

In *Holidays in Hell*, P. J. O'Rourke describes time spent in a host of uncongenial locations, from Christmas in El Salvador to a visit to Cold War Warsaw.

Ernest Hemingway's *Death in the Afternoon*, about bullfighting in Spain, is a true classic of its kind.

True crime

Truman Capote's *In Cold Blood* and Norman Mailer's *The Executioner's Song* have long been considered classics of the genre. *In Cold Blood* tells the story of a multiple murder and presents the horrifying facts while trying to examine the reasons behind the crime. Mailer's book, which he described as a 'true life novel', describes the nine months between Gary Gilmore's release on parole for the shocking murders of two strangers and his eventual execution.

Chapter 20

Travel Writing: Tales for Armchair Explorers

*T*he world has never been smaller and travel easier, which perhaps explains why so many people want to read about travel. Travel writing ranges from newspaper and magazine articles to narrative non-fiction accounts of exotic places and challenging journeys.

Because the world's shrunk and everyone travels, being a successful travel writer is harder than ever before. Finding new places to write about is also increasingly difficult. An important distinction needs to be made between travel guides – books that tell you how to get somewhere, offer some facts and history, and list hotels, restaurants and sites of interest – and travel literature, which involves narrative and provides deeper insights into the place and its people. Travel writing should always reveal something new – perhaps some neglected aspect of a place or an unexpected insight into it.

Reporting about Places: Travel Journalism

Many travel writers start with journalism. In theory, going off for some great holiday, all expenses paid, and writing a short article about it for a good fee seems easy. Travel journalism is, however, rarely that simple. And, although some people do make their living as travel writers, they're a very small minority.

Firstly, very few newspapers or magazines pay anyone to go travelling. If they do, they almost always send someone on their own staff or with an existing reputation. Secondly, most destinations have been written about before. You really have to find a new place, or a new angle on an old place, to have any chance of interesting an editor.

If you hope to break into this area, remember you're competing against:

- ✔ Highly competent journalists who have specialised in travel and already have good links with the newspaper or magazine you're pitching to.
- ✔ The celebrity writer who provides the basis for an article, which is then knocked into shape by an experienced sub-editor.
- ✔ A junior member of staff who wants a pay rise but instead has been placated with a trip that doesn't suit the editor's schedule.
- ✔ Hobby writers who are happy to travel and produce unpaid articles for the pleasure of seeing their name in print.

However, don't be too discouraged. You can try several ways to get those first crucial pieces published and become a professional travel writer:

- ✔ **Start a travel blog:** Pick a theme and get writing. Consider covering a specific place, the difficulties of travelling with small children, the people and customs of a country. A professional-looking blog and good writing can be an excellent showcase for your work.
- ✔ **Write for a travel website:** You can upload travel articles onto Internet sites. A few of them even pay you. Some sites are more interested in where you've travelled than your writing experience, so can be a way of breaking in. Try websites such as Travelmag (www.travelmag.co.uk) or Matador Network (www.matadornetwork.com) or the Travelers' Notebook (www.thetravelersnotebook.com), which currently pays a non-negotiable $25 per article.
- ✔ **Approach your local newspaper:** Most local newspapers don't employ dedicated travel writing staff. Contact your paper's feature editor about writing articles on destinations of interest to the readers. You'll almost certainly be asked to write *on spec* initially, which means you get paid only if your article's accepted. Try to find some kind of local link for your travel story.
- ✔ **Pitch to smaller magazines:** One of the many smaller travel magazines, or small magazines with travel sections, is much more likely to publish the work of a new travel writer. Specialist and trade publications may also provide opportunities. Don't expect to be paid much if you do get into print.
- ✔ **Make your piece stand out:** Pay attention to your writing and your readers by following these tips:

- Use a clear writing style. Know the point of the story, get to it quickly and convey it to the reader.

- Remember that you're part of the story. Make sure you create a strong sense of your personality, and what you thought or felt about the destination.

- Add life and colour. Use anecdotes, events and quotations to keep the article lively.

- Use all the senses. Recreate the total travel experience – sights, sounds, smells, textures and tastes – for your readers through the use of words alone.

- Include precise, practical and accurate information. Give readers information they can use.

Travel writing should be light, bright, lively and fun in tone – don't be afraid to make people laugh. When you leave your familiar world and go to new places, misunderstandings can lead to humorous events. Incorporate these mishaps into your pieces – people like to read about them, and can also use the information to avoid such things themselves. Farce and slapstick aren't in keeping, though, so do keep a sense of proportion.

Doing the Actual Travelling

Going travelling involves a number of choices: whether to do so cheaply or luxuriously, alone or with an organised group. These choices depend on your personality and the kind of travel writing you want to do. If you want to write something original, you almost certainly have to stray from the beaten track. But as most travellers want something safer and more structured, you might also do well to write about the kind of travel that most people want to take part in. Most travel writers want to keep their costs to a minimum.

Finding free or cheap travel

According to myth, travel writing entails lots of free trips to exotic locations. Unfortunately, this usually isn't so. Most travel writers get a small fee for their work, which doesn't even cover the cost of the journey.

Arranging free travel isn't easy but is sometimes possible. Many of the tips below apply to previously published writers – although not necessarily travel writers. Try one of these ploys:

- ✔ Offer to write an article for an airline's in-flight magazine in return for free or cheap tickets.

✔ Be part of a free press trip offered by a holiday operator – although you usually need to be on a list of known journalists.

✔ Ask for a free place on an activity holiday in return for writing about it. This ploy usually involves a double-bluff whereby you tell the magazine you're going on the holiday and the holiday people you're writing for the magazine. Sometimes the holiday organisation will agree to give you a free place only if the promised article actually appears.

Tickets bought online from specialist travel agencies rather than tour operators are often much cheaper. Round-the-world tickets are also a good deal – they just need organisation and planning. Avoid peak times such as school holidays.

Finding a good destination

Most people think they need to go somewhere really obscure to get started on their travel-writing career – Myanmar, a tiny island off the north coast of Norway or the depths of Borneo. This approach isn't always necessary – not many people want to travel to these places, and sometimes political reasons make it inappropriate to write a jolly travel piece about them.

Don't overlook the obvious. Sometimes people avoid the more common destinations because they're sure they've been written about before. However, these destinations are also more popular; far more people are going to plan a weekend to Paris than a trip to the North Pole. So, if you can find a new angle, a hidden place in Paris or an aspect of the city most people don't know, you may have more chance of selling it – and Paris is cheaper to research, too.

Research as much as possible about the place and the specific angle you're covering in advance to avoid wasting time (and money) on the trip trying to find out things you could have discovered at home. Hitting the ground running means you can get as much as possible out of the days actually in the location.

Read the travel pages of the newspaper or magazine you want to write for. Work out which places and angles have already been covered, so that you can identify a gap.

If you've already decided on your destination, try to find an off-beat place to visit or an unusual activity to try when you're there. You then have a new angle or experience to offer.

If something particularly interesting or dangerous happens to you, you may be able to write about the experience on your return. Obviously, though, you can't plan for this eventuality!

Travelling essentials

If you're travelling somewhere remote, take the following:

✔ **A money belt:** This should contain your tickets, passport, immunisation records, emergency cash, credit and debit cards, medication, travel insurance information, and emergency contact numbers. Keep your memory card here too so you don't lose all your pictures if your camera's stolen. If you're going somewhere particularly crime-ridden, keep a photocopy of everything in your money belt in your luggage. Also leave copies with someone who can fax or email them to you in an emergency.

✔ **Water purifying tablets:** These are cheaper than buying bottled water, and you're never at risk of running out.

✔ **Sunglasses and a spare pair of prescription glasses:** Always carry them in a rigid, crushproof case.

✔ **An adequate supply of any regularly taken or emergency medications:** Keep them in the original bottles, with prescription labels for identification. Also take useful medications such as painkillers. Antibiotics and syringes and needles may also be useful in some places.

✔ **A tiny compass:** This can be useful for urban as well as jungle navigation!

✔ **Comfortable, durable footwear:** Well-fitting shoes are a necessity and may be hard to find where you're travelling.

✔ **Long ultra-lightweight silk or synthetic underwear:** This garment can be worn under almost anything, and can double as pyjamas in cold climates or air-conditioned hotels, on trains and so on.

✔ **Safe sex supplies:** Sexually transmitted diseases are the most common health hazard for travellers, and condoms may not be easy to buy in some places.

Writing on the journey

Keep a notebook and record all the details of your trip. You may think you'll remember, but you often won't. You forget names and places, exactly how long a journey took, what things cost and the names of restaurants and hotels.

Also take time to describe small details: the exact colour of the rocks, scent and sight of a flower, sound of street vendors. Remember to use all your senses and record how it actually feels to be in a particular place. Describe times or places when you feel scared, lost, lonely, exhilarated or exhausted. Make sure you get the raw material down before you lose it.

Write down what people say and how they say it. Again, you may forget conversations and end up with cardboard characters spouting pidgin platitudes.

Be open to the unexpected. Sometimes things going wrong leads to the most exciting or interesting parts of a piece of travel writing. Getting arrested and describing the inside of a police station, your car breaking down and you spending the night sleeping under the stars in the desert, taking a wrong turn, getting lost and stumbling across a remarkable new and unspoiled place are just some examples.

Try to offer your reader something out of the ordinary; something that only someone who's been to the location would know. Take part in unusual activities or make an effort to meet and talk to new people to discover what life is like for them. Be curious. Penetrate below the surface seen by most tourists just passing through.

Stop at an Internet café periodically, type up your notes and email them home. If you lose or have your notebook stolen, only the most recent material will be lost.

Tackling a Travel Book

If you've managed to write some travel pieces, consider trying your hand at a book.

Travel classics

Read a selection of these classic and contemporary travel books to get a feel for the genre:

- Laurence Sterne's *A Sentimental Journey through France and Italy* (1768) is usually described as a novel but is arranged as a travelogue and is clearly based on his own experiences.

- Robert Louis Stevenson's *Travels with a Donkey in the Cévennes* (1879) recounts his 12-day, 120-mile solo journey through the sparsely populated and impoverished areas of south-central France and is one of the earliest accounts of hiking and camping outdoors as a recreational activity.

- Laurens van der Post's *The Lost World of the Kalahari* (1958) is a fascinating attempt by the South African soldier/explorer/writer to capture a forgotten way of life.

- Lawrence Durrell's *Bitter Lemons of Cyprus* (1957) blends the story of beginning a new

life in this beautiful place with an account of the beginnings of the conflict there. This narrative retains political relevance today.

- Eric Newby's *A Short Walk in the Hindu Kush* (1958) is an account of how Newby and his friend Hugh Carless set out to scale Mir Samir, an unclimbed glacial peak of 20,000 feet in Afghanistan. Newby's style was inspired by comic portraits of Englishmen abroad, which were popular at the time.

- Peter Matthiessen's *The Snow Leopard* (1978) is the story of his trek in Nepal with the zoologist George Schaller in search of the elusive snow leopard, using all the skills of a novelist to create a beautifully written and gripping narrative. His journey becomes a spiritual odyssey and the leopard becomes a metaphor for revelation.

- William Dalrymple's *From the Holy Mountain* (1997) describes a pilgrimage taking the author through a bloody civil war in eastern

Turkey, the ruins of Beirut, the vicious tensions of the West Bank and a fundamentalist uprising in southern Egypt. His book is a memorial to the slowly dying civilisation of Eastern Christianity and those who struggle to keep it alive.

✔ Bruce Chatwin's *In Patagonia* (1977) is an exquisite account of his journey through a far-off, rarely seen land, involving evocative descriptions, notes on the odd history of the region and anecdotes about the people he met.

✔ Heinrich Harrer's *Seven Years in Tibet* (1954) tells the story of how he was imprisoned by the British while mountain climbing in India at the outbreak of the Second World War and escaped into Tibet, where he met the young Dalai Lama, becoming his tutor and friend.

✔ Isak Dinesen's *Out of Africa* (1937) is a lyrical meditation, under a pen name, on Karen Blixen's life on her coffee plantation in Kenya, as well as a tribute to some of the people who touched her life there. It is also a vivid snapshot of African colonial life in the last decades of the British Empire.

✔ Peter Mayle's *A Year in Provence* (1989) spawned a thousand imitations. Chronicling his year as a British expatriate living in the village of Menerbes, it became an international bestseller.

✔ Rory MacLean's *Stalin's Nose* (1992) is a black and surreal travelogue through Eastern Europe after the fall of the Berlin Wall. It was followed by *Magic Bus* (2006), a history of the overland hippie trail through Asia.

✔ Bill Bryson's *Notes from a Small Island* (1995) describes his final trip around the UK, his home for over 20 years, before returning to his native United States. It provides a wonderful insight into the country and its people.

✔ Paul Theroux's *The Great Railway Bazaar* (1977) describes the writer's circular train ride from London via Iran, India, south-east Asia, Japan and Russia.

✔ P. J. O'Rourke's *Holidays in Hell* (1989) is a classic, bestselling guided tour of the world's most desolate, dangerous and desperate places. He provides an insight into the history and politics of his destinations, as well as what being there was actually like.

Choosing a genre

Books describing travel experiences have become incredibly popular in recent years. Consider these different categories:

✔ **The adventure journey:** This takes the reader to wild, far away and remote places, with an element of danger. It can involve extreme sports, or arduous journeys in difficult weather conditions or dangerous terrain.

In the past, such books tended to be written by serious explorers, mountaineers and so on. Now, with the strong demand for alternative travel experiences – driven partly by gap year students wanting excitement and adventure, and partly by older travellers who want to explore the world after their children have left home – books about adventure travel have become far more common.

✔ **The travelogue:** This offers a memoir or account of a journey, sometimes through one country and often across several continents. Examples include Dervla Murphy's *Full Tilt: Ireland to India with a Bicycle* (1965), in which she describes her adventures on a journey through Europe, Turkey, Iran, Afghanistan, and over the Himalayas into Pakistan and India, and *In Ethiopia with a Mule* (1969).

✔ **The relocation book:** This describes someone's experience of leaving one type of life behind and going off to embrace another, usually abroad. The narrative details how the expatriate adapts.

Peter Mayle's *A Year in Provence* kicked off this trend. Nowadays, finding a location that is popular enough to sell in reasonable quantities but hasn't already been done several times over isn't easy.

✔ **Serious reportage:** This is written by travel writers who've spent many years living and working in the country they describe; they speak the language and have many friends there. Journalists who've reported seriously on a country for a long time often write these books. Examples include Fitzroy Maclean's famous *Eastern Approaches* (1949) and Colin Thubron's *In Siberia* (1999).

Getting a concept

Nowadays, some new angle or concept appears the prerequisite for making your work stand out in the crowd. This notion has become so much a feature of travel writing that some authors parody the idea – consider Tony Hawks's bestselling book *Round Ireland with a Fridge* (1999). Travelling through Iceland on stilts, Paraguay with an elephant or Tibet by hang-glider is almost necessary before anyone will take notice of your idea.

Don't be cynical, though. Taking the journey that you want to, in the way you want to, is probably better than trying to do something highly gimmicky in the hope of landing a book contract. If you write well and find interesting things to say about your travels, someone may well show interest.

Chapter 21

All About Blogging

*T*he word blog has become so familiar in its short life (it emerged in the mid-1990s) that many people don't realise that it comes from the contraction of two words, 'web' and 'log'. A *blog* is a series of posts on a website arranged in reverse chronological order, so the most recent entry is displayed first and you scroll down to see the earlier ones.

Most blogs are personal observances or opinions, and most enable readers to respond to them, so that a conversation can develop between the reader and the blogger, and also between the readers themselves. In this sense, blogging is a unique, interactive medium for the new computer age.

Writing a blog allows everyone who has access to a computer to have a voice, which can potentially reach almost everyone in the world. It also acts as a great marketing tool for writers who want to promote their work online.

Making Your Blog Work for You

Blogging can be a great way to get started as a writer. It gives you an audience (even if only a small one at first) and a format in which to work. Most blogs are fairly short, which is also encouraging for a new writer. Blogging can be both a way to develop yourself as a writer and to market your writing.

Choosing a format

Blogs come in different genres:

✔ **Journalistic:** Many blogs are written by journalists reporting on a situation or story and updating it regularly. Others are more like comment pieces or columns.

If you refer to anything factual, always check your sources. You may like to include links and references, too.

✔ **Diary:** Diaries and autobiography are an obvious way of blogging, but you need more than 'something interesting happened to me yesterday' to keep readers hooked. You may be telling the story of your struggle with cancer; your search for a job, Mr Right or a missing child. As long as you offer a narrative thread, readers will come back for more.

Some journals or diaries are very funny, too; if people get a good laugh, they're much more likely to return to your site.

✔ **Fiction:** Some people write fiction blogs, delivering regular instalments of their novels. Others post short stories or vignettes. Some blogs even tell stories in comic book form.

Don't make your entries too long; short fiction works best in blog format.

Finding a clear and interesting title

The title is the most important part of your blog. Readers find your website via a search engine and decide to visit it based on its title. A *blog post* is similar to an article in a magazine – your most recent post is what visitors to your blog see first, but they can dig deeper to find earlier writings. The title for each post needs to be clear and inform the reader what it concerns – use the title like a headline to attract interest.

Avoid vagueness and ambiguity in your headlines. With millions of blogs and masses of new content being uploaded daily, readers often skim, scan and jump around from one site to another. Make your titles informative and interesting enough to entice readers to your blog. Give each post a title that attracts attention and is still relevant to the content.

Include keywords related to its subject in the title of your post. *Keywords* are those that people type into search engines to find information on a topic.

Make your title no longer than 10 to 12 words.

Paying attention to your posts

You can make your blog more appealing to attract and keep an audience. Try these tips:

- **Stay on topic:** Be clear about what kind of blog you're writing and your main topic. Most of your readers will be interested in what you write about a specific theme or area of interest. Don't be tempted to sidetrack about something that isn't relevant, no matter how funny or interesting it is – you risk losing a large chunk of your readership. Instead, define a topic and stick to it to create a loyal following of interested readers.

- **Be informative:** Keep up to date with the latest news and opinions on your topic. Before you write, check your facts; your reputation's at stake. If you're offering an opinion, be sure to qualify your post and make clear that it's a personal view.

- **Know that old news isn't news:** While blogging every day may be too much of a commitment for you, whatever you say must be current and accurate. If you leave too long a period between postings, your blog starts to look out of date and won't attract readers. Further, if you update frequently, search engines tend to pick up the pages more regularly.

- **Stick to a schedule and write regularly:** An occasional lapse or holiday is generally understood, but readers returning to find stale, outdated content are going to find another blog with similar content instead. The more regularly you post, the more your readership will grow.

  Surveys show that the most popular blogs tend to be updated once or twice a day, while the least popular offer new content only a few times a month.

- **Keep the writing clear and simple:** Make your posts easy to understand. Remember that the web's global and that some expressions, idioms and acronyms don't translate well to readers outside the UK; explain anything that isn't obvious.

- **Make an archive:** Archive old blog posts to develop a large resource of information about your topic, or to create a story or history. Make it easy for people to find what they're looking for – consider archiving your posts by topic rather than date. (Date order may be appropriate for personal journal rather than topic-driven blogs.) Along with the archives, include a search feature if you can.

- **Spell check and proofread before you post:** Reading through your post and correcting any mistakes before you upload it takes only a few extra moments. Doing so can save you the necessity of offering embarrassing explanations or apologies later. Remember that whatever you publish on the Internet can be found by others and archived, so even if you correct a mistake later, some damage will have been done.

✔ **Think before you post:** If you're writing something controversial, always give yourself a minute before uploading it. And never post late at night when you've had a few drinks or are very tired – you may regret what you've written in the morning!

✔ **Encourage comment:** Allow comments on your posts and always respond to them – blogs are all about dialogue. Half the point of having a blog is lost if you don't allow comments. They give you something to respond to, help you with new thoughts and contribute to a higher level of analysis. You also benefit from the additions, corrections, tips and other feedback from readers.

To encourage comments, don't require a sign-in, as this feature puts people off. Also, use spam-screening software.

Consider rewarding comment by displaying the names of people who do so most frequently, or by highlighting their responses. Commenting is the simplest way to create your own community of readers with similar interests.

✔ **Use visual images:** Long blocks of text often aren't read. Break up your post with visuals – graphs, charts, photos and even videos – as appropriate.

Avoiding pitfalls

A blog can be a dangerous tool: your current employer, future employer, mother, brother and previous lover can all read it.

To save yourself and others from embarrassment, or worse, avoid posting:

✔ Work-related items that are confidential, rude, company-related or otherwise self-damaging and unprofessional.

Some employees have been fired because of the content of their blogs. Respect your company's information restrictions, and don't jeopardise future employment opportunities.

✔ Personal information about other people. For example, your father may object to you publicising that he's an alcoholic! If you do describe something personal, avoid using names or surnames, or make up names.

Be wary of posting too much information about yourself – blog stalking is a reality. Don't give out personal information such as your full name, where you live or work, or details of your child's school.

Be prepared for some nasty comments or emails if you're blogging about controversial issues such as animal rights, religion or politics. If they threaten you directly, contact the police.

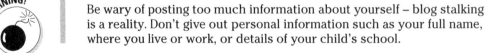

Always back up your commentary with reliable and varied sources.

Setting about Blogging

You can set up a blog page on your own website or use a blogging platform. A *blogging platform* is the software used to publish your content on the web. Just like choosing a word-processing program or web browser, you can select from a range of different blogging platforms.

Some blogging platforms are free; others charge a monthly or yearly subscription fee. Some are hosted online for you; others require you to host them on your own web server. Some are meant for individual bloggers; others for group publishing or small networks of bloggers.

Most blogs clearly display a time and date so that the reader can see exactly when each item was posted. You can update your blog daily or only when you want to record a specific event or something important.

Opting for a hosted blog

Using a hosted blogging platform is by far the easiest way to get started. www.Blogger.com, Wordpress.com, www.TypePad.com and www.xanga.com are the most popular. These services are free or charge a nominal fee, and getting started is very easy, involving minimum setup.

Don't be put off because getting started sounds technical – it isn't. You don't have to be a geek to be a blogger – even complete technophobes can follow the simple steps.

These platforms provide you with plenty of options for displaying your blog and text. Decide how you want your blog to look, including use of colour, number of columns and visuals. You can also usually include your own photo.

Check out other people's blogs to see how they organise the space, and to ascertain what you do and don't like about them. Pay attention to how easy – or difficult – finding information on each site is. Use this information to inform the layout of your own page.

Usually, you blog within your web browser and type online while connected to your site. You log in to your blog and create a new post just like writing an email, providing a subject line or title, followed by a body of text.

When writing online, remember that browsers can crash or web connections suddenly cut out, meaning you lose your material. Consider writing offline and then uploading your post when you connect to the Internet.

Desktop blogging applications are one solution to the problem of losing text. These applications – of which BlogJet (www.codingrobots.com/blogjet) is the most popular – act very much like word-processing and desktop publishing programs but upload your finished work onto your blog.

Unfortunately, on most hosted blogging services, you can't use your own domain name.

Read the small print of your blogging program. The copyright of your blog's content may be 'owned' by the company that puts it on the web for you.

Blogging on your own website

If you already have your own website, you can create a page for your blog and add to it as you go along. If you have a website designer or editor, he'll be able to advise you on presentation.

Write the content and then send it to your designer/editor to upload or do so yourself if you know how. For more technical aspects of blogging, see *Blogging For Dummies, 2nd Edition* by Susannah Gardner and Shane Birley.

Making your first post

After you've set up your website or hosted space, you're ready to write your first post. If you haven't done much writing, this piece can seem hard. Even if you've written a lot, though, making your first post special and unique isn't easy.

Don't put too much pressure on yourself. If your blog's factual, think about the main thing you want to say and then say it. Keep your posts fairly short and not too complicated, and try to express yourself simply and clearly. If you're writing a diary or comment blog, imagine that you're talking or writing a letter or email to a friend.

Write in your own voice. Don't be afraid to be individual, but avoid being too mannered or wacky – unless this really is your thing – because such a persona may put people off. Readers come back because they like the way you come across or they're getting something unique.

Start with a simple 'Welcome to my blog' post. Say why you've set it up and give a brief overview of the subjects you'll be covering. Doing so helps you to focus your own mind as well as that of your readers.

Publicising Your Blog

Spending a lot of time on your blog is pointless if nobody's going to read it, so taking a few basic steps to help connect your blog to other web users is important.

You can publicise your blog by *pinging* the major weblog tracking sites. Don't worry if you don't understand the process – it simply means that your service or software sends a signal to the tracking sites to alert them to the fact that you've posted a new entry. Most blogging services handle pinging automatically. If your software doesn't ping, try Ping-O-Matic (www.pingomatic.com), a service sending signals to 14 different sites. You can also find a list of ping services online, for example at www.dailyblogtips.com/ping-list/.

Making use of RSS feeds

RSS (Really Simple Syndication) is a widely supported format for feeds. A *feed* delivers regularly updated summaries of web content, including headlines, which link to full versions of that content. You need to include your blog's content in an RSS feed to increase readership and distribution.

When you subscribe to a feed using a feed reader, you can quickly see summaries of new information in one place. You can go to a free website (such as www.feed43.com) that enables you to download the RSS symbol with a link to your page. People can then subscribe to a download of new items from your page when they click on it.

Do whatever you can to help your readers find you and navigate around your site. Make subscribing to your feed easy by placing the orange RSS button in a highly visible location.

Telling your old friends and making new ones

When you're ready, tell friends about your blog and ask them to pass the information on. Link to each other's blogs and comment on posts.

Visiting, reading and commenting on other people's blogs, whether you know them or not, is a good way to make yours popular. Link to other sites covering the same or related topics. On most sites, a link to your blog is automatically included in your comment; thus the more blogs you comment on, the more people can link to yours.

Linking to other established websites is also a good way to network and make yourself known in your niche. Building a network with other people in the blogosphere is the best way to attract readers. Making friends online is a great way to meet people you'd otherwise never come into contact with while simultaneously expanding the reach of your blog.

Most blog audiences are small, but with time and regular updates audiences grow. Bloggers may never have more than a few hundred readers, but the people who return regularly are generally interested in what you have to say.

Using your blog to publicise you

While you need to publicise your blog, your blog can also work to publicise you. Many businesses, artists and writers blog regularly on their websites to keep bringing people to them. Search engines favour websites that are updated regularly, and blogging is a great way to make sure that your content's always new. Posting new material also increases your chance of appearing high on search-engine list results.

Include an 'about' page. Your blog reveals your personal views, so introduce yourself to your readers. Don't blog anonymously.

Turning blogs into books

Some people write a blog with the intention of later getting their work into print; others find that their blog is successful and want to get it to a wider audience through bookshops. You can turn your blog into a book by publishing it yourself or, if you have enough readers, finding a commercial publisher interested in your product. Many successful bloggers have been offered book deals.

One of the first blogs to make the transition to a book, in 2003, was that of a Baghdad blogger known as Salam Pax, who wrote an online war diary from Iraq. Ahdaf Soueif's *Baghdad Burning: Girl Blog from Iraq* (2005) is another example.

Belle de Jour's *The Intimate Adventures of a London Call Girl* (2005) had already caused a blogging sensation. Writing under a pseudonym, her posts revealed intimate details about her working life.

Other bloggers have self-published or used online publishers Lulu.com. The Blooker Prize is a competition run by Lulu.com for the best book created from a blog. The 2007 winner was Colby Buzzell's *My War: Killing Time In Iraq*. Julie Powell's 2006 winner, *Julie and Julia: 365 Days, 524 Recipes, 1 Tiny Apartment Kitchen* has been made into a film by Nora Ephron, starring Meryl Streep and Amy Adams.

Part V
Finding an Audience

'It's not grabbing you is it?'

In this part . . .

It doesn't matter how brilliant your work is if nobody is ever going to hear or read it. Getting your work published is tough – you have a lot of competition. This part helps you to understand how the publishing industry works and why things are as challenging as they are. Printing a book, putting on a play, or making a film costs a lot of money and people in the industry want to be fairly sure they're going to get a return for their investment, so you need to listen to what they have to say.

This part explains how the whole scene works and gives you some tips to help you to break through.

Chapter 22

Finding Professionals to Publish Your Book

In This Chapter

▶ Meeting publishers

▶ Seeing how publishing works

▶ Working out the maths

▶ Going through the process

▶ Looking for agents

▶ Consulting the pros

▶ Publishing yourself

*I*f you've done a lot of writing, inevitably, at some point, you start thinking about how to get your work published.

You may have been writing from the beginning with a bestseller in mind, or you may have written for yourself with no thought of finding an audience until someone responds warmly to your work and suggests that you send it off somewhere. Whatever the case, you need to research all the possibilities thoroughly before you approach an agent or publisher.

Let me be completely honest about the situation from the outset. Your chance of being accepted by a reputable publisher is small. Far more people write books than outlets exist for publication. Agents and publishers are awash with unpublished manuscripts, and many talented writers are out there competing for a small number of slots.

Even if you do manage to get published, your book is unlikely to be a bestseller. The great majority of published books sell a few hundred or thousand copies, get a few small or even no reviews, go out of print fairly rapidly, and make very little money for the authors – or publishers.

On the other hand, every publisher's dream is to find a new talent, publish the book, win a major prize and launch a starry career. Agents and publishers are actively looking for that special book. They don't always know which book it will be, and often don't even recognise it when they find it. So don't despair – a very small chance exists that your book might just be the one.

Getting to Know the World of Publishing

Before setting out to sell your work, familiarise yourself with the process of publishing, both from an editorial and commercial angle. With this knowledge, you know where agents and publishers are coming from and why they make the decisions they do.

The publishing world is divided into the world of the big commercial publishing houses, with huge budgets, many imprints and long lists of titles, and the small independents, which publish a handful of titles a year and scrape by on goodwill and sometimes with the help of limited Arts Council grants. Most of the former are part of huge media empires and are international in scope, dealing with newspapers, journals and films, as well as books. Many of the latter are run from home or small shabby offices, and many of the staff are on tiny salaries or are even unpaid. In the middle are a few independent houses that make enough money to run an office and pay staff, but aren't able to spend large amounts of money on marketing or advances to authors.

Being absorbed in mainstream publishing

Big names you're familiar with, such as HarperCollins, Random House, Macmillan, Pearson (Penguin) and Hodder Headline are considered mainstream publishers with a fair amount of money and generally a considerable history behind them.

Each major publisher has a number of imprints. An *imprint* is a division within a publishing house, a kind of brand name that appears on the cover of the book. Each imprint may act like a small publishing house within the bigger company, with its own editors, unique design and particular philosophy. Many imprints are publishing houses bought up by the big companies in the 1980s, and well-known examples such as Arrow, Chatto & Windus, Doubleday, Harvill Secker, Hutchinson, Jonathan Cape and William Heinemann are now all fiction lists owned by Random House.

A number of publishers specialise in specific types of books, such as those for children and non-fiction areas like military history, health and do-it-yourself. A number of specialist poetry publishers also exist.

Go to the publishers' websites to identify their various imprints and work out what kinds of books they publish.

Alternatively, visit a bookshop, choose the kind of books you like and identify the imprint on the spine. Next, check the *copyright page* (the page near the front carrying all the copyright and publishing information) to see which big company the imprints are part of. Have a good browse to see which publishers own which imprints.

One of the problems of the big publishers buying up small imprints is that only about five major houses now exist in the UK. And while you may believe that you can send your book to the editors at all the different imprints, in fact they all share information with one another and use the same sales and marketing staff. So if your book is turned down by one of these imprints, all the others will probably follow suit.

Because you get so few chances to submit your book to the big publishing houses, make sure your manuscript is your absolute best effort – don't squander the opportunity.

Adding in the advantages of a smaller publisher

Many writers think that being published by the big houses is best, but this isn't necessarily the case. Significant advantages to being published by a smaller reputable independent publishing house include:

- ✔ The big houses have *front list* titles that are heavily promoted, and other books are then left to sink or swim mostly on their own. For a smaller house, every book they publish is a big book and they spend time and effort marketing it.

- ✔ You usually have a closer relationship with the staff, who have fewer authors to handle and often take more time and trouble over the editing process and getting publicity for your book. At the big houses, your first book competes for publicity with those by big-name authors who inevitably are put forward for review slots, interviews and so on.

- ✔ Every publisher can enter a limited number of books – usually just two or three – to the big literary competitions such as the Man Booker and Orange Prizes and the Costa Award. Big houses tend to put forward their well-known authors. Some smaller independents may enter your book for these prizes – and almost every year books from small presses make it at least onto the longlist, giving a real boost to these books' chances for winning and increasing the attention they attract.

Examining the selection process

Understanding how books are selected by publishing companies can be a big help when you come to submit a book for publication. Focus your energies on negotiating your way through the hurdles.

Dealing with mainstream publishers

Most big publishers don't read unsolicited manuscripts. You need an agent to submit manuscripts to them (see the 'Finding Out About Agents' section later in this chapter). If you submit your manuscript on the off-chance, the best outcome is that it is returned straightaway with a standard letter – if you provided a stamped addressed envelope. The worst is that your work is simply recycled or binned.

Publishers used to keep a *slush pile* – manuscripts sent in without an agent or personal recommendation. Once a month the pile of manuscripts would be tipped onto the boardroom table to be sifted through. Editors would read the first and last paragraph and a page or two in the middle, and if the material didn't strike them as exceptional, out it would go. Usually only one or two in a hundred would be selected for further attention. Now agents are the ones sitting on slush piles.

You can sometimes get a manuscript read without an agent if you're fortunate enough to know an editor or member of staff at a publishing company. Maybe you're acquainted with an author who's already published by them, who can recommend your work. Manufacturing such relationships isn't really possible, however.

If a book is submitted to a publishing house via an agent, it will be read. How quickly this reading happens depends on the reputation of the agent and the closeness of the relationship between that particular person and the editor.

Commissioning editors are responsible for buying books. Usually, they send books out to reliable and trusted readers – the editors themselves don't have time to read everything they're sent. If the book comes back with a good report, the editor then reads it.

In the past, if the editor liked the book that was the end of the story – it was published and promoted. Now, however, the book has to be pitched to a big editorial board or at an acquisitions meeting, involving not only the editors, but also the sales and marketing staff. The latter haven't read the book, but must take a view on its saleability based on the editor's pitch. The sales and marketing team estimate how many copies the book's likely to sell and if it can be promoted well.

Sometimes the publishing house decides that they'll only take a book if their US counterpart also wants it (meaning a bigger audience and *print run* – the number of copies printed – which make the book more profitable). The book is then reviewed by the US editors and you have to await her decision.

If the UK editor gets the go-ahead, they then offer you a deal. Authors are usually paid on a royalty basis. They receive a percentage of the cover price or the sums received by the publisher from the bookshops when a book is sold. As sales figures take a long time to come through, authors are usually offered a down-payment, which is an advance on royalties. The size of the advance is linked to the number of copies the publishing house thinks they can sell. You get to keep the advance even if the book doesn't sell as well as expected.

Looking at the process in a small publishing house

In smaller independent presses, usually someone does read unsolicited manuscripts. These publishers can't afford to compete with the big houses on advances for the more profitable-seeming novels, so they're always looking out for hidden gems.

They use readers, too, though often unpaid; many small publishers ask students to go through manuscripts for them. If they have a pile of manuscripts to wade through, these readers often just read the first few pages before making a decision.

If a reader likes the book, it goes to the editor. If the editor also really likes it, he can usually make the decision to publish, although sometimes he needs to consult with the director or other members of the team.

Small publishing companies can't usually offer much of an advance, even if they think the book will sell well, as they don't have the cash flow.

Fitting into slots and schedules

Getting published is sometimes just a matter of luck. All publishing houses have a schedule or timetable of the books that they plan to publish, and they work quite a long time in advance. In practice, these schedules are always slipping and changing. A major author may become ill or develop an intractable case of writer's block and deliver his book late, leaving a gap in the schedule. The editor may then be frantically casting about for a book to fill it. If your book crosses the editor's desk at this point, and he likes it but is hesitating, the need to fill a slot may tip him over into taking it.

Sometimes a publisher really likes a book, but their lists are full for the moment and they can't really see when they can slot it in. With small publishers, other factors may also be relevant; for example, if they have a small list and published a holocaust-related novel last year, they may not want to do another one this year, even if the manuscript's very good.

Look at the titles released by a particular publisher to make sure that they take the kind of book you've written. Also check out if they've published something very similar to yours in the last year or two. If they have, your book has practically no chance of being accepted.

Looking at How Publishing Houses Are Organised

Large and medium-sized publishing houses have certain departments, which I explain in the following sections. You won't be in direct contact with all of them; you generally deal with the editorial department. You also liaise with the publicity department about promoting the book and may occasionally meet the sales and marketing team at a sales conference or book launch.

Editorial

The editorial people are responsible for reading, commissioning and editing books and dealing with the authors. At the top are the *commissioning editors,* who take on a book and champion it, the *desk editors* or *copy-editors* who work closely on the manuscript and then come the *editorial assistants* who help them out and are often training to move up the ladder.

Never neglect the editorial assistants. Often new and keen, they can sometimes give you access to people higher up. Always be polite and try to create a good relationship with them.

Publicity

The press office staff contact journalists and literary editors to solicit reviews. They also organise appearances at literary festivals, bookshop readings and signings, and radio interviews.

If your book has a newsworthy angle, the press office staff try to get news or feature coverage.

Art

The art department decides on the look and style of a book, and designs its jacket and other marketing materials. This area is highly specialised, and a great deal of thought goes into the design, especially of the jacket. *Roughs* – the sample designs and mock-ups – are presented to the editorial and marketing departments, and often the sales team are consulted too, before a final decision is taken.

Marketing

The marketing staff work out how to promote the book and design marketing and advertising campaigns.

The marketing department prepares all the advertising, such as ads in the book trade magazines or even, for major titles, in the mainstream press. They organise the sales conference where the book is presented to the sales team. They also work with the sales team in meeting the buyers for major bookshops and try to get the book into special promotions.

Production

The production team organises the typesetting (laying out the text and artwork on the pages) and printing of the book. They find a reliable, competitively priced printer and arrange for delivery of the completed books to the warehouse.

The sales team

A large publisher has a team of sales representatives who sell books to the buyers in bookshops. Smaller publishers usually use specialised sales teams representing several companies; the sales staff earn money on commission.

Increasingly, sales are dictated by the key buyers for large bookshop chains, who take books centrally. Few individual shops manage their own buying nowadays.

Bookshops chains often use a central stock system. If a book is in *core stock*, every branch must order it and re-order a copy automatically every time one sells. This system can make a huge difference to the sales of a book.

The reps also put books forward for special promotions, such as Book of the Month and 'three for the price of two' offers. The bookshops make the final choice, though.

The distributor

Large publishers distribute their own books from computerised warehouses. Small independent presses usually use a specialist book and/or magazine distributor to warehouse and send out theirs. Because they're small and have a number of clients, these distributors often take longer than a big publisher to get the books into the shops.

The rights team

Sometimes when you sign a contract, the agent keeps the rights to publish your book in foreign countries – *foreign rights* – and tries to sell them to overseas publishers. Not all agents sell foreign rights, though, and not all books are agented, so each publisher has a team to do so.

Translation costs are so high – a good literary translation of an average length book costs about £10,000 – that most books have to have sold in considerable quantities in the home market before a foreign publisher will express interest.

The rights team also deal with domestic rights; serialisations in newspapers, book clubs, audio, large print and digital.

Tallying the Mathematics of Publishing

Unfortunately, the money made from the sale of each book has to be split so many ways. Table 22-1 gives you a rough breakdown of the costs associated with selling a £7.99 paperback.

Table 22-1	Cost Breakdown of a £7.99 Paperback
Type of Cost	*Cost Per Copy*
Production: typesetting, jacket design	40p
Printing	£1.00
Royalties (your money!)	60p
Salesforce distribution	£1.00
Trade discount at an average of 50%	£4.00
Publisher's overheads	50p
Publisher's profit	49p

Print runs

The more books you print in one go, the cheaper the unit price becomes. Printing only 1,000 paperbacks of average length costs about £2,000 – or £2.00 a copy – which is really too expensive. Printing 10,000, however, means the cost is about £6,000, or 60p a book – much better.

So, if the publisher sells 1,000 books, they make only £490 profit. Publishing is thus a high volume business – you need to sell lots of books to make money. Unfortunately, most books don't make money. However, once in a while a book sells by the bucket-load, and this highly successful title subsidises all the others.

Publishers seldom know which books are going to be successful. Books by well-known authors are usually a fairly safe bet – and publishers can use sales figures from their previous titles to predict the success of new ones. New authors are a complete unknown – so publishers keep publishing their novels in the hope that a few win prizes or become popular by word-of-mouth and become bestsellers.

Understanding trade discounts

When books are sold into bookshops, the latter takes a proportion of the money made on the sale – the *trade discount*. In the past, about 35 per cent of cover price was the standard discount, leaving a reasonable share for the publisher. Now, however, bookshops demand bigger discounts to make more profit. If the publisher doesn't agree, the bookshops don't stock the book. Bookshops also increasingly order from big wholesalers, who also take a cut, making the discount around 50 or 55 per cent.

When a book is sold in a big 'three for two' promotion, the discount rises to 60 per cent, and some shops demand as much as 70 per cent. When a book is sold at high discount, the author's royalty has to be adjusted downwards or the publisher would make a loss on every sale.

Being Accepted into the Publishing Process

Having your manuscript accepted for publication starts a process of engagement with contracts, publishers and editors. This is a time of anticipation – and hard work. The process goes something like this:

Bookshops and the book trade

If you think trying to get a book accepted by a publisher is hard, then spare some thought for the publisher, who's trying to get their books taken notice of by the book trade. The sales reps are the people on the ground who trudge from bookshop to bookshop, showing the buyers the advance information sheets and book jackets and talking each title up.

The senior rep and marketing people also talk to the chief buyer at Waterstone's, Borders and other bookshop chains, and also the big wholesalers that stock books and send them – usually within 24–48 hours – to the small independent bookshops who can't hold much stock and need to order titles at short notice.

Recently, the big bookshops have begun to diversify, selling stationery, magazines, CDs and DVDs, some gifts and even offering coffee shops. Bookshops are now threatened by Internet sales, following the success of Amazon and other online bookstores; 2 per cent of books were sold online in 1999 and nearly 10 per cent a decade later.

Independent bookshops can still thrive and be an invaluable support to a local author. Buy all your books in these shops and attend events – if you support them, they'll support you and reward you by hosting launches, readings and signings.

1. **You receive a letter of acceptance.**

   The publisher writes to you – or your agent – accepting the book (possibly on certain conditions, like carrying out some edits) and stating the advance and royalties payable. If you find the terms acceptable, you move on to Step 2.

2. **You and the publisher negotiate a contract.**

   The contract lays out all the terms on which the book will be published, such as copyright, the date of publication, arrangements for accounting, terms for royalties in the home market and for translations and foreign editions, and for all the subsidiary rights, such as audio books, book-club editions, serialisations and large print editions. It spells out arrangements for *remaindering* (selling unsold books at remainder bookshops) and reversion of rights if the book is allowed to go out of print, which means that you take back the rights to the book and are free to sell it elsewhere.

   The Society of Authors offers a free contract-reading service to members. If you're offered a book deal, joining is well worthwhile, especially if you don't have an agent to vet a contract for you. Check out www.societyofauthors.org.

3. **The editing process begins.**

   The editor usually does an initial structural edit and may suggest major changes, such as deleting or adding some material, changing the order of the chapters or writing additional scenes.

When you submit your manuscript or computer file, a copy-editor goes through it correcting spelling, punctuation and grammar errors, checking the accuracy of any names, places and other factual text, paying attention to continuity issues and applying the *house style* – the preferred spelling, punctuation and printing rules the publisher uses.

4. **The editors prepare an *advance information sheet.***

   This sheet contains all the book's details; its length, format, ISBN (*International Standard Book Number* – a unique identification assigned to every published book), a *blurb* (a short summary) and author biography. This sheet goes to the publisher's sales team so that they can start selling the book to the bookshops.

5. **The finished manuscript is typeset.**

   As the author, you're sent proofs to check. *Proofs* are the pages of the typeset book, which show the author and editor exactly what the pages look like in the finished book.

   You're allowed to make reasonable changes; huge amounts of rewriting at this stage aren't usually acceptable. You usually get three weeks to read and correct the proofs.

6. **You're approached to help with the writing of the back cover blurb, although the publisher has the final say.**

   You also need to write a biography and perhaps provide a photograph of yourself.

7. **You're sent the designs for the cover.**

   Although your opinion is sought, you don't have the last say on how your book looks. Book jacket design is a highly specialised business and can be very expensive, so your amateur opinions and likes and dislikes aren't usually appreciated.

8. **The book is printed and advance copies are sent out to the press for review.**

   Advance copies can be special proof copies with marketing information on the back jacket. Sometimes the finished copies are used, but sent out ahead of the official publication date.

   If you have any contacts in the press or with book reviewers, now is the time to use them!

   You receive a limited number of free copies, usually 10 or 12; you can also buy copies at author discount.

9. **The book is officially published and available in bookshops.**

   Most books by new authors don't receive a proper *launch* – a party, reading or event celebrating the publication, which can be a good marketing opportunity. If you want a launch, you may be expected to organise it yourself at your own expense. Bookshops are usually happy to host an event as they get to sell lots of books. Sometimes the publisher chips in to help with the costs of wine and nibbles. Invite all your friends and relatives and make sure they don't leave without buying your book!

Finding Out About Agents

As most publishing houses don't read books that aren't recommended to them by literary agents, you need to get taken on by an agent if you're serious about getting published.

Literary agents aren't hard to find, many of whom used to work in publishing and know other editors and agents. You can fairly easily get hold of a list of agents, but knowing which to approach can be difficult.

Most agents now have websites, so look them up and see which authors they have on their lists and what kind of writing they take on. Some agents, for example, don't handle children's fiction, while others specialise in crime or literary fiction. Don't waste agents' time by sending them material they don't handle.

Approaching an agent who publishes a writer you like or admire, or who publishes the kind of books that you like to read is a helpful approach. Choosing a book is highly subjective, so picking an agent whose taste is obviously very different to your own is pointless. Most writers have websites and list their agent under their contact information, and all agencies have websites listing their authors.

Many agents belong to the Association of Author's Agents. In order to join, an agent must have been established for at least one year and be earning commissions of at least £25,000 a year. A young, new agent may thus not be able to register yet, so the fact that she's not a member doesn't automatically mean she's no good. However, approaching an agent who's a member of the AAA does give you some confidence that she's established and abides by a professional code of conduct.

Realising how agents work

Some literary agents work for huge agencies, such as Curtis Brown, PFD or AP Watt. Others work in small agencies of just a few people. Some agents work alone, often from home. No particular advantage is gained by selecting one over the others, as long as you and the agent get on well, he has a good reputation and is prepared to work hard to get your book published.

Finding someone you like and respect and can have a good working relationship with is crucial when choosing an agent. The relationship won't work if the agent thinks he's a supreme being and you're too terrified to phone him, or if you're too familiar and think you can ring him every day and witter on.

Always meet potential agents in person to ensure you can establish a good relationship with them. Don't commit until you know the chemistry's right.

An agent needs to protect her reputation in the business and maintain good relationships with the editors of the major publishing houses. As a result, in a dispute between you and your publisher, your agent may in fact take the publisher's side over yours, even though she's meant to be representing you. She may calculate that she has more to lose in alienating the editor who publishes several of her authors and might buy more books from her than in falling out with you, especially if you're an unproven, first-time author. Put yourself in your agent's shoes and understand why she's acting in a certain way, even if it doesn't appear to be in your interests.

Be clear about the agreement you have with the agent and be conscious of what you can reasonably expect from her. You may need to accept at the outset that your agent holds all the power; she won't like it if you try to boss her around and tell her where you want her to send your book. You have to be a successful author who's making lots of money for your agent before the power balance shifts in your favour.

Be aware that the literary world is a small one, and people know and talk to one another. You need an agent precisely because she has all these contacts. Publishers and agents may seem to be rivals, but many are friends and meet one another at literary lunches, book fairs, prize ceremonies and book launches. You can't afford to get a reputation for being a difficult author. But you don't want to be a doormat either. Maintaining equilibrium in the author–agent relationship isn't easy!

An intrinsically awkward relationship

I think the author–agent relationship is intrinsically awkward. In normal situations when you employ someone to work for you, you may take their advice but you know you're the boss. A lawyer, builder or estate agent is taken on and fired by you. With a literary agent, however, the relationship's usually the other way round. He takes you on, and you're eternally grateful to him for doing so. You feel that he's in the driving seat, not you – yet you're the one who pays him out of your earnings if you do get published.

Approaching an agent

Being completely straightforward is the best way to approach an agent.

First, ring up and talk to the agent's assistant or secretary; say you've written a book and are looking for someone to represent you. Ask if he's taking on new authors. An agent usually likes to have a limited number of clients, say about 20; if he represents more than this, he can't do a decent job for each author. If you ring a big agency, they may say that their senior agents aren't available, but they do have more junior agents who are looking for new clients.

Junior staff can be very helpful in providing information, and can make all the difference to getting your book read. Also, some of them may become agents themselves later on.

Having a personal contact in the world of publishing is priceless. Most bookshops hold regular events where authors read or launch their books, and many of these are open to the public. Often the author's agent or publisher is present. Attend these events and don't be afraid to approach the author, agent or publisher. Don't bore him senseless about your book – just say simply that you've written a novel (or memoir or whatever it is) and you'd be thrilled if he'd take a look at it. People are generally amazingly open and friendly at these events.

Avoid sending your manuscript to agents at their busiest times of year:

- ✔ Not during the first week of September; the agent will just be back in the office after the summer holiday and be overwhelmed.
- ✔ Not just before, during or immediately after the Frankfurt Book Fair in October (you can look up the dates on the Internet).
- ✔ Not just before, during or immediately after the London Book Fair (usually in April).

You also need to avoid the summer and Easter holidays and the run-up to Christmas.

Sending in your manuscript

Most agencies want to see a synopsis and the first three chapters of your book. You also need to write a covering letter. The next sections cover these in detail.

Don't send in your submission by email unless specifically asked to. Doing so puts the onus on the agent to print it out, which is time-consuming and expensive. Most agencies delete email submissions unread or send a polite reply rejecting it.

The synopsis

The *synopsis* is a factual summary of your book, demonstrating how the material is organised. For a non-fiction book, you can provide a chapter by chapter breakdown, with a few sentences explaining the contents of each. For a novel, keep the synopsis brief, and don't so much describe the theme as the way the story unfolds.

Try to keep your synopsis to one page, and certainly no longer than two. Don't use tiny type so that you can cram more details in – keep it short and simple.

The three chapters

Even if the agent doesn't make this clear, she wants to see the first three chapters – don't send chapters 9, 17 and 33 because you think they're better!

Make these first three chapters as good as you possibly can before you send them out into the world.

The covering letter

The simpler this letter is, the better. It must just:

- ✔ State if the book's a novel, memoir or autobiography, for example.
- ✔ Give an idea of the length (as a word count).
- ✔ Reveal the title, and one or two sentences describing the book.

Say a few words about yourself if they're relevant; for example, if you're professionally involved in the subject matter or the book's based on your personal experience. If you've already had something published, say so; explain when and by whom it was published, and provide a web address if relevant.

Don't make value judgements. Your role isn't to say how good you think your book is; the agent needs to make her own assessment. In particular, don't boast – but don't put yourself down either. Avoid telling agents that you think the book would make a great film with your favourite film stars as the main characters.

Never give an agent a deadline for getting back to you. She won't appreciate an attempt to bully her into prioritising your work over all the other people in the queue.

Below is a sample covering letter that may well inspire the agent's interest:

Dear *(Agent's name, correctly spelt)*

I enclose a synopsis and the first three chapters for my debut novel, *The Stars are Shining*. This is an 80,000-word novel about the life and loves of a young girl growing up in wartime Britain who trains as a nurse and volunteers to work with wounded soldiers.

The novel draws on my experience working overseas reporting on the work of the International Red Cross in various war zones and on my mother's wartime diaries.

I have written for *Medical News* and my articles have occasionally been published in *The Independent* and *The Observer*, and one of my short stories was shortlisted two years ago for the Asham Award. A piece of my short fiction was published in *Mslexia*.

I do hope you will enjoy the novel, and I look forward to hearing from you.

Best wishes

(Name)

 If, after six weeks or so, you haven't heard from the agent, chase her up. A postcard asking politely if she's had time to read your book is an appropriate approach. If you still hear nothing, forget about it and send the book off to someone else. Don't withdraw the book from the first agent – she may come back in three months' time and say she loves it!

Sending the book out to three or four agents at once is fine, as each may take time to assess it; contacting agents one at a time may take several years!

Getting Your Book Ready to Send Out

Publishers used to be in a position of recognising raw talent and inviting a promising new author to lunch to talk about his writing. They'd offer encouragement and comment on manuscripts, and often put in a lot of work nurturing talent and knocking a book into shape. Sadly, those days are long gone. Editing books is a highly skilled job, and is expensive, so publishing houses are cutting costs wherever they can. Nowadays, most books are expected to come in ready to go and receive just a cursory edit.

Knocking your book into tip-top shape

Agents now often employ editors to work with authors to get their books in shape before they're offered to publishers. Some agents, especially those who used to be editors in publishing houses, do the job themselves. Nowadays agents want a manuscript to be as polished as possible before they send it out, to safeguard their reputations and give the book the best possible chance of being accepted.

However, agents themselves are under pressure and receive large numbers of manuscripts, especially now many of the big publishers refuse to read manuscripts themselves. So the onus is on you, the writer, to get your book into shape before you submit it to agents.

Consulting an editorial consultancy

An *editorial consultancy* is an agency set up to advise authors and assess manuscripts so that writers can improve their books before sending them out to agents and publishers. Some of these agencies are quite big and employ a large number of skilled readers, most of whom are published novelists with a good reputation.

The consultants charge a standard fee based on word length.

The Literary Consultancy (TLC) is probably the best known. Based in London, it provides editorial advice to writers at all levels. TLC has over 50 expert readers, representing a wide range of literary styles, who write a detailed and constructive five- to ten-page report on each book. Check out www.literaryconsultancy.co.uk.

Some authors, however, want to work more closely with a reader or editor. A more personal service is sometimes offered where, in addition to a written report, you meet the reader to discuss her comments. In addition, many novelists – most of whom receive very little in terms of advances and royalties from their published work – work as teachers in adult education and are happy to read and assess a student's work for a suitable fee.

You can end up paying out a lot of money for these services. Always remember that, while a good critique can help, you do need to do most of the work yourself. No one's going to write your book for you, or turn a hopelessly disorganised manuscript into a brilliantly tight narrative. Writing is hard work and inescapably so.

Always get a written quote before sending your work off for appraisal, so that you know exactly what you are committing yourself to.

Doing It Yourself: Self-Publishing

Because so many people are now writing and getting published by mainstream presses is so difficult, self-publishing has become much more respectable. Be aware, though, that self-publishing isn't the same as vanity publishing.

Vanity publishing

In response to the many people who want to be published, a whole industry of conmen and sharks has sprung up in which people offer to publish a book for a (usually hefty) fee. They usually refer to themselves as 'subsidy publishers'.

As a rule, writers should never pay to have their work published. In this situation the publisher doesn't care about the quality of the work or if bookshops are likely to stock it. The bigger the fee, the more you need to worry. Vanity publishers can charge anything from £2,000 to an astonishing £20,000 to publish your work.

Further, many vanity presses issue dodgy contracts involving you handing over copyright of the work to them – something no writer should ever do. Sometimes they contract only to print a small number of books, and charge exorbitant fees for producing further copies.

Unfortunately, people in the trade also always recognise vanity published books. They never get reviewed, and bookshops aren't interested in taking them. Most of these publishers don't have a sales team and do nothing to get the books sold into the shops. Some of them don't even list the book on online book retailer Amazon or make any attempt to get publicity.

A book produced by a vanity publisher may be:

- ✔ Poorly designed, with an amateurish cover, type that's too small and badly laid out on the page with poor margins.

- ✔ Printed on the wrong type of paper, which is too thick, stiff or shiny so that the book is heavy or just feels wrong when handled.

- ✔ An odd size rather than one of the standard formats, making bookshops reluctant to take it.

- ✔ Missing obvious details such as the ISBN or barcode, meaning bookshops can't stock it.

Vanity publishers aren't interested in the quality of the work; they just use authors' desire to see their work in print to make money out of them. Because the money is almost always paid upfront, the publisher has no interest in attempting to sell the book, unlike a conventional publisher. Some vanity publishers have been known to refuse to speak to the author after they've printed a few copies and delivered them. Some even declare bankruptcy on a regular basis and then reappear under another name.

Since self-publishing became respectable, some vanity publishers have tried passing themselves off as such. Don't be fooled. If someone asks you to pay for publication, don't do it. You'll face disappointment, possibly heartbreak – and a large hole in your pocket.

Self-publishing

Effectively setting up a small company is the best way to publish your book. You assume responsibility for every aspect of the design, you get the book typeset, find a printer, organise the production, store the printed books, market and sell them – and you pay for the whole thing.

As a business, you need to keep proper accounts and get advice on legal matters. You're taking the risk of investing your money and may not get much of a return.

On the plus side, you can control every aspect of the process, including the jacket. More importantly, as the publisher you could make far more money than you would ever get from author's royalties.

Be clear that publishing your book yourself involves an enormous amount of work. For a publisher the task is hard enough, but at least they've done it all before and know what they're doing; you'll be learning from scratch. You need to:

- Set up a company. Seek advice from an accountant or your local business agency.

- Buy an ISBN – a unique 13-digit number identifying your book to bookshops, libraries and so on. Go to www.isbn.nielsenbookdata.co.uk for information.

- Register the book with Nielsen's book data at www.nielsenbookdata.co.uk.

- Organise the design, jacket, typesetting and printing.

- Store the books and post them out.

- Get your books accepted by the book wholesalers or buyers at the big bookshop chains.

- List your book on Amazon and other online bookshops – www.amazon.co.uk has a section for publishers.

- Send copies to the main copyright libraries – the British Library (www.bl.uk) and the Agency for the Legal Deposit Libraries (www.legaldeposit.org.uk), which is a legal requirement.

- Send copies to reviewers. Many libraries contain up-to-date press guides such as *Benn's Media Directory* or *Willing's Press Guide* (you can buy these yourself but they're expensive). These press guides list all the media outlets and identify the literary and arts editors.

- Organise publicity.

- Arrange events and readings.

Each one of these tasks is time-consuming – put together they can be a nightmare. What's more, getting to see the buyers in the bookshops is very difficult – most will refuse to see you. The big chains can't spare time to deal with all the thousands of tiny publishers springing up – they like to deal with a few big publishers and the book wholesalers.

Discover as much as you can about the mechanics of printing and publishing. Get a selection of quotes for printing and ensure that all the costs are completely clear from the outset. You need to find out about the standard book formats – A paperback, B paperback, trade paperback, demi – types of paper, types of binding, lamination, spot varnishing and other printing technicalities. Talk to bookshops about the formats they like and printers about the printing techniques – if possible, show them a sample of the kind of book you'd like them to produce.

Talk to other people who've self-published and get tips from them. Doing so can save you a lot of grief and ensure you don't repeat their mistakes.

Be prepared for disappointment – unless you have contacts among journalists and reviewers, getting your book reviewed will be very difficult, as will placing it in bookshops. Making any real impact won't be easy. Many literary prizes no long accept self-published books, and libraries may also be reluctant to stock them.

If you have a captive audience – for example, you teach a regular supply of students – are a huge self-promoter, don't mind always carrying a couple of copies around with you so you can sell your book to anyone who's interested, will consider renting a market stall and selling direct to passers-by, and are prepared to work incredibly hard – then maybe self-publishing's for you.

Printing on demand

New printing technology has made a difference to the huge cost of producing a book. Printing on demand means that you can get orders for books and print them as you need them.

Print-on-demand technology is an advanced form of photocopying. The quality isn't yet quite as good as traditional litho printing, although it has improved – and you have a much more limited range of paper stock.

Unfortunately, print on demand involves high unit costs – perhaps £3.00 to £5.00 per book – and doesn't vary with the number of copies printed. So selling your book at a profit is difficult if the usual bookshop paperback price applies.

A number of outlets, such as Lightning Source (www.lightningsource.com) and Lulu.com (www.lulu.com), provide an electronic print-on-demand service. You send in your typeset pages and jacket design, and they print the book and fulfil orders. They supply the ISBN, organise printing, list the book on Amazon and other online bookshops, and save you a great deal of time and trouble. Should your book sell well, though, you won't make much money from it.

Chapter 23

Becoming a Professional

· ·

· ·

*W*hen you're writing regularly, you can do a lot to help yourself feel that you're really a writer and to be accepted as one. To 'professionalise' yourself as a writer, you need to take yourself seriously so that others can too.

Of course, some people write in a garret by themselves, produce a book, send it off and get it published. However, this scenario is becoming increasingly rare. Today's publishers want authors with contacts, who attend events, readings and festivals, and interact with their readers. They want authors who consider their work a job and put in the effort.

Today, more than ever, you have many opportunities for meeting up with other writers and readers. This chapter covers how to go about it.

Joining a Writing Circle

Linking up with other writers is the best thing you can do. This has always been the case. Writers J. R. R. Tolkien and C. S. Lewis formed the Inklings, a group of writers who met at the Eagle and Child pub in Oxford in the 1930s and 1940s to read and share their work. The Bloomsbury Group of the early twentieth century included the writers Virginia Woolf, E. M. Forster, Mary McCarthy and Lytton Strachey, as well as a number of influential artists and critics.

You can get together with friends who write and start your own circle, meeting regularly in one another's houses and reading your work. If you don't know other writers, try to meet some. Many libraries advertise local writers' circles and various websites list them throughout the UK; try `www.write words.org.uk/directory` or `www.writers-circles.com`.

Make sure that the dynamics of the writers' circle suit you. Choose one in which people are writing the same kind of material – if everyone else is penning literary and experimental fiction and you're attempting a commercial blockbuster, you'll probably feel uncomfortable. Also make sure that the group's supportive rather than critical. You may need to try out two or three circles before you find the right one for you.

If you join an existing writing circle, go gently at first and try to fit in with the way the group's run. If you set up your own, set some initial ground rules. These may include:

- **Maintaining confidentiality:** This means not talking to others outside of the group about what people have written or said. Confidentiality is particularly important if people are writing about their personal experiences.

- **Offering constructive criticism:** People often need to put some thought into the type of criticism appropriate in the group. Banning the words 'good' and 'bad' is a good idea, so that people have to think more carefully about what they think is or isn't working in the piece of writing. All criticism should be geared towards how the piece can be improved.

- **Setting time limits:** Use a timer so that everyone has a fair chance to present and receive feedback on their work. This approach prevents some individuals from dominating the sessions.

- **Respecting differences:** Writers aren't all the same and people also like to read different things. Make sure that you support each other's work rather than impose your own views and prejudices on it.

- **Banning intoxicants:** Asking people not to drink before or during a meeting is a good idea – of course, socialising afterwards is fine. Alcohol and other intoxicants can cloud judgement and make people say things they later regret.

Attending Writing Courses

Everyone can improve their writing, and a vast number of writing courses are available. Some are run by local authorities and are subsidised; others are private and quite expensive. Most employ tutors who are published writers and very generous both with their time and in sharing their skills with others.

Providing an overview

So many courses offer so many different programmes that generalising about what to expect is difficult. However, most writing courses stick to this basic format:

- ✔ Everyone introduces themselves. The tutor usually says a few words about herself and then you're asked to state your name, where you're at with your writing and what you're hoping to achieve as a result of attending the course.

- ✔ You may look at short literary passages to see how they work. The tutors usually have the skills to talk intelligently and analytically about pieces of writing in such a way that you can learn from them.

- ✔ You take part in short writing exercises in class. These often focus on a particular theme and are specific, timed exercises to help you develop particular techniques.

  Sometimes you're asked to do exercises in pairs and small groups. Doing so means you can often learn from one another; you also discover that writing can be sociable and fun!

- ✔ You're asked to read your exercise and the tutor and group give you feedback. This isn't aimed at grading your piece but looks at what you communicated well or was unclear and confusing, and at ways to improve it.

  Students are usually shown how to give constructive feedback and to avoid making hurtful or over-critical comments.

Evaluating criticism

Trusting the tutor and group to manage feedback effectively is important. Never accept criticism from a group that discourages you. Feedback should always be given in a supportive, encouraging and helpful way and never be harsh or completely negative. Sometimes more advanced writers say they want to know the 'truth' about their work and to be 'torn to pieces'. I've never seen students who've received truly negative criticism be anything other than devastated, though; they've always suffered an immediate setback in both their confidence and writing.

Over-negative criticism doesn't work. The writer is hurt and often withdraws into his shell. He thinks that the critic doesn't really understand what he's trying to do. The writer stops listening – and stops learning.

This situation doesn't mean you need to praise work that needs a lot of improvement – far from it. You can offer a great deal of criticism if you do so within a supportive and caring context, which helps the student to hear what you're saying. Every piece of writing contains something praiseworthy and you can couch your criticism in such a way that the student can learn from it and grow as a writer.

If you're giving feedback in a group, consider different ways of phrasing your comments. Always think of something positive to say first, then about how to convey your point without hurting the writer. Also, make your comments very specific so that the writer knows what to look at and improve. Instead of:

> I couldn't understand what was going on. It went on for too long and was a bit boring.

Say:

> I can see you've worked really hard on this piece. I really liked the way you described the main character, but I was a bit confused about where she was and how many people were there. I also think the piece could be more effective if you edited it down a bit, so I could focus on what was most important in the scene.

For more advanced students, writing courses often consist of a series of workshops in which students simply read out their work in progress and receive critical feedback. If the course continues for some time, the students get to know one another and their works quite well, which makes the feedback they receive increasingly meaningful.

Signing on for adult education courses

Many further education colleges offer daytime and evening courses on a wide range of subjects, including languages, the arts and creative writing.

A wide range of creative writing courses is available at all levels – beginner, intermediate and advanced. You can focus on children's fiction, short stories, novels, real life accounts, travel writing, journalism, screenplays and playwriting.

Your library is a good place to start your search for writing classes, or contact local colleges directly. Many courses are taught by tutors who are experts in their own field. You may sometimes be awarded a certificate to show you've taken part.

The tutors' schemes of work and lesson plans are subject to government inspection. Most courses are accessible to those with disabilities.

Consider these points when sourcing a suitable course:

✔ Is it a one-off or does it offer a continuation route as you improve?

✔ How many students will be enrolled? Some classes have up to 25 students, making it difficult for everyone to participate fully.

✔ Are refreshment facilities available? Chatting over a cup of tea can help you to build relationships within the group and get more out of the sessions.

Taking certificate and MA courses

Creative writing is a relatively new academic subject in the UK. In the US, creative writing undergraduate and Masters degree programmes have been established for some time. In addition, universities offer courses in journalism, life writing, screen and play writing. Some of the leading courses publish their own quarterly magazines, which have launched a great many writing careers. In the UK, the growth of such courses has been much more recent. In 1990, UK universities offered only a handful of MA (Masters) writing courses, one undergraduate degree and a sprinkling of creative writing modules within English degrees. Now, UCAS, the university applications organisation, lists over 80 institutions throughout the UK offering writing courses at all levels.

The courses

Some universities offer a creative writing module as part of a traditional English Literature degree course. A few offer creative writing as a degree in its own right. Most popular are the certificate and diploma courses and the MA-level postgraduate courses, which attract a greater number of mature students. You can even do a PhD in creative writing, which is likely to consist of writing an entire novel.

Many courses are run by enthusiastic writers and lecturers who have their own, very individualistic, take on how to teach, assess and grade creative writing. Each institution and, in many cases, each tutor, can decide on the style, structure and content of the course.

Conduct research to find a course that seems right for you. In particular, check out the tutors' published writing to get a flavour of their styles and approaches.

A creative writing course should:

✔ Provide a supportive environment in which you can write among your peers.

✔ Offer inspirational talks, workshops and readings.

✔ Increase your awareness of how literature works.

✔ Give you access to skilled writers and informed critical opinions.

✔ Help you to identify problems in your work and give you tools to address them.

University courses are aimed at students who want to take writing seriously. They give you a chance to learn, experiment and take risks with your writing in a supportive and creative environment. However, much of the support you'll receive will be from your peers; these are university-level courses that rely on students getting on with the work in a mature and independent fashion.

None of these courses promise to turn you into a bestselling writer but all can enable you to stretch yourself, explore the writing process and learn about writing through the example of others.

Most of the courses teach you through lectures, seminar discussion, workshops and individual tutorials. You're normally assessed by a combination of creative and critical samples of writing. Although each module includes a theoretical component, mostly these courses award marks on the basis of your creative work.

How to apply

You have to apply through UCAS for some courses. All the information you need is on the UCAS website at www.ucas.ac.uk. You usually need to send in a sample of your work, complete an application form and provide two references.

Although you're usually expected to already have an undergraduate degree, in practice many universities are keen to widen access so it may not be necessary. Consult the websites of the universities concerned, and contact the admissions staff, who are usually extremely friendly and helpful.

Levels of qualification

Higher education qualifications are awarded at five levels by universities and colleges in England, Wales and Northern Ireland. In ascending order, these are:

✔ Certificate – usually a Certificate of Higher Education

✔ Intermediate – Foundation degrees, ordinary Bachelor (BA) degrees and Diplomas of Higher Education

✔ Honours – Bachelor degrees with honours, Graduate Certificates and Graduate Diplomas

✔ Masters – Master (MA) degrees, Postgraduate Certificates and Postgraduate Diplomas

✔ Doctoral – doctorates such as PhDs

Ensure that you understand the level of course you're applying for – getting confused between undergraduate and postgraduate certificates and diplomas, for example, is all too easy.

The Open University offers a wide range of courses at every level, which can suit those who live in remote places, have severe constraints on their time or find it hard to travel. If you work long hours or have small children, the Open University may be your best option.

Paying for private courses

Many private writing courses are available throughout the UK. Some of these are affiliated with institutions or held in public buildings; others take place in hired venues such as clubs and hotels; still others are run from tutors' own homes.

The value of these courses depends entirely on the quality of the tutors, so careful research is necessary. Before choosing a course, consider the type of environment you prefer, accessibility of venues and suitability of dates and times. Read novels and scripts by the tutors to see if they write the kind of material you like.

I set up the Complete Creative Writing Course ten years ago in London, in response to the need for a professional and imaginative course for people who want to write fiction. The course is run in a variety of upmarket venues in central London, including the Groucho and New Cavendish Clubs. I now offer beginner, intermediate and advanced courses for prose writers, as well as courses in screenwriting and children's writing. See www.writing courses.org.uk for details.

You can find writing courses on the Internet and in reference works such as the *Writers' and Artists' Yearbook* (www.writersandartists.co.uk) and *The Writer's Handbook* (www.thewritershandbook.com).

Going on a residential course or writing holiday

For some people, getting away from home is the only way to get some serious writing done. Nowadays you can go on activity holidays to focus on learning a skill – and meet new people into the bargain.

Many private courses and residential writing holidays take place abroad. Generally in warm climates, these run during spring, summer and autumn in countries such as France, Spain, Portugal, Italy and Greece. Such holidays are also available in the UK. Go to www.travel-quest.co.uk for details on writing holidays.

The London Book Fair

Frankfurt and London are the two international book fairs on every publisher's calendar. The London Book Fair is usually held in April and has exhibitors from all over the world. Lots of seminars and events take place, involving authors, agents and publishers discussing a variety of topics from marketing digital media to teenage fiction. Book launches, signings and interviews with well-known authors are part and parcel of the event.

Under one roof you can visit all the major publishers' stands to find out what new books they're releasing and which titles are selling

well. You can also catch up on the smaller independent publishers. Tickets are available for all the events, or you can hang out at the main café and see interviews with a range of authors talking about their work.

The London Book Fair is open to the public, with the exception of the International Rights Centre where agents and publishers buy and sell foreign rights. It offers a fantastic opportunity to pick up catalogues, look at forthcoming titles and get a feel for what's going on in the world of publishing.

How useful these courses are depends very much on the teachers and types of programme. Some are holidays with a bit of writing on the side; others are much more serious, offering a tight programme and less free time. Some enable you to have access to restaurants, beaches and nightlife when you're not writing or attending workshops, while others are situated in remote locations. Choose the programme and location that best suit your needs.

Stealing away to a writers' retreat

Some venues run writers' retreats during which you don't receive tuition but are supported in finding time to write. Often meals are provided so that you have nothing to do but focus on your work.

A writers' retreat may seem ideal, but before you opt for one, ask yourself some hard questions:

- Do you like being alone and can you manage with only your own company for most of the day?
- Can you survive away from family and friends for a whole week, fortnight or month?
- Can you manage without your cat, books and familiar things around you?
- Will you feel guilty about abandoning your partner or children?
- Can you manage without phone calls, emails or the Internet?

If your answer to all these questions is an unqualified 'yes', take a look at the following:

> ✔ **The Arvon Foundation:** www.arvonfoundation.org
>
> ✔ **Hawthornden Castle:** Lasswade, Midlothian EH18 1EG, Scotland; Tel: 44 (0) 131 440 2180
>
> ✔ **Ty Newydd Writers' Centre:** www.tynewydd.org

Religious retreats also enable you to get away from everything; you can write in your room while you're there.

Focusing on Literary Festivals

Literary festivals provide an opportunity to hear well-known writers reading from and talking about their work, and to meet with other people interested in literature and the arts.

A diary of UK festivals

Below is a list of the largest literary festivals. You can find details of each on the British Council's website: www.britishcouncil.org. *The Writer's Handbook* and the *Writers' and Artists' Yearbook* also list literary festivals.

✔ The Bath Literature Festival (February–March)

✔ Jewish Book Week (February–March)

✔ Words by the Water, Keswick (February–March)

✔ York Literature Festival (March)

✔ The *Sunday Times* Oxford Literary Festival (April)

✔ Cambridge WordFest (April)

✔ Charleston Festival (May)

✔ *The Guardian* Hay Festival (May)

✔ The London Literature Festival, Southbank Centre, London (June)

✔ Dartington Hall Festival, Ways with Words (July)

✔ Theakston's Old Peculier Crime Writing Festival, Harrogate (July)

✔ Edinburgh International Literature Festival (August)

✔ Wigtown Literary Festival (September)

✔ Cheltenham Festival of Literature (October)

✔ Ilkley Literature Festival (October)

✔ Aldeburgh International Poetry Festival (November)

In the past, literary festivals were small humble gatherings of authors and their fans. Now, they're booming, with new events opening each year, attracting celebrity authors, politicians, prize-winning novelists and poets, and even stars of stage and screen. Currently, over 100 literary festivals take place in the UK. Most are held annually or every other year; some are small local events and others attract international acclaim.

Most literary festivals are held in venues with plentiful bookshops, restaurants and cafés. You may get the opportunity to meet authors directly and ask them questions.

Frequently, publishers, publicists and agents attend these festivals with their authors, thus providing an opportunity to make contacts and maybe even find someone who'll agree to look at your work.

In addition, many literary festivals now organise workshops for writers, often with published novelists as tutors. These offer a fantastic opportunity to get feedback from well-known writers – and a chance to get talent-spotted.

Attending Bookshop Readings, Events and Launches

Events at your local bookshop, library and similar venues put you in contact with other writers – often well-known authors. Look out for these events and go along. Hearing writers read and talk about their work is good experience, and you may get an opportunity to ask questions and even to approach a writer directly.

Larger bookshops issue a programme of events and talks, giving you a chance to read the relevant books in advance.

Agents and publishers also sometimes attend these events to support their authors. Again, you can get into conversation with them if an opportunity arises – don't be too pushy, though.

If you do summon up the nerve to approach agents or publishers at an event, bear these tips in mind:

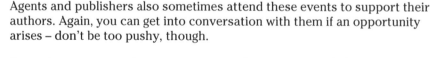

- ✔ Check the person's identity before you launch in. Try 'I didn't quite catch your name' if you're not sure.
- ✔ Say how much you enjoyed the reading or the author's previous book if you're at a launch. Praise always helps.

Reading literary magazines

Literary magazines feature book reviews, articles about writing and publishing, and interviews with well-known writers, agents and editors. Buy your own subscription or read them in your local library to find out more about the world of writing and publishing.

The Bookseller, the main magazine for the book trade, provides lots of information about what's going on – which titles are doing well, what deals have been struck, what kind of advances are being paid to writers.

You can glean information on new publishing initiatives and developments, such as print on demand, and discover which publishers are doing well and which are in trouble.

✔ Ask permission to do so before you launch into talking about your book. Stating 'I've just completed my first novel; may I tell you a little about it?' gives them the option of saying that now isn't a good time – they may then suggest you email or phone them at another time.

✔ Practise summarising your book in a few words for precisely this occasion. If you talk for too long or try to describe the entire plot you'll scare them off. Just say a sentence or two – whet their appetite and hopefully they'll start asking you about it.

✔ Don't put on airs or sell yourself too strongly – be natural, simple and direct.

✔ At a launch, always buy the book. You have an opportunity to say something to the author when he or she signs it. Also, if you aren't prepared to buy someone else's book, why do you think people will be willing to buy yours?

Getting Your First Work into Print

Nothing's more thrilling than seeing your work in print. You don't have to wait until your first novel's published, though. You can start small, and practise getting your work out there and read.

Letters

Newspapers, magazines, journals and literary magazines always have a letters page. Write to them. Write about writing or reading. Comment on reviews of books, films and plays. Disagree with the critics. Write about political issues that affect you.

Make your letters brief, concise and interesting. You may have a letter published straight away or have to wait awhile – it doesn't matter. Newspapers and magazines always welcome letters and from time to time you'll get one into print – and you may even win a 'star letter' prize.

Life articles

Many newspapers and magazines feature readers' experiences, often under titles such as 'First person' or 'It happened to me'. Read a selection of these. Work out the word count of such articles, and identify topics that haven't been covered and which you have the experience to write about.

If a national magazine or newspaper turns down your article, try a local one. Write about local issues that concern you.

Some writers attract agents on the basis of such pieces written in daily newspapers and magazines. A positive response from the public to such an article can prove an audience exists for your book.

Literary magazines

Polishing your pieces and sending them off to literary magazines is your best approach as a writer. Getting an article published will really help you on your way. Many of the smaller literary magazines take short pieces and poems from unknown writers.

Go to `www2.eng.cam.ac.uk/~tpl/lit/ukmags.html` for a list of literary magazines.

Read a selection of magazines and only submit your work to those which publish similar material.

Literary magazines vary from large, established publications such as the quarterly *Granta*, published by Penguin, to small publications run by tiny arts organisations.

Anthologies of new writing

Occasionally, publishers or literary organisations publish anthologies of new writing. These are often advertised in literary magazines or in the press. Keep your eye out.

Entering Competitions

Writing for competitions is a great way to hone your skills as a writer and become more professional in your approach. A large number of competitions are held every year, and many of them offer cash prizes. In addition, they offer you an opportunity to get your work in print.

Occasionally, really high profile writing contests are televised or featured in the press – don't miss out on the opportunity to take part. For example, in 2008 the *Daily Telegraph* ran the Alexander McCall Smith challenge, in which authors were asked to submit a minimum of ten separate blogs (online diary entries) to create a story or novel of between 10,000 and 100,000 words. Television hosts Richard and Judy ran a 'How to Get Published' competition for aspiring novelists, with the winner being offered a publishing deal by Pan Macmillan. The competition received over 40,000 entries – but somebody has to win!

Before you enter a competition, remember:

- **Choose a competition in the right genre for you:** Don't enter a sci-fi writing competition if you usually write romance – the gamble's unlikely to come off.

- **Read all the rules carefully:** Each competition's different, and you can come unstuck if you don't read the small print.

- **Write to the theme:** Don't make a tiny adjustment to an existing story in the hope that it meets the criteria – it probably won't.

- **Stick to the word length:** Don't go more than a handful of words over. You may think the judges won't count, but professional editors are practised at estimating length and will spot a story that's more than a few words too long.

- **Meet the deadline:** You'd be amazed at how many people still send in stories weeks after a competition has closed. Don't leave it until the last minute in case of postal strikes and other mishaps.

Chapter 11 covers entering short story competitions. Competitions for novels and poetry also exist. Look out for competitions on literary websites such as `www.writewords.org.uk` and `www.theshortstory.org.uk`, in magazines like *Mslexia* (`www.mslexia.co.uk`) and in *The Writer's Handbook* (`www.writershandbook`).

And if you fail . . .

This is a true story.

John Kennedy Toole wrote his novel, *A Confederacy of Dunces*, in the 1960s. He submitted it for publication but no publisher showed the slightest interest. Toole fell into a deep depression and finally killed himself in March 1969, using a garden hose hooked up to the exhaust of his Chevrolet. He was just 31.

His suicide would've been the end of the story if Toole's mother hadn't found a smeared carbon copy of the manuscript. She took it to Walker Percy, an author and college instructor at Loyola University in New Orleans, and asked him to read it. Initially reluctant, Percy became increasingly impressed by the manuscript. He sent it to a publisher with a letter of recommendation. *A Confederacy of Dunces* was finally published in 1980, 11 years after the author's tragic death.

The book went on to win the Pulitzer Prize the following year, making Toole the first writer to receive the coveted award posthumously. It has gone on to become a classic, which is still in print today.

Always maintain hope — you never know what's round the corner!

Part VI
The Part of Tens

'Any interesting manuscripts waiting for me
in reception, Miss Mauleverer?'

In this part . . .

Every *For Dummies* book has a few short chapters at the end to give you a quick burst of inspiration. Here you'll find ten top tips for writers, ten ways to get noticed, and ten works of literature that you should definitely never be without.

Chapter 24

Ten Top Tips for Writers

....

....

*W*hen you start writing, you may face many pitfalls. Take the advice of other writers who've gone before you and experienced the same difficulties and problems. Below are the ten most important things to bear in mind.

Write for Yourself

Writing to please yourself is the most important aspect of becoming a writer.

Far too many writers worry about other people's opinions of their work. You'll never write something that everybody loves – someone will always criticise your work. All that matters is that you like and are involved with what you're writing.

So shut your mind to your family and friends, and thoughts of agents, publishers and reviewers – and just concentrate on writing what interests you, and doing the best you can.

Enjoy the Journey

Rome wasn't built in a day, and nor is a story, book or collection of poetry. Writing takes time – to explore your characters and understand them fully, and to work out a plot. Your writing needs time to ripen. You need to draft, rewrite and edit. Sometimes you have to put your work aside for awhile and then come back to it afresh. So don't hurry or push yourself too hard.

Developing a Buddhist mindfulness about your writing can be helpful. Slow down; take deep breaths; look out of the window; stare into space. Write slowly. Enjoy the feel of the pen on the page or the sound of your fingers tapping on the keyboard. Savour your choice of words and how they sound when read aloud. Don't worry about the end point; enjoy the process of writing, and the taking of small steady steps towards your goal.

Be Specific

Your writing communicates best when you avoid generalisations. You're inviting the reader into your own world, created in specific, concrete detail. Characters are defined by what they do, by small, concrete acts that you can describe. Your character lives in a house, town and country; by offering vivid details you make the character's circumstances real to your reader.

Being specific about details makes a huge difference to your writing. Don't use a general word like 'tree' when you can say 'oak' or 'hazel'; write 'apple' or 'cherry' rather than 'fruit'.

When you're writing about a car, state its make, colour and condition. Consider what statement a particular car makes about its owner – a smart red Audi versus a battered old Ford.

Be specific about characters' clothes, mannerisms and personal grooming – again, these speak volumes about their personalities.

Consider how things move, whether they creep, scurry, glide or jerk. Specify exact temperatures and their effects on the characters' environment – whether a day is hot enough to melt the tarmac or cold enough to create frost flowers on the window. Don't be afraid to be bold.

Show, Don't Tell

When you *tell* readers something, you make a statement they have to accept as true. When you *show* them something, you describe and dramatise it, allowing readers to see what's happening and draw their own conclusions.

Telling doesn't let readers use their imaginations; it doesn't engage or arouse them.

Consider these examples of showing and telling:

✔ **Telling:** 'Susan was a very lazy person. People already found her attractive so she didn't bother to make herself look good. Although her clothes were very unfashionable, men were always chasing after her.'

This description doesn't actually provide a clear picture of Susan. In what way is she lazy? What kind of unfashionable clothes does she wear – starchy suits, clashing patterns, last year's colours? In what way is she attractive? What kind of men chase after her?

Also, this passage doesn't reveal anything about Susan. You don't know what age she is or what kind of life she leads, and you don't really care.

✔ **Showing:** 'Susan liked to lie in bed until around noon, dozing and listening to the radio, long after the other students had gone out. Her clothes lay in a hopeless jumble at the end of the bed; old frayed jeans, crumpled shirts, baggy jumpers with holes in the elbows. When she finally got up, she'd pull on some random clothes from the top of the pile and run her fingers through her long, thick hair, which seemed to arrange itself into luxuriant curls with no effort; she never bothered to comb it. When she went out, people would turn to look at her, and she was never seen at college without one or two young men in tow, offering her a cigarette, sharing their lecture notes or asking her out to see a film.'

Here, you can see Susan in action, observe her directly and make your own judgements, instead of having the author telling you what to think.

In reality, you do need to tell your readers some details to move the narrative from one dramatic passage to another. But mostly you need to build up a vivid picture, which the reader can visualise like a film passing before their eyes.

Dialogue is an exception – you must tell readers exactly what the characters say. For example, 'Jo and Simon were always arguing' is much less effective than actually describing one particular row, enabling the reader to really see what's going on between them and to feel angry or saddened by their behaviour.

In plays and screenplays, you tell everything about your characters through dramatic dialogue and specific actions. In prose fiction, you need to work harder at dramatising your story.

Read and Re-read

Becoming a good writer is impossible without reading, re-reading and thinking about what you read. Don't be afraid to be influenced by really good writers; they will have done the same.

Read widely, in all genres. You can learn much about plotting a narrative from a potboiler thriller, and about imagery from a great poem. Newspaper headlines and advertising slogans can demonstrate clarity and conciseness. Narrative non-fiction can show you how to make hard facts interesting.

Don't be afraid to experiment in your reading. Go to a bookshop and ignore the piles of three-for-two offers and titles that you've already heard of. Read the blurbs on the back of books and consider which ones appeal to you and why. Browse the shelves and pick something obscure that for some reason appeals to you.

When you read, do so slowly and really think about how the author achieves the effects you enjoy or find interesting.

Copy out or photocopy passages that you really like and put them in a scrap-book to consult when you hit a problem in your own writing. If you're wondering how to make a piece of dialogue sound natural or convey a personality in a few phrases, you can take a look at how the experts have done it and learn from them.

Carry a book with you wherever you go. Read the poems on the Tube. Read in libraries and bookshops, on the bus, in bed and in the bath. Just read!

Be Open to What's Around You

As a writer you need to be open to the world around you, to draw on it for your inspiration. You need to be curious in particular about people and what makes them act the way they do.

Look around you. Observe how people dress, move and behave. Listen to conversations and note people's vocabulary, phrasing, accents and subject matter. Consider their motivations, hopes and fears. Be aware of human frailty.

Look at both the natural and man-made world around you. Observe colours, feel textures, be aware of smells and sounds. Create images to capture and convey these details to others.

Be a magpie. Collect objects, photos and props to help you in your writing. Put them in your notebook. Study maps and guidebooks to find tucked-away corners in cities or the countryside. Develop a nose for unusual settings and locations.

Nothing is ever too trivial or unimportant to use in your writing.

Learn from Others

You don't only learn from reading and observing the world around you. You can actively research events, places and people you can't otherwise describe or write about. If you're writing a scene in your novel involving a doctor, for example, talk to one. Read medical books. Interview people who've experienced the kind of illness or accident you're writing about to gain their perspective.

You can learn from other beginner writers, too. Listen to their work and take note of mistakes that you've also made. Consider what does and doesn't communicate well. Discover how to shape your work, delete the parts that don't ring true, cut scenes or verses that go on for too long or provide the crucial information that's missing.

Also learn from published authors. Go to readings and read articles about how writers work. Listen to interviews with authors on television or radio or live at literary festivals.

Write and Rewrite

Remember that drafting is just the beginning. Drafting resembles producing the clay from which you go on to shape your pot. Never be satisfied with what you've written the first time; push yourself on to enrich and develop your work.

Writing really is rewriting. A brief survey of authors revealed that, on average, a published novel has been rewritten 20 times.

The more you rewrite, the easier your work is to read. You can tell when a piece of writing has been edited because it reads so smoothly and easily, as if no effort were taken at all.

Steel yourself for the long haul.

Accept Rejection

When you start offering your work, expect rejection. Accept it, and don't get wound up about it. You're just beginning. Your novel is very unlikely to be accepted first time.

Be business-like about submitting your work. Keep track of who you've sent out pieces to and file feedback, especially positive comments. When a story or poem is rejected, just send it to the next person on your list; keep going until no options remain.

After you've finished a piece, start something new. Put the old one aside for now. Remember that plenty of novelists have two or three unpublished manuscripts under the bed.

Don't Give Up

If you want to be a writer, then write. Don't give up because you're not successful. You never know what will happen later in life or even after you're dead. A historian in times to come may discover your diary and recognise its unique insight into twenty-first-century life. A poem you wrote many years ago may suddenly appeal to someone and be published or get chosen in a competition. A novel that was rejected 30 times might get dusted down and see the light of day many, many years after you first wrote it.

Plenty of good novels don't get published and lots of indifferent ones do. That situation isn't fair, but neither is life. Don't get mad about it.

Being realistic about your aims mean you're less likely to be disappointed. Keep going, live in hope and be open to whatever happens.

Chapter 25

Ten Ways to Get Noticed

In This Chapter

▶ Keeping your message simple

▶ Sending your work out

▶ Staying positive

Sometimes you may feel as if everyone's writing a novel, penning a poem or trying to sell their screenplay. Pretending that you don't face a huge amount of competition out there is pointless. To get yourself noticed, do the best work you can and be as professional as possible in the way you handle yourself. Here are a few tips.

Practise Your Pitch and Keep it Short

Prepare a short pitch to use whenever you meet someone who may be able to help you professionally – just a simple sentence or two, summarising your work and the general area it covers.

For example:

> I'm writing a short novel for teenagers about a young man who discovers that his father is not the man he thought he was. He sets out on a quest to find his natural father and finds himself in a world of criminals and drug-pushers and his life is endangered.

Or:

> I'm writing a biography of my great-grandmother, who set off on a journey through Africa and ended up working as a missionary in Tanzania. I've just spent two months there researching the background and come up with some amazing discoveries.

Practise saying your pitch, using no more than 50 words or lasting no longer than 30 seconds. Hone and polish it. Practise it on your friends. Listen to the questions they ask you and think of short, simple answers to those too.

Ignore the Opinions of Family and Friends

You'd be amazed at how many writers approach agents by saying that their family and friends love their book. Well, they would do, wouldn't they? What mother, father, partner, lover or friend is going to destroy their relationship with you by announcing that they really can't stand your book? In addition, family and friends are very unlikely to be writers or critics or to have any of the skills needed to make constructive comments about a book. They won't know what to say about it and you shouldn't put them in the awkward position of having to try.

I'm always a bit wary if people just say 'I enjoyed your book'. If they can't think of anything more specific to say, I don't think they can have got much out of it. Maybe they haven't even read it and are just being polite.

The only opinions about your book that matter are those of:

- ✔ Other writers
- ✔ Editors and agents
- ✔ Publishers

Be Focused

When offering your work, whether to agents, publishers, newspapers or magazines, be focused. Consider the most suitable places to send it. Do your research: work out which authors that agent represents, find books published by that imprint, read the newspapers and magazines.

Don't submit your work willy-nilly. Busy people feel annoyed when you send them the kind of book they don't publish or handle. Never use a standard letter addressed to 'Dear Sir or Madam' and don't send a piece of work to dozens of publishers, agents or publications all at the same time.

Do research into the best person or people to offer your work to. Find out a little bit about them and their organisation on the Internet. Make your approach personal. Follow it up.

Perfect Your Work First

One of the biggest mistakes beginner writers make is sending their work out too early, before they've polished and finished it. Submitting a rough draft is almost always a big mistake. Nowadays very few publishers are looking for raw talent. They don't have the time to work with authors, encouraging them and offering advice.

Agents and editors have long memories. If they reject your work the first time, they're likely to remember this fact if you send it in again. They won't be as interested as if they hadn't seen it before. You've already entered their memory as someone who wasn't good enough.

Sending in the first three chapters before you've finished the book can work against you too. If an agent or publisher likes it, they're likely to ask for the rest. If you haven't written it, they'll be disappointed that they can't read it straight away.

Also, you're immediately under pressure. The agent or editor may start nagging you, ringing you up to see how you're getting on and asking to see some more. This situation may make you send your work in before you're ready to do so. The agent or editor may then be disappointed with the result and turn your book down. Wait until you've completely finished and then submit the first three chapters.

The first time you offer a really good product is its best chance of being accepted. Agents, publishers and magazines are all looking for that new writer, fresh book, article or play. Don't spoil this unique opportunity by sending out material before you've perfected it.

Don't Argue with Editors and Agents

Editors and agents are professionals and are likely to have been working in the world of publishing for some time. They know the publishing scene and have seen everything before. If they give you advice about your work, you may find yourself in a dilemma. Do you listen to them and make the changes they want or stick to what you really intended?

On the whole, taking the editor or agent's advice is best. Often you can't see your work as an outsider can. An editor or agent can often spot things that you're blind to. Maybe a scene in a book or a poem in a collection doesn't work – one that you're particularly fond of. This part may work for you because it links to a specific memory, event or feeling. But that relevance to you doesn't mean it belongs in the finished book, and an editor may ask you to take it out. This process is known as 'killing your darlings'.

Editors and agents like writers who are prepared to be edited. They don't want someone who is going to argue about every comma and full stop. For this reason, book publishers really like working with journalists, who've been edited before and are usually very open to suggestion.

Publishing is a commercial marketplace. If you want to get published, you have to abide by its rules and fit in with the way it functions. Publishers are taking the financial risk on printing a book, and they want to give it the best chance of making a return. If you don't want to accept advice, leave your book under the bed – or publish it yourself.

Be Modest

Don't go around boasting about how brilliant you are; doing so just annoys people. You may think the book you're writing is a work of unsurpassed genius but in all likelihood others won't agree. If you talk up your work too much, people may be disappointed when they finally come to read it.

In particular, if you make spectacular claims about your writing to agents and publishers, they're likely to look for ways to shoot your work down. They'll read it and think, it's not *that* good. If you make no particular claims, they may think, actually, this is really not bad.

Apart from anything else, being modest is polite, and people respond better to it.

Just concentrate on your writing and leave others to make judgements on it.

Attend Events and Maintain Your Profile

Going to literary events, readings, festivals, and other places where writers get together and talk is always a good idea. Many libraries and bookshops organise events; get in touch with them and find out when they are. Put them in your diary. Go, even if you don't feel like it on the night.

Talking to other writers can be your biggest source of support and help. Join a writers' circle. Organise your own events and readings.

Attend festivals and readings where agents and publishers are likely to be present. Don't be afraid to talk to them. Don't push yourself forward in a brash and obvious way, but don't be a wallflower and keep away from them either.

If you get a chance to talk to a well-known author, agent or publisher, don't pass it up. Be interested in him or her. Ask questions first before you launch into a description of your own writing. If you decide you want to make a pitch, keep it short (see the first tip in this chapter).

Network Like Mad

Never underestimate the value of contacts. Meeting people in the world of publishing and keeping those contacts open is important.

- ✔ **Hand out business cards.** Just provide your name and what you do – 'Writer', 'Freelance journalist', 'Poet', 'Novelist' – together with your postal and email addresses and phone numbers. Elaborate or costly ones aren't necessary; some organisations and Internet sites provide them for free.

- ✔ **Set up a website.** Provide some information about yourself, a good photo and examples of your best work. Think about starting a blog.

- ✔ **Get in touch with your local arts organisations.** Some of these provide bursaries for writers and organise readings and events.

- ✔ **Find out if any small independent publishers are located in your area.** If so, get in touch with them or go to events that they organise.

- ✔ **Pass on information and share it with other writers in your position.** Do other writers a favour, and they may do the same for you.

Don't Take a Rebuff Too Personally

Some rebuffs and rejections are inevitable when you're trying to put yourself forward and sell your work. Don't take them personally. Remember that a lot of the professionals you come across are very busy people, and are constantly being pitched ideas and projects.

Newspaper editors are under the greatest pressure and often work to very tight deadlines. If you ring them at the wrong time, they'll be incredibly brusque and may even refuse to talk to you at all. Finding out in advance the best time to ring is an idea, but even so, something urgent may come up. If you sense that you've phoned at the wrong moment, ask when to call back.

Just because one poem, story or article is rejected doesn't mean that others will be. Stay calm and professional. Accepting rejection of a whole book is harder because of the time you've invested in it, but you can listen to feedback, do more work and send it out again.

When you meet editors, agents and publishers in the flesh, they're almost always polite and interested. Only authors in the abstract tend to elicit brusqueness. So never miss an opportunity to meet up in person.

Stay Positive and Believe in Yourself

Obviously, at times you'll feel down about your writing, and lonely and rejected. In fact, if you're prone to melancholic thinking, maybe being a writer isn't good for you.

You need to find ways to stay positive about your writing even when things aren't going well, to bounce back from rejections and enough self-confidence to keep going. Develop some kind of inner strength to see you through the bad times.

If you don't believe in yourself, why should anyone else? So believe!

Chapter 26

Ten Pieces of Writing to Inspire You

In This Chapter

▶ Reading to learn

▶ Reading for enjoyment

▶ Reading to change your life

*T*his selection of books is indisputably a personal list, although all the works are critically acclaimed and widely read. Consider making your own list of favourite works, and add to and change it as you continue to read.

Short Story: 'The Dead' from Dubliners by James Joyce

James Joyce, best known for his novel *Ulysses*, is one of the most important and influential writers of the first half of the twentieth century. His virtuoso experiments in prose helped to redefine the limits of language and the form of the modern novel. Those who find his novels difficult or even impossible to read can try his short stories instead.

'The Dead' is the last and longest story in his collection *Dubliners* (1914), a series of character portraits that reveal everyday life in turn-of-the-century Dublin. 'The Dead' has been described as one of the most beautifully executed stories in the English language, and I wholeheartedly agree.

The story describes a party to celebrate the feast of the Epiphany, 6 January, when the Three Kings were meant to visit the infant Jesus. The choice of this feast emphasises that the whole story is an epiphany, or moment of revelation. In the story, Gabriel Conway realises the shallowness of his relationship with his wife, Gretta, who was once in love with a man called Michael Furey, now dead.

'The dead' can be seen to refer to the dead characters in the story, especially Michael Furey, but it can also mean the other shallow characters at the party or even the state of Ireland. 'The Dead' is a beautifully written story, told in poetry-like prose, and like the best art is capable of multiple interpretations. And the ending will make you cry.

Classic Novel: Emma by Jane Austen

You either love Jane Austen or hate her, but you can't mistake the skill with which she writes. *Emma* (1815) is the story of an opinionated young woman who's blind to her own feelings while constantly trying to manipulate those of others. Anyone who thinks Austen's novels are romantic should think again after reading this one. The hero is no dashing young beau, and Emma's dawning realisation that she loves him is as much a recognition of her own folly and lack of self-knowledge. The climactic moment when she realises her mistakes is one of the greatest in English literature.

Emma is the opposite of a Cinderella story, in which a poor girl marries a rich man; Emma is independently wealthy from the beginning. And Emma is far from being a romantic heroine; instead, she has to be humbled to find true happiness.

Austen's ironic tone is funny and light, disguising the seriousness of the underlying moral of the story. Her gift for reproducing conversations and her insights into human frailty are unsurpassed. The way the plot twists and turns, keeping the reader in suspense, is masterly.

Less read than the more famous *Pride and Prejudice*, *Emma* has often been preferred by the critics. In his introduction to the 1966 Penguin Classics edition, Ronald Blythe states that the book is 'the climax of Jane Austen's genius and the Parthenon of fiction'. I agree with him.

Contemporary Novel: The Remains of the Day by Kazuo Ishiguro

This novel won the Booker Prize in 1989 and went on to become an Academy Award-winning film. In a couple of decades *The Remains of the Day* has become one of the most highly-regarded post-war British novels.

The novel is written in the first person by the narrator, Stevens, a butler who worked for a Lord Darlington. The butler is reflecting on his life and recalling in particular his relationship with a member of the staff at the house, Miss Kenton, whom he is travelling to meet after many years. *The Remains of the Day* is a classic example of the unreliable narrator – as you read, you gradually realise that Stevens is blinkered and cannot admit to the truth of what happened or acknowledge his real feelings. Ishiguro skilfully uses the butler's description of events to reveal the truth to the reader.

The Remains of the Day was both a critical and commercial success on its first publication. Reviewers praised its characterisation, language, tone and thematic content. Lawrence Graver, writing for the *New York Times Book Review*, called the novel: 'a dream of a book: a beguiling comedy of manners that evolves almost magically into a profound and heart-rending study of personality, class, and culture.'

Play: Hamlet by William Shakespeare

Okay, I can hear you all groaning, but surely *Hamlet* (believed to be written between 1599 and 1601) is one of the most amazing plays ever written. Much of the language of the play, so vital and original in its time, has entered into everyday usage and is still powerful today. (And I love the story about the man who went to see *Hamlet* and came out saying, 'It's a great play – pity it was full of clichés'!)

For years I was obsessed with *Hamlet*. I saw every film and theatre production that I could. I was amazed at how, every time I saw it, the play was different. Every actor interprets the role in his own way and each interpretation adds to the whole. You never tire of it.

I've seen *Hamlet* in traditional dress, in modern dress, set in wartime and in an office. I've seen a production in a park, in a school and on a beach; in black and white and Technicolor; in Russian and German; in a basement theatre in Mexico City. I've seen actors' interpretations of Hamlet as mad, cold and calculating, in love and in the grip of Oedipal passion. And every time I'm gripped.

Hamlet is a perfectly composed play. The balance between Hamlet's inner dilemma, revealed through the *soliloquies* (utterances or discourses by a person who's talking to himself – often used as a device in drama to disclose a character's innermost thoughts), and the way this dilemma is acted out in the action of the play is brilliant. Hamlet is a fully-formed, divided, flawed human being, capable of all human emotion. In fact, I'm in love with Hamlet. And Hamlet, deep down, is me.

Screenplay: Butch Cassidy and the Sundance Kid by William Goldman

William Goldman is a legend in the world of screenwriting. *Butch Cassidy and the Sundance Kid* won him an Oscar for original screenplay in 1969 and he went on to write the screenplays for many well-known films, including *The Stepford Wives*, *Marathon Man*, *All the President's Men* and *A Bridge Too Far*.

Butch Cassidy and the Sundance Kid was a completely original concept. Unlike any other Western ever made, it was simultaneously serious and humorous. The film tells the story of the Hole in the Wall gang, led by Butch Cassidy with the help of the gunslinger known as the Sundance Kid. The gang rob trains until a super posse is hired to hunt them down, at which point they decide to start over in Bolivia.

The story concerns in part the legend of the American West and the coming to a close of the lawless era. The two main characters are anti-heroes, loveable rogues with whom the audience can identify. A female interest is provided by Sundance's girlfriend, Etta, played by Katharine Ross.

While much of the film's success can be ascribed to the chemistry between the two lead characters, played by Paul Newman and Robert Redford, their lines define their characters perfectly and stay in the mind long after the film's over. Some of the lines – such as 'Who are those guys?' are catchphrases still in use today.

Poetry: The Oxford Book of English Verse and The Oxford Book of Twentieth Century English Verse

As selecting just one poem from the many hundreds in the English language written by a host of brilliant poets is impossible, I suggest you buy anthologies of classic and modern poetry. *The Oxford Book of English Verse* contains five of my favourite poems:

- ✔ John Donne's 'Death'
- ✔ Andrew Marvell's 'Thoughts in a Garden'
- ✔ William Blake's 'The Tiger'
- ✔ Gerard Manley Hopkins's 'Pied Beauty'
- ✔ Wilfred Owen's 'Anthem for Doomed Youth'

The Oxford Book of Twentieth Century English Verse, chosen by Philip Larkin, features five other favourites:

- ✔ W. B. Yeats's 'Sailing to Byzantium'
- ✔ D. H. Lawrence's 'The Mountain Lion'
- ✔ Siegfried Sassoon's 'Everyone Sang'
- ✔ T. S. Eliot's 'Journey of the Magi'
- ✔ Stevie Smith's 'Not Waving But Drowning'

Why not read a poem a day? Choose a short one, read it aloud and think about it. Doing so is good for your soul!

Journals: The Diary of Anaïs Nin (Volume One) by Anaïs Nin

Writer and feminist Anaïs Nin began her diary at age 11 in 1914 during a trip from Europe to New York. Nin later said that she began the diary as a letter to her father, the Cuban composer Joaquín Nin, who'd left the family a few years earlier.

Nin had sought to have the diary published as early as the 1930s. Due to its size (in 1966, the diary contained more than 15,000 typewritten pages in some 150 volumes) and literary style, she wouldn't find a publisher until 1966, when the first volume, covering the years 1931–1934, was released. Six more volumes of her diary would follow, and the more sexually explicit 'unexpurgated' versions followed later.

The first volume is probably the most interesting and deals with the author's relationship with American novelist Henry Miller and his wife, June. Most of the entries concern the period when she was living in Louveciennes near Paris, and contain long accounts of her struggles as a writer and her experience of psychoanalysis.

How truthful Nin's accounts are remains controversial; in fact, she left a great deal out, including any references to her husband, possibly at his own request or to protect other people.

The subject matter is fascinating in itself, but Nin's prose style is what makes this book so exciting, ravishing, totally original and truly inspirational.

Travel Writing: In Patagonia by Bruce Chatwin

In Patagonia (1977) is a beautifully written account of the author's journey through 'the uttermost part of the earth', at the southern tip of South America, where bandits were once made welcome and Charles Darwin formed part of his theory of the 'survival of the fittest'.

Chatwin's evocative descriptions, notes on the odd history of the region and enchanting anecdotes make *In Patagonia* a unique insight into a place that very few people have visited. While some Patagonians have claimed he invented some of his anecdotes, the book still retains an aura of authenticity and his descriptive writing is superb. *In Patagonia* became an instant classic.

Narrative Non-Fiction: In Cold Blood by Truman Capote

This book is credited with creating the whole genre of narrative non-fiction. Truman Capote decided to bring all the skills of fiction writing into this investigation of a seemingly motiveless crime in Kansas, when a wealthy wheat farmer, his wife and their two young children were shot to death in their home. The killers were arrested not long after the murders, but Capote was to spend six years working on the book.

Together with his childhood friend and fellow author Harper Lee (author of *To Kill a Mockingbird*), Capote interviewed local residents and the investigators on the case and took thousands of pages of notes.

In Cold Blood was first published as a four-part serial in the *New Yorker* magazine, beginning in September 1965. The piece was an immediate sensation, particularly in Kansas, where the issues sold out immediately. *In Cold Blood* was first published in book form by Random House in January 1966, and was hailed by critics as a masterpiece.

Although you know the outcome of *In Cold Blood* from the start, Capote still manages to build incredible narrative suspense. He also somehow creates a degree of sympathy for the murderers while describing all the horrific details of the crime. The ending is surprisingly lyrical.

Autobiography: I Know Why the Caged Bird Sings by Maya Angelou

The author of this classic autobiography is an American poet, playwright, actress, author, producer and important figure in the Civil Rights movement. *I Know Why the Caged Bird Sings* (1969) is the first – and almost certainly the best – of five autobiographical volumes and is a remarkable retelling of the turbulent events of her childhood, during which she shuttled back and forth between dramatically different environments in rural Stamps, Arkansas and St. Louis, Missouri and San Francisco, California in the 1930s and 1940s.

The book describes the life of a precocious but insecure black girl in the American South and her relationships with a vividly described and diverse cast of characters, including her determined, strict but wise grandmother, Annie Henderson, her bitter, crippled uncle, Willie Johnson, her bright and imaginative brother, Bailey Johnson Junior, her playboy father, Bailey Johnson, and her brilliant, beautiful and worldly mother, Vivian Baxter Johnson.

As young children, Maya and Bailey simultaneously struggle with the pain of having been rejected and abandoned by their parents and of being black in a world of deep-seated racism. When Maya is raped by her mother's boyfriend, she also has to deal with her own shame of having been sexually abused. Despite the harshness and difficulties she experiences, Angelou's book ends on a note of confidence and hope.

Index

• V •

FOR DUMMIES®

Making Everything Easier! ™

UK editions

BUSINESS

978-0-470-51806-9

978-0-470-77930-9

978-0-470-71382-2

FINANCE

978-0-470-99280-7

978-0-470-74324-9

978-0-470-69515-9

HOBBIES

978-0-470-69960-7

978-0-470-77085-6

978-0-470-75857-1

Body Language For Dummies
978-0-470-51291-3

British Sign Language
For Dummies
978-0-470-69477-0

Business NLP For Dummies
978-0-470-69757-3

Cricket For Dummies
978-0-470-03454-5

Digital Marketing For Dummies
978-0-470-05793-3

Divorce For Dummies, 2nd Edition
978-0-470-74128-3

eBay.co.uk Business All-in-One
For Dummies
978-0-470-72125-4

English Grammar For Dummies
978-0-470-05752-0

Fertility & Infertility For Dummies
978-0-470-05750-6

Flirting For Dummies
978-0-470-74259-4

Golf For Dummies
978-0-470-01811-8

Green Living For Dummies
978-0-470-06038-4

Hypnotherapy For Dummies
978-0-470-01930-6

Inventing For Dummies
978-0-470-51996-7

Lean Six Sigma For Dummies
978-0-470-75626-3

**Available wherever books are sold. For more information or to order direct go to www.wiley.com
or call +44 (0) 1243 843291**

05380_p1

FOR DUMMIES®

A world of resources to help you grow

UK editions

SELF-HELP

978-0-470-01838-5

978-0-7645-7028-5

978-0-470-75876-2

Motivation For Dummies
978-0-470-76035-2

Personal Development All-In-One
For Dummies
978-0-470-51501-3

PRINCE2 For Dummies
978-0-470-51919-6

Psychometric Tests For Dummies
978-0-470-75366-8

Raising Happy Children
For Dummies
978-0-470-05978-4

Reading the Financial Pages
For Dummies
978-0-470-71432-4

HEALTH

978-0-470-69430-5

978-0-470-51737-6

978-0-470-71401-0

Sage 50 Accounts For Dummies
978-0-470-71558-1

Study Skills For Dummies
978-0-470-74047-7

Succeeding at Assessment Centres
For Dummies
978-0-470-72101-8

Sudoku For Dummies
978-0-470-01892-7

Teaching Skills For Dummies
978-0-470-74084-2

Time Management For Dummies
978-0-470-77765-7

Understanding and Paying Less
Property Tax For Dummies
978-0-470-75872-4

Work-Life Balance For Dummies
978-0-470-71380-8

HISTORY

978-0-470-99468-9

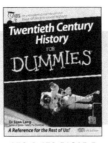

978-0-470-51015-5

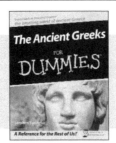

978-0-470-98787-2

FOR DUMMIES

The easy way to get more done and have more fun

LANGUAGES

978-0-7645-5194-9

978-0-7645-5193-2

978-0-471-77270-5

MUSIC

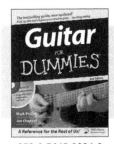
978-0-7645-9904-0

978-0-470-03275-6
UK Edition

978-0-7645-5105-5

SCIENCE & MATHS

978-0-7645-5326-4

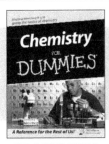
978-0-7645-5430-8

978-0-7645-5325-7

Art For Dummies
978-0-7645-5104-8

Baby & Toddler Sleep Solutions
For Dummies
978-0-470-11794-1

Bass Guitar For Dummies
978-0-7645-2487-5

Brain Games For Dummies
978-0-470-37378-1

Christianity For Dummies
978-0-7645-4482-8

Filmmaking For Dummies,
2nd Edition
978-0-470-38694-1

Forensics For Dummies
978-0-7645-5580-0

German For Dummies
978-0-7645-5195-6

Hobby Farming For Dummies
978-0-470-28172-7

Index Investing For Dummies
978-0-470-29406-2

Jewelry Making & Beading
For Dummies
978-0-7645-2571-1

Knitting For Dummies, 2nd Edition
978-0-470-28747-7

Music Composition For Dummies
978-0-470-22421-2

Physics For Dummies
978-0-7645-5433-9

Schizophrenia For Dummies
978-0-470-25927-6

Sex For Dummies, 3rd Edition
978-0-470-04523-7

Solar Power Your Home For Dummies
978-0-470-17569-9

Tennis For Dummies
978-0-7645-5087-4

The Koran For Dummies
978-0-7645-5581-7

FOR DUMMIES

Helping you expand your horizons and achieve your potential

COMPUTER BASICS

978-0-470-27759-1

978-0-470-13728-4

978-0-471-75421-3

DIGITAL LIFESTYLE

978-0-470-25074-7

978-0-470-39062-7

978-0-470-42342-4

WEB & DESIGN

978-0-470-39700-8

978-0-470-32725-8

978-0-470-34502-3

Access 2007 For Dummies
978-0-470-04612-8

Adobe Creative Suite 3 Design
Premium All-in-One Desk Reference
For Dummies
978-0-470-11724-8

AutoCAD 2009 For Dummies
978-0-470-22977-4

C++ For Dummies, 5th Edition
978-0-7645-6852-7

Computers For Seniors For Dummies
978-0-470-24055-7

Excel 2007 All-In-One Desk Reference
For Dummies
978-0-470-03738-6

Flash CS3 For Dummies
978-0-470-12100-9

Green IT For Dummies
978-0-470-38688-0

Mac OS X Leopard For Dummies
978-0-470-05433-8

Macs For Dummies, 10th Edition
978-0-470-27817-8

Networking All-in-One Desk Reference
For Dummies, 3rd Edition
978-0-470-17915-4

Office 2007 All-in-One Desk Reference
For Dummies
978-0-471-78279-7

Search Engine Optimization
For Dummies, 3rd Edition
978-0-470-26270-2

The Internet For Dummies,
11th Edition
978-0-470-12174-0

Visual Studio 2008 All-In-One Desk
Reference For Dummies
978-0-470-19108-8

Web Analytics For Dummies
978-0-470-09824-0

Windows XP For Dummies, 2nd Edition
978-0-7645-7326-2